Everyday Assessment for Special Education and Inclusive Classroom Teachers
A Case Study Approach

Series Editor
Dee Berlinghoff, PhD

Everyday Assessment for Special Education and Inclusive Classroom Teachers
A Case Study Approach

Frank O. Dykes, EdD
The University of Texas at Tyler
Tyler, Texas

Jessica A. Rueter, PhD
The University of Texas at Tyler
Tyler, Texas

Staci M. Zolkoski, PhD
The University of Texas at Tyler
Tyler, Texas

Routledge
Taylor & Francis Group
NEW YORK AND LONDON

Instructors: *Everyday Assessment for Special Education and Inclusive Classroom Teachers: A Case Study Approach* includes ancillary materials specifically available for faculty use. Included are test bank questions and PowerPoint slides. Please visit www.routledge.com/9781630919504 to obtain access.

First published 2024 by SLACK Incorporated

Published 2024 by Routledge
605 Third Avenue, New York, NY 10158

and by Routledge
4 Park Square, Milton Park, Abingdon, Oxon OX14 4RN

Routledge is an imprint of the Taylor & Francis Group, an informa business

Copyright © 2024 Taylor & Francis Group.

Drs. Frank O. Dykes, Jessica A. Rueter, *and* Staci M. Zolkoski *reported no financial or proprietary interest in the materials presented herein.*

All rights reserved. No part of this book may be reprinted or reproduced or utilised in any form or by any electronic, mechanical, or other means, now known or hereafter invented, including photocopying and recording, or in any information storage or retrieval system, without permission in writing from the publishers.

Trademark notice: Product or corporate names may be trademarks or registered trademarks, and are used only for identification and explanation without intent to infringe.

Library of Congress Control Number: 2023945661

ISBN: 9781630919504 (pbk)
ISBN: 9781003524069 (ebk)

DOI: 10.4324/9781003524069

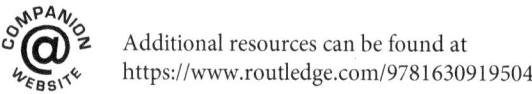

Additional resources can be found at
https://www.routledge.com/9781630919504

Contents

Acknowledgments .... *vii*
About the Authors .... *ix*

Chapter 1	Overview of Assessment 1
Chapter 2	Basic Concepts of Measurement 13
Chapter 3	Legal Issues in Assessment 31
Chapter 4	Norm-Referenced Assessment 53
Chapter 5	Formative and Summative Assessments 71
Chapter 6	Progress Monitoring and Response to Intervention 89
Chapter 7	Assessing Behavior 107
Chapter 8	Assessments of Reading 135
Chapter 9	Assessments of Writing 151
Chapter 10	Assessments of Mathematics 167

Appendix *183*
Index *201*

Instructors: *Everyday Assessment for Special Education and Inclusive Classroom Teachers: A Case Study Approach* includes ancillary materials specifically available for faculty use. Included are test bank questions and PowerPoint slides. Please visit www.routledge.com/9781630919504 to obtain access.

Acknowledgments

First, we acknowledge our families for their unwavering support, especially when we were not available on weekends and holidays. Thanks to Griff, Dean, Sean, Zoe, Colton, and Bull. A special thanks to the Molina family for your unfettered access and for allowing your children to participate in our journey. We would also like to acknowledge the school districts and children with whom we have had the joy of working for the past several years. Our case study scenarios would not have been possible without you. Thanks to Sean Zolkoski for editing our sundry mistakes. Finally, we would like to thank Lori Anderson for the amazing job she did in preparing the resource materials for our textbook.

About the Authors

Frank O. Dykes, EdD, has more than 35 years of experience in education as a general education teacher, special education teacher, educational diagnostician, central office administrator, and university professor. He maintains an active role in public education as an educational consultant in the areas of assessment, evidence-based strategies, cultural diversity, and learning disabilities. Dr. Dykes has several publications to his credit and is a speaker at the international, national, and state levels. His research interests include special education assessment, learning disabilities, teacher training, RTI, minority overrepresentation in special education, and LGBTQ youth issues. Dr. Dykes is the past state treasurer for the Council for Exceptional Children (CEC)–Texas and is a past member of the CEC Elections Committee. At the time of the publication of this book. Dr. Dykes was serving as the past president of the Teacher Education Division of CEC.

Jessica A. Rueter, PhD, is an associate professor of special education at the University of Texas at Tyler (UT Tyler). Dr. Rueter has 30 years of experience as a special education teacher, educational diagnostician, and university professor. Dr. Rueter has several publications to her credit and is a frequent speaker at the international, national, and state levels. She is an assessment consultant to school districts in East Texas and in the Dallas–Fort Worth metropolitan area and has served as an expert witness in due process hearings. Her research interests include best practices of assessment of students with disabilities and translating assessment results into evidence-based instructional practices. Dr. Rueter serves as program coordinator for the educational diagnostician program at UT Tyler, former cochair for the Small Special Education Program Caucus (SSEPC) Symposium, past president of the Council for Educational Diagnostic Services (CEDS), past president of the Texas Council for Exceptional Children (CEC), and continues to be an active member of CEC, CEDS, TED, and SSEPC.

Staci M. Zolkoski, PhD, is an associate professor of special education at the University of Texas at Tyler (UT Tyler). She earned her bachelor's degree in early childhood education from the University of Toledo in Ohio. She earned her master's degree and PhD from the University of North Texas in special education with an emphasis in behavior disorders. Prior to working at the collegiate level, Dr. Zolkoski taught kindergarten and fourth grade. She teaches classroom management at the undergraduate and graduate levels as well as courses in special education, behavior disorders, and educational strategies. She has won Kappa Delta Pi International Honor Society Teacher of the Year for the School of Education at UT Tyler two times and received the Teacher of the Year award for the Department of Education and Psychology at UT Tyler. Dr. Zolkoski is a member of Council for Exceptional Children (CEC) and is an active member of the Division of Emotional and Behavioral Health (DEBH), where she serves on the publications and professional development committees. She serves as the treasurer of the DEBH Foundation and is the editor of the DEBH newsletter, *Behavior Today*. Dr. Zolkoski has presented and published her research in resilience and social emotional learning at the national and international levels. She has worked with local school districts in implementing social emotional learning and has done trainings supporting teachers and schools in social emotional learning and classroom management. Dr. Zolkoski has also presented for ElevateTXed, which is a collaborative effort across the University of Texas system.

Overview of Assessment

CHAPTER OBJECTIVES

- Define assessment.
- Review the history of educational assessment and intelligence testing.
- Identify purposes of assessment.
- Differentiate between assessment and testing.
- Describe formal and informal assessment.
- Examine test bias.
- Describe multidisciplinary assessment.

KEY TERMS

- **anecdotal:** Referring to factual claims relying on observation rather than scientific evidence.
- **assessment:** The gathering of information to make an informed decision.
- **bias:** A prejudice or favor for or against a person or group compared to another.
- **curriculum-based assessment (CBA):** Assessment utilizing direct observation and recording of a student's performance as it relates to the curriculum.
- **curriculum-based measurement (CBM):** Assessment that measures a student's progress through the direct assessment of academic skills using probes or timed samples.
- **multidisciplinary assessment:** Assessment conducted by a variety of professionals, along with the parent.
- **portfolio assessment:** A compilation of student work completed over a specified time period.
- **probe:** A brief, timed curriculum assessment tool.
- **test:** Sample of student behavior collected under specified, standardized conditions.

KEY ABBREVIATIONS

- CBA: curriculum-based assessment
- CBM: curriculum-based measurement
- NCLB: No Child Left Behind

CASE STUDY

Ms. Wang is a first-year third-grade teacher at Pineview Elementary, a Title I school in a suburban area. She has several students in her class who have specific deficits in phonemic awareness. During the day, she pulls the students into small groups for 30 minutes of instruction targeting phonemic awareness skills, particularly segmenting the first sound in words. After 3 weeks of group instruction, she is concerned that Michael and Jazmine are making limited progress. Ms. Wang meets with the school's reading coach, Mr. Evers, to discuss the students and their lack of progress. When they meet, Ms. Wang has no specific data to share with Mr. Evers; however, she does have some anecdotal records. She has kept notes indicating that Michael is unable to identify the first sound in words such as mop, cot, fat, rat, and ham. Jazmine is able to identify the first sound in rat and ham, but not mop, cot, and fat. The students have been working on identifying the first sounds in the words for the past 3 weeks. After they review and discuss the anecdotal observations, Mr. Evers explains it would be best if Ms. Wang would conduct an assessment to determine the specific difficulties the students are having with phonemic awareness skills. As a first-year teacher, Ms. Wang is hesitant to ask what Mr. Evers means by assessment. She thanks him for his help and returns to her classroom wondering what he means by assessment and where she can find help.

WHAT IS ASSESSMENT?

Still confused by Mr. Evers's vague explanation, Ms. Wang reaches out to a veteran teacher on campus who provides her with an overview of assessment. Assessment can be defined as the gathering of information to make an informed decision. Lawrence (2013) defined the purpose of academic

TABLE 1-1. PURPOSES OF ASSESSMENT

ASSESSMENT PURPOSE	EXPLANATION	EXAMPLE
Identify strengths and weaknesses	Used to gather information across a wide variety of areas such as reading, writing, math	Ms. Wang could examine Jazmine's performance across all academic areas to ascertain her intra-individual differences.
Determine relative standing	Compare one student's performance to that of other students	Ms. Wang uses a norm-referenced reading assessment to compare Michael's performance to other students in his class.
Inform instruction	Using assessment data to inform student instruction	Ms. Wang could have Jazmine read a list of words aloud and identify the first sound in each word. The sounds she is not able to identify would be appropriate to target for instruction.
Grading	The most common form of assessment used by teachers	Ms. Wang assigns a numeric value to a worksheet assessing Michael's ability to identifying beginning sounds.

assessment as (1) identifying student strengths and weaknesses, (2) monitoring student progress, and (3) assessing students' prior knowledge. Bryant et al. (2020) noted the purposes of assessment are to identify strengths and weaknesses, determine relative standing, inform instruction, documenting progress, and for grading. A summary of the purposes of assessment is provided in Table 1-1.

Ms. Wang had conducted assessment through her anecdotal observations. She gathered data about her students to make an informed decision related to the students' challenges with phonological processing. The information gleaned through observation can yield worthwhile information. In her role as a teacher, Ms. Wang acts much like a detective. She looks at the facts and makes a determination based on the evidence she has gathered. While she has some information, Ms. Wang lacks data regarding the specific phonological skills that would assist her in developing a targeted plan to address the challenges faced by her students. Before she seeks out specific measures to use in her classroom, Ms. Wang decides to pull out some of her former college textbooks to review the history of assessment.

HISTORY OF EDUCATIONAL ASSESSMENT

Educational assessment practices have been shaped by a variety of disciplines, forces, and trends. "Changes in education, psychology, and medicine, and in the beliefs that society holds regarding the educational process continue to influence how schools go about gathering assessment information to make decisions about students they serve" (McLoughlin et al., 2018, p. 5). Legislation leading to mandating accountability testing in school was precipitated by the publication of *A Nation at Risk* (National Commission on Excellence in Education, 1983). Prior to that time, local communities were primarily responsible for designating what should be taught in schools. Americans began to see the significance of education in earning a living during the crash of the stock market in 1929 and the subsequent sense of nationalism brought about by World War II. With the launch of the Russian spacecraft *Sputnik*, Americans began to blame schools for the lack of science and technology training, and developed the belief that the American school system should be the "ultimate achiever among the nations of the free world" (Lichter, 2017, p. 44). With the release of *A Nation at*

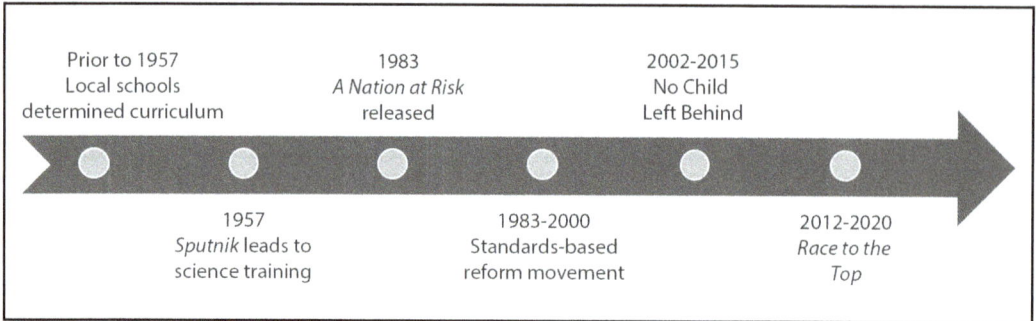

Figure 1-1. Educational assessment timeline.

Risk, a renewed focus was placed on education, and a series of reforms began. One of the first reactions was to increase high school graduation rates, raise the standards for admission to educator preparation programs, and strengthen local school initiatives such as more homework and stricter attendance policies. In the 1980s and early 1990s, state governors heralded a need to go "back to the basics," and a clarion call was made to require tougher state oversight and state achievement testing systems.

As the early 1990s progressed, a new reform in education began to take root. It was known as standards-based reform. Proponents of standards-based reformed called for states and districts to develop content standards that would lead to a creation of a curriculum that would delineate learning objectives by subject and grade level. As Bill Clinton assumed the presidency, he sought to institute federal implementation of standards-based reform with the creation of "Goals 2000," which aimed at requiring states to submit standards to a national council for approval; however, this did not materialize (National Association of Special Education Teachers, 2022).

Following the election of President George W. Bush, the *No Child Left Behind Act* (NCLB; 2001) was signed into law. This law established an accountability system with sanctions. NCLB requires frequent administration of achievement tests, as well as the disaggregation of test scores by race, and it requires adequate yearly progress. School districts that were not able to meet this criterion faced sanctions such as the reconstitution of a school with new teachers and administration. NCLB remained at the forefront of education policy while President Bush served his two terms in office. Critics of NCLB sought a change with the election of Barack Obama.

Deeming the sanctions of NCLB too deleterious, President Barack Obama appointed his Secretary of Education to devise a new method to assist schools in improving student outcomes. The *Race to the Top* (U.S. Department of Education, 2009) program provided states with additional funding to create more charter schools and to provide pay incentives to teachers based on student achievement scores. Additionally, competing states were required to join a multistate consortium to develop assessments. This led to the creation of the Common Core, which is a national set of standards for subject areas taught in schools. See Figure 1-1 for a timeline summary of educational assessment events.

CHECK FOR UNDERSTANDING

What publication lead to an increased focus on school accountability?

Despite the numerous reforms that have been implemented for the past 40+ years, assessment practices are out of step with best education practices (Kaestle, 2013). Current assessment reforms are aimed at integrating what is known about teaching and learning. "Recent research in brain and cognitive science provides an impetus for shifting the nation's schools away from a single-minded focus on current testing models and performance assessments that measure and encourage deeper learning" (Conley, 2015, p. 1). Hamilton et al. (2008) suggest advances in technology and psychometrics "offer the possibility of new assessment methods that would tap a broader range of skills and knowledge than today's multiple-choice tests, and do so more efficiently and at a reasonable cost" leading to "high-quality assessments that require students to apply complex problem-solving and reasoning skills" (p. 11).

HISTORY OF INTELLIGENCE TESTING

In most states, traditional intelligence quotient (IQ) tests continue to be used as part of the assessment process (Overton, 2016). Coined by the German psychologist, William Stern, IQ is a score from one of a number of standardized tests designed to assess one's intelligence. Alfred Binet was the first to design an IQ test. Binet was asked by the French government to develop a mechanism to determine which students might struggle in school. Binet sought help from his colleague, Theodore Simon, to develop a test with questions focusing on attention, memory, and problem solving. Binet and Simon (1905) developed the first standardized intelligence test, the *Binet-Simon Scale*. In 1916, a psychologist at Stanford University, Lewis Terman (Warne, 2018), adapted the *Binet-Simon Scale*, which became the *Stanford-Binet Intelligence Scales*, the premier instrument used for several decades in the United States.

"Probably the most important event in the spread of intelligence testing was the testing program carried out by the U.S. Army during the first world war" (Boake, 2002, p. 389). During this time, a committee of testing experts was formed to design tests, known as the Army Alpha and Beta tests, to determine if army recruits were fit for military service. The army testing program established credibility of testing and provided training for many psychologists in test construction and interpretation. These early efforts became the prototypes for many current individual and group assessments. One individual who worked with the army testing was David Wechsler. Wechsler enlisted in the army and helped score examination protocols and attended the School of Military Psychology to train as a psychological examiner (Boake, 2002). Following his military service, Wechsler joined Bellevue Hospital in New York City as chief psychologist and developed a battery of intelligence known as the *Wechsler-Bellevue Intelligence Scale* (1939), which became a widely used adult intelligence test. Wechsler went on to revise the *Wechsler-Bellevue Intelligence Scale*, and in 1949 he published the *Wechsler Intelligence Scale for Children* followed by the *Wechsler Adult Intelligence Scale* in 1955. See Figure 1-2 for an evolution of intelligence testing. Rather than scoring based on chronological or mental age, Wechsler developed instruments counted by comparing the test taker's score to others in the same age group. This method is the standard used by all intelligence testing instruments. Besides the Wechsler scales, other common instruments used to measure intelligence include the *Universal Nonverbal Intelligence Test*, *Differential Ability Scales*, *Woodcock-Johnson IV Tests of Cognitive Abilities*, and *Kaufman Assessment Battery for Children*.

CHECK FOR UNDERSTANDING

Why did the U.S. Army assess recruits with the Army Alpha and Beta tests?

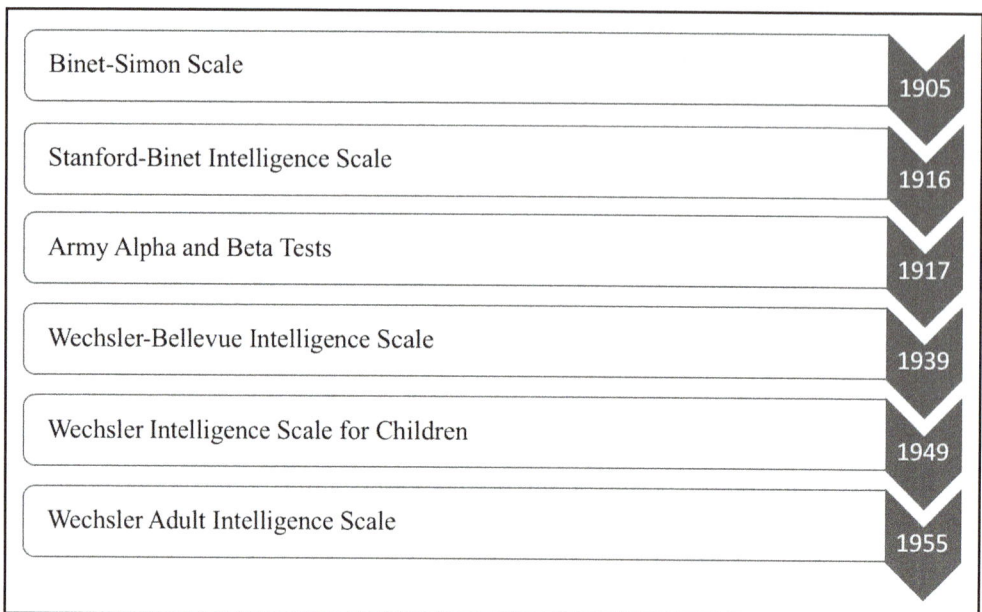

Figure 1-2. Evolution of intelligence testing development.

While some believe IQ tests offer value, there are controversies surrounding IQ testing. For example, IQ testing was used to screen new immigrants as they entered the United States. These tests were administered in English to non–English-speaking immigrants, leading to inaccurate generalizations about entire populations of people. Additionally, critics of intelligence testing posit that IQ tests are inherently biased against Black and Hispanic Americans, and the bias can result in discrimination and question the reliability and validity of assessment instruments. The issues of intelligence testing have led to litigation, which will be highlighted in Chapter 3 of this book.

With the increased attention to the disproportionality of marginalized groups with regard to placement of students with cultural and linguistic differences, it is important to use assessment instruments free from ethic, cultural, and linguistic bias. Even though IQ testing has received much criticism, it is still used in most states to determine if a student meets eligibility for special education services (Overton, 2016). The most important consideration for school personnel remains using or interpreting IQ scores as only a small part of the information gathered to make educational decisions.

INFORMAL ASSESSMENT

After reviewing her college textbooks, Ms. Wang realizes there are many ways to assess student progress in the classroom. One method used is informal assessments, which are nonstandardized measures often developed by the teacher to evaluate student progress. Informal measures might include observations, interviews, curriculum-based assessments (CBAs), or curriculum-based measurements (CBMs).

Curriculum-Based Assessment

CBA is used when a teacher takes frequent measurement of a student's classroom performance on the curriculum being taught. CBA refers to informal measurement using "direct observation and recording of student's performance in the local curriculum as a basis for gathering information to make instructional decisions" (Deno, 2003, p. 185). CBAs are a student-centered approach for documenting progress and provide valuable information for planning, delivering, and assessing instruction. Examples of CBAs include worksheets, rating scales, quizzes, and class projects. CBA is used primarily to design and deliver instruction and allows the teacher to identify specific deficits in need of remediation (VanDerHeyden & Burns, 2005). CBA emphasizes direct, repeated assessment of academic behaviors utilizing probes such as math facts, spelling lists, and reading passages (Little & Akin-Little, 2014). Through frequent collection of data, the curriculum can be monitored, and modifications can be made to daily instruction to improve academic performance. CBAs are quick to develop and easily scored, which make them advantageous to use in for data collection purposes. Harris (2013) noted "assessment will become the intimate companion of instruction, and, in fact, it should become as intrinsic part of instruction" (p. 16). Advantages of CBAs include that they are teacher made, may be administered in groups, and assess specific content taught during an academic period. However, there are disadvantages of using CBAs. The CBA may not have adequate reliability and validity and might not be considered an appropriate measure for students who are ethically or linguistically diverse.

Check for Understanding

What is one advantage and one disadvantage of using a CBA?

Curriculum-Based Measurement

In addition to using CBA, Ms. Wang might implement a CBM to assess the student's ability in phonological processing. CBM is a method of measuring student progress through direct assessment of academic skills. In CBM, the teacher gives the student brief, timed samples, or probes, created from academic material taken from the school's curriculum (McLane, n.d.). The probes are timed and last from 1 to 5 minutes and are administered one to two times per week. Specific skills that can be measured through the use of a CBM include reading fluency, letter sequences, math facts, and word recall. These repeated measures of academic skills have technical adequacy and validity and are standardized. The data from the probe are charted in a graph to provide a visual record. The visual record allows the teacher to evaluate student progress and make needed changes in instruction. While the CBA compares a student against a standard of mastery, the CBM compares the student with their own performance on a specific skill. McLane (n.d.) highlights that the visual record provided by the CBM allows students to keep track of their own progress, and it evaluates the success of the instruction. Another advantage of CBM noted by McLane is that it is easily understood and interpreted, in contrast with typical standardized scores.

Portfolio Assessment

Ms. Wang may also use portfolio assessments to gauge student progress. Portfolio assessments are a "compilation of work a student completes over a period time" (Powell, 2019, p. 122). Portfolios contain student-selected work samples and sometimes student notes explaining how the samples were created and edited. Portfolios are often scored using an evaluation rubric that specifies the evaluation criteria needing to be considered when evaluating the work products. *Ms. Wang might want to keep work samples to show how students are progressing in the area of phonological processing.* For example, she might compile a portfolio including student work samples, teacher-made tests, homework assignments, error analysis of work samples, and running records with miscue analysis.

TEST VERSUS ASSESSMENT

The terms *test* and *assessment* are often used interchangeably by educators; however, the two terms are not synonymous. As noted earlier, assessment can be defined as the gathering of data to make an informed decision. Testing is one method that can be used to gather data. A test can be defined as "a sample of student behavior collected under standard conditions" (McLoughlin et al., 2018, p. 8). Testing can be informal, such as using a CBA or CBM, or it can be formal. Formal assessment, often referred to as norm-referenced or standardized assessment, requires one to follow procedures that contain specific rules for administration, scoring, and assessment. Informal assessments do not require rigid administration, scoring, and interpretation procedures. Data from informal assessments can be used to inform a cycle of continuous improvement (Gersten et al., 2009).

CHECK FOR UNDERSTANDING

How are an assessment and a test different?

FORMAL ASSESSMENT

Formal assessment is often referred to as standardized or norm referenced. This type of assessment is given with specific instructions and procedures and is most often administered by individuals trained in tests and measurements. These measures are used to compare the performance of one individual to that for a normative group. Formal and informal assessment are fully detailed in Chapters 4 and 5.

CHECK FOR UNDERSTANDING

How are formal and informal assessments different?

CULTURAL BIAS IN ASSESSMENT

As Mrs. Tonka, the veteran teacher, explains assessment to Ms. Wang. She is very explicit with her explanation of bias that may occur in assessment. Culture and background may lead to inaccuracies in assessment. Performance gaps on standardized tests between minority and nonminority groups in the United States prevail despite the efforts to reduce them (Kim & Zabelina, 2015). Cultural and social norms may impact how test takers understand and interpret wording of test questions. The norming process used in the United States takes into account the scores of the majority group populations. This norming process often does not take into account the various racial or ethnic groups. Padilla and Borsato (2008) noted that if the cultural and linguistic backgrounds of individuals being tested are not represented in the group used in the norming process, the validity and reliability of the tests are questionable. For example, test item interpretation can impact test questions written in a language that is different from the language of the test taker. Moreover, words used in test questions may have different meanings for different cultures. Villegas and Lucas (2002) caution that broader cultural factors should be considered when examining test bias. Other factors may include but are not limited to religion, gender, age, social class, sexual orientation, and others.

While progress has been made in developing unbiased tests, other bias may present challenges when working with students from culturally and linguistically diverse backgrounds. There is a tendency within human decision making to subconsciously make attributions about people (Dee & Gershenson, 2017). These attributions can lead to unconscious bias. When the unconscious bias of well-intentioned teachers influences judgment toward particular groups of students, it can influence instructional practices, student expectations, and recommendations like course placement, special education, and discipline (Dee & Gershenson, 2017). *In her discussion with Ms. Wang, Mrs. Tonka emphasizes the need to have high expectations for all students.* Ladson-Billings (1995) noted that teachers may lack the knowledge and skills to successfully interact with students who are different from themselves. Teachers need to examine their own expectations for students of various racial or social classes to ensure appropriate and effective instructional strategies. In addition, parental involvement in assessment may assist consideration of cultural and language factors and the role they plan in interpreting assessment data (McLeskey et al., 2017). Proactive educators are aware of potential biases so they can fully support all students both academically and psychologically. One method to help alleviate bias in assessment is through the implementation of multidisciplinary assessment.

Check for Understanding

How might bias impact assessment of a student?

Multidisciplinary Assessment

Given the increasing diversity of the population, it is necessary to include various professionals in the assessment process to eradicate bias. One method to use is a multidisciplinary assessment. In this assessment model, a team is comprised of teachers, specialists, administrators, and parents who provide data to assess a child's needs. *Based on the challenges Ms. Wang is noting with the children experiencing reading challenges, she could reach out to various professionals on the campus to provide a wide range of expertise and experience to facilitate support for students.* Nellis et al. (2014) proposed that the "use of multidisciplinary teams provide a context for consideration of a variety of barriers to learning that may be impacting the student's performance. Barriers might include instructional, curricular, environmental or learner factors" (p. 113). The use of a multidisciplinary approach to assessment is predicated on the critical role of collaboration. School collaborative practices can increase student achievement and improve education practices (Nellis et al., 2014). Waldron and McLeskey (2010) noted higher quality of instructional practices when collaborative school practices are utilized. They indicate the practice of collaboration promotes trust and respect among colleagues.

One multidisciplinary assessment approach used by school professionals is response to intervention. Response to intervention is regarded as a "multitiered, problem-solving approach that addresses the learning of all students through educational teams that identify areas of concern about specific students as well as the core instructional process" (Nellis et al., 2014, p. 118). Within this problem-solving method, data are used to fully understand the nature of the student's difficulty, and a plan is developed to ameliorate the difficulties. The team focuses on identifying the problem and understanding the factors contributing to the student's challenges. This process provides a route to prescribe individualized interventions targeting the student's needs (Thomas et al., 2020).

The use of the team approach to address student learning issues is not a new concept. Other iterations of the team approach have been used in schools for decades. These include Teacher Assistance Teams (Chalfant et al., 1979), Child Study Teams (Moore et al., 1989), Prereferral Intervention Teams

(Graden et al., 1985), Mainstream Assistance Teams (Fuchs et al., 1990), and Instructional Support Teams (Kovaleski et al., 1995). Within each of these approaches, the goal is to identify and develop a plan of action to address the academic and/or behavioral challenges faced by students.

Check for Understanding

How might a multidisciplinary team ensure that bias is not present in assessment?

Summary

Teachers use assessment data on a daily basis as they conduct their instructional duties. Assessment data may be formal, such as reviewing scores from a standardized test, or it may be informal, such as charting a student's progress on a CBM. Whatever method of assessment is utilized, it is important to keep it free from bias and to involve as many personnel as necessary to provide a multidisciplinary assessment to provide a true picture of a child's educational strengths and weaknesses in order to develop a plan of action to meet the unique learning needs of the student.

This textbook provides novice teachers with a practitioner-friendly text that describes topics related to assessment and provides practical applications for the classroom setting. Understanding that assessment is the foundation of effective instruction, the authors pair rationale and research with real-life case studies to guide the reader in extracting data to inform everyday teaching practices. Each chapter begins with a case study that introduces in a personal and engaging manner the topics that will be discussed. The following is a synopsis of the content for each chapter:

Chapter 2: Focuses on descriptive statistics that help teachers understand the terminology often used in assessment

Chapter 3: Discusses the legal issues and court cases focused on assessment

Chapter 4: Reviews norm-referenced assessments used for eligibility and placement decisions

Chapter 5: Analyzes both formative and summative assessments and their practical application to the classroom setting

Chapter 6: Identifies progress monitoring measures and the response to intervention model

Chapter 7: Highlights methods for assessing behavior and the development of functional behavior assessments and behavior intervention plans

Chapter 8: Provides a review of various formal and informal assessments of reading

Chapter 9: Introduces formal and informal writing assessments used in schools

Chapter 10: Highlights the various formal and informal assessments for mathematics

Case Study Wrap-Up

After the meeting with Mrs. Tonka, Ms. Wang understands more about assessment and uses the information to devise a plan of action to assess phonological processing skills for Michael and Jazmine. She decides to implement a CBM to conduct daily probes of learning and to devise an individual plan for each student based on the information gleaned from the probes.

CHAPTER REVIEW

1. Why does a teacher need to conduct assessment?
2. How are assessments and tests different?
3. Differentiate between a curriculum-based measurement and a curriculum-based assessment.
4. What is test bias, and how does one avoid test bias in assessment?
5. Explain one difference between formal and informal assessment.

REFERENCES

Binet, A., & Simon, T. (1905). New methods for the diagnosis of the intellectual level of subnormal. In H. H. Goddard (Ed.), *Development of intelligence in children (the Binet-Simon Scale)* (pp. 37–90). Williams & Wilkins.

Boake, C. (2002). From the Binet-Simon to the Wechsler-Bellevue: Tracing the history of intelligence testing. *Journal of Clinical and Experimental Neuropsychology, 24*(3), 383–405. https://doi.org/10.1076/jcen.24.3.383.981

Bryant, D. P., Bryant, B. R., & Smith, D. D. (2020). *Teaching students with special needs in inclusive classrooms* (2nd ed.). Sage.

Chalfant, J. C., Pysh, M. V., & Moultrie, R. (1979). Teacher assistance teams: A model for within-building problem solving. *Learning Disability Quarterly, 2*, 85–96.

Conley, D. T. (2015). A new era for educational assessment. *Education Policy Analysis Archives, 23*(8), 1–40. http://dx.doi.org/10.14507/epaa.v23.1983

Dee, T., & Gershenson, S. (2017). *Unconscious bias in the classroom: Evidence and opportunities.* Google's Computer Science Education Research. https://cepa.stanford.edu/content/unconscious-bias-classroom-evidence-and-opportunities

Deno, S. L. (2003). Developments in curriculum-based measurement. *Journal of Special Education, 37*, 184–192.

Fuchs, D., Fuchs, L. S., & Bahr, M. W. (1990). Mainstream assistance teams: A scientific basis for the art of consultation. *Exceptional Children, 57*, 128–139.

Gersten, R. M., What Works Clearinghouse (Institute of Education Sciences), & National Center for Education Evaluation and Regional Assistance (U.S.). (2009). *Assisting students struggling with reading: Response to intervention and multi-tier intervention in the primary grades.* U.S. Department of Education, National Center for Educational Evaluation and Regional Assistance, Institutes of Education Sciences.

Graden, J. L., Casey, C., & Christenson, S. L. (1985). Implementing a prereferral intervention system: I. The model. *Exceptional Children, 51*, 377–384.

Hamilton, L. S., Stecher, B. M., & Yuan, K. (2008). *Standards-based reform in the United States: History, research, and future directions.* Center of Education Policy, RAND.

Harris, C. (2013). *Curriculum-based assessment: A primer* (4th ed.). Charles C. Thomas.

Kaestle, C. (2013). *Testing policy in the United States: A historical perspective.* Gordon Commission.

Kim, K. H., & Zabelina, D. (2015). Cultural bias in assessment: Can creativity assessment help? *International Journal of Critical Pedagogy, 6*(2), 129–147.

Kovaleski, J. F., Tucker, J. A., & Duffy, D. J. (1995). School reform through instructional support: The Pennsylvania initiative (part I). *Communiqué: National Association of School Psychologists, 23*(8), 1–8.

Ladson-Billings, G. (1995). But that's just good teaching! The case for culturally relevant pedagogy. *Theory Into Practice, 34*, 159–165.

Lawrence, B. M. (2013). *What is the purpose of classroom assessments?* http://www.ehow.com/facts_7651703_purpose-classroom-assessments.html#izz2UbwxvTEh

Lichter, J. M. (2017). *A history of the legislation leading to the federally-mandated assessments in education from A Nation at Risk to the conclusion of No Child Left Behind* (Doctoral dissertation, University of Nebraska). Proquest Dissertations.

Little, S. G., & Akin-Little, A. (2014). *Academic assessment and intervention.* Routledge.

McLane, K. (n.d.). *Fact sheet: Benefits of curriculum-based measurement.* The National Center on Student Progress Monitoring, American Institutes for Research.

McLeskey, J., Barringer, M. D., Billingsley, B., Brownell, M., Jackson, D., Kennedy, M., Lewis, T., Macheady, L., Rodriguez, J., Scheeler, M. C., Winn, J., & Ziegler, C. (2017). *High-leverage practices in special education.* Council for Exceptional Children & CEEDAR Center.

McLoughlin, J. A., Lewis, R. B., & Kritikos, E. P. (2018). *Assessing students with special needs* (8th ed.). Prentice Hall.

Moore, K. J., Fifield, M. B., Spira, D. A., & Scarlato, M. (1989). Child study team decision making in special education: Improving the process. *Remedial and Special Education, 10*, 50–58.

National Association of Special Education Teachers. (2022). *Special Education Law Goals 2000 Educate America Act.* https://www.naset.org/professional-resources/special-education-and-the-law/goals-2000-educate-america-act

National Commission on Excellence in Education. (1983). *A nation at risk: The imperative for educational reform.* U.S. Government Printing Office.

Nellis, L. M., Sickman, L. S., Newman, D. S., & Harman, D. R. (2014). Schoolwide collaboration to prevent and address reading difficulties: Opportunities for school psychologists and speech-language pathologists. *Journal of Educational and Psychological Consultation, 24*, 110–127.

No Child Left Behind Act of 2001: P.L. 107–110, 20 U.S.C. 6319 (2001).

Overton, T. (2016). *Assessing learners with special needs: An applied approach* (8th ed.). Pearson.

Padilla, A. M., & Borsato, G. N. (2008). Issues in culturally appropriate psychoeducational assessment. In L. A. Suzuki & J. G. Ponterrotto (Eds.), *Handbook of multicultural assessment* (pp. 5–21). John Wiley & Sons.

Powell, S. D. (2019). *Your introduction to education: Exploration in teaching.* Pearson.

Thomas, E. R., Conoyer, S. J., & Lembke, E. S. (2020). Districtwide evaluation of RTI implementation: Success, challenges, and self-efficacy. *Learning Disabilities Research & Practice, 35*(3), 118–125. https://doi.org/10.1111/ldrp.12226

U.S. Department of Education. (2009). *Race to the Top program executive summary.* U.S. Department of Education.

VanDerHeyden, A. M., & Burns, M. K. (2005). Using curriculum-based assessment and curriculum-based measurement to guide elementary mathematics instruction: Effect on individual and group accountability scores. *Assessment for Effective Intervention, 30*(3), 15–31.

Villegas, A. M., & Lucas, T. (2002). Preparing culturally responsive teachers: Rethinking the curriculum. *Journal of Teacher Education, 53*(1), 20–32.

Waldron, N. L., & McLeskey, J. (2010). Establishing a collaborative school culture through comprehensive school reform. *Journal of Educational & Psychological Consultation, 20*, 58–74. https://doi.org/10.1080/1047441090353564

Warne, R. T. (2018). An evaluation (and vindication?) of Lewis Terman: What the father of gifted education can teach the 21st century. *Gifted Child Quarterly, 63*(1), 1–19. https://doi.org/10.117/0016986218799433

Wechsler, D. (1939). *The measurement of adult intelligence.* Williams & Wilkins.

Wechsler, D. (1949). *Wechsler Intelligence Scale for Children. Manual.* Psychological Corporation.

Wechsler, D. (1955). *Manual for the Wechsler Adult Intelligence Scale.* Psychological Corporation.

Basic Concepts of Measurement

CHAPTER OBJECTIVES

- Describe the following types of scores: raw scores, scaled scores, standard scores, percentile ranks, age, and grade equivalents.
- Identify similarities and differences between scaled scores and standard scores.
- Create the normal curve using standard scores and scaled scores.
- Apply the normal curve to classroom settings (PK–12 to college classrooms).
- Define reliability and identify the four types of reliability.
- Explain standard error of measurement.
- Define validity and identify the three types of validity.

KEY TERMS

- **age equivalent (AE):** The median raw score for a particular age level.
- **concurrent validity:** Involves comparing scores from a new assessment measure with scores from a similar measure that includes the same content.
- **confidence intervals (CI):** Range of scores around an obtained score.
- **construct validity:** Evaluates whether the standardized assessment measures the trait or characteristic it was intended to measure.
- **content validity:** How well an assessment measure represents the domain or learning area that is being evaluated.
- **correlation:** A statistical method used to measure the relationship between two variables.
- **correlation coefficient (r):** The relationship that is expressed between two variables.
- **criterion-related validity:** The relationship between the results of the assessment measure and results of a comparable measure.
- **derived scores:** Scores that are obtained using the raw score and expectancy tables that are included in the back of standardized assessment manuals. Two types of derived scores include (1) standard scores and (2) scaled scores.
- **educational diagnostician:** An assessment professional who is trained to administer and interpret standardized assessments.
- **equivalent forms reliability:** A form of reliability in which different versions of the same assessment are designed to be equivalent to one another.
- **examiner:** A person who is specifically trained to administer standardized assessments. These individuals include educational diagnosticians and/or teachers who have training in administering standardized assessments.
- **grade equivalent (GE):** The median raw score for a particular grade level.
- **internal consistency:** The process of assessing the relationship between multiple items on a single test using one administration of the test.
- **interrater reliability:** The process by which an impartial examiner assesses the phenomenon that has already been evaluated by another examiner. The phenomenon is then compared to determine how much variability exists between the two test scores. That is, it is the degree to which two or more examiners agree with each other.
- **mean:** Arithmetic average of a set of scores.
- **measures of central tendency:** Mean, median, and mode.
- **median:** Middlemost score in a set of data.
- **mode:** Most frequently occurring score in a set of data.
- **normal distribution or curve:** A distribution in which all three measures of central tendency fall exactly at the same point on the curve.
- **obtained score:** The number obtained by an examinee on a test.
- **percentile ranks:** Scores that express the percentage of students who scored as well as or lower than a given student's score.
- **predictive validity:** Refers to how effective a test is in predicting future performance.
- **raw scores:** The number of items correct on a standardized assessment measure.
- **reliability:** Consistency of assessment results. In other words, results are consistent over time and are repeatable.

- **scaled scores:** A type of a derived score that has a mean of 10 and a standard deviation of 3.
- **standard deviation (SD):** Represents the variability of a set of data. Standard deviations are determined during the standardization process and will always contain the same share of the population being measured.
- **standard error of measurement (SEM):** Represents the amount of error that is determined to exist in an assessment measure.
- **standard scores:** A type of a derived score that has a mean of 100 and a standard deviation of 15.
- **standardized assessments:** Assessment measures that are administered and scored in a consistent or standard manner.
- **terms of technical adequacy:** Reliability and validity.
- **test–retest reliability:** The consistency of test results across time. It is the consistency of scores from repeated test administrations of the same assessment.
- **true score:** A hypothetical value that represents the observed score and the score that would be earned if the entire domain of items were evaluated.
- **validity:** The accuracy of an assessment measure and the degree to which the assessment measures what it is supposed to measure.

KEY ABBREVIATIONS

- AE: age equivalents
- CI: confidence intervals
- GE: grade equivalent
- *r*: correlation coefficient
- SD: standard deviation
- SEM: standard error of measurement

CASE STUDY

Madison is a 10-year old female student who is in the fourth grade at The Greatest Elementary School Ever. Madison resides with her biological parents and is the only child in the Farnin household. Joe and Tamara Farnin (Madison's parents) are self-employed and obtained some college credits. Mr. and Mrs. Farnin are concerned about Madison's progress in school. They reported to the school that Madison has an aunt who experienced difficulties with reading. Mr. and Mrs. Farnin reported Madison is a positive influence with her friends, encouraging, and has been complimented on her mannerly behavior.

Health History

According to Mr. and Mrs. Farnin, Madison met her developmental milestones, and there were no complications during pregnancy or birth. Her medical history is significant for ear infections. Madison has had all her immunizations and sees her physician regularly for routine medical checkups. According to the health and vision screening dated September 25, 2020, Madison's vision and hearing are within normal limits.

Educational and Programming History

Madison's educational and programming history is varied. Madison transferred to The Greatest Elementary School Ever in May 2020. Madison had previously attended The Learning Center from 2016 to April 2020. The Learning Center is a private, tuition-based school created to meet the learning needs of children with a variety of identified language-based disorders such as dyslexia, dysgraphia, dyscalculia, auditory processing, receptive/expressive language deficits, and/or ADD with any of the three types: inattentive, impulsivity, or combined inattentive/impulsivity. Prior to attending The Learning Center, Madison attended XYC Elementary (2015). Mr. and Mrs. Farnin reported Madison ended first grade highly discouraged and did not want to attend school any longer. They are concerned Madison is having difficulty identifying letters, decoding words, and enunciating (especially p, b, and d).

Reason for Referral

Madison has been struggling to learn to read. Her teacher, Mr. Saunders, referred her for an evaluation to see if Madison has a learning disability in the area of reading. Ms. Collins, who is an educational diagnostician, has been asked to complete the assessment. An educational diagnostician is an assessment professional trained to administer and interpret standardized assessments.

WHY MEASUREMENT MATTERS

Psychoeducational assessments using standardized measures has a long-standing history in the educational decision-making process (Overton, 2016). Standardized assessments are assessment measures administered and scored in consistent or standard manner (Popham, 1999). Moreover, these assessments help families and educators identify areas of strength and weakness for the child being evaluated. Understanding a child's strengths and weaknesses helps teachers select instructional strategies and design lessons specifically crafted for the child who is struggling. Understanding basic concepts of assessment, such as the different types of scores, reliability and validity, and application of the normal curve, offers teachers a deeper understanding of the educational performance of the children in their classroom.

DIFFERENT TYPES OF SCORES

Raw Scores

This chapter presents the common types of scores that are obtained on standardized measures. The first score that is obtained on a standardized measure is the raw score. Raw scores represent the number of items correct (Overton, 2016). In the classroom, all the teacher needs to do is add the number of items correct on a test to get the raw score. For example, if there are 10 questions on the test, and Madison answers 7 out of 10 items correct, the raw score is 7 (Table 2-1). However, on standardized measures, raw scores cannot be used to compare a child's performance to another child's performance. The process of comparing scores is through an understanding of derived scores.

CHECK FOR UNDERSTANDING

Raw scores represent the number of items answered correctly. Raw scores are not used to compare performance on standardized assessments.

TABLE 2-1. An Example of Calculating the Raw Score

QUESTION NUMBER	STUDENT SCORE
1.	1
2.	0
3.	1
4.	1
5.	1
6.	0
7.	1
8.	1
9.	1
10.	0

Each time Madison answers correctly she receives a score of 1. Raw score = 7.

Derived Scores

Derived scores are scores obtained using the raw score and expectancy tables that are included in the back of standardized assessment manuals (Wiebe, n.d.). Two types of derived scores include (1) standard scores and (2) scaled scores. Standard scores represent equal units of data. Standard scores have a mean of 100 and a standard deviation of 15. Scaled scores also represent equal units of data and have a mean of 10 and a standard deviation of 3. Standard scores and scaled scores are interpreted through the normal "bell" curve, which will be discussed later in this chapter.

Check for Understanding

Derived scores are used to compare scores and have equal units of measure. Two types of derived scores include:

1. Standard scores (mean of 100 and standard deviation of 15)
2. Scaled scores (mean of 10 and standard deviation of 3)

Percentile Ranks

Percentile ranks and age and grade equivalents are additional ways to look at data from a standardized assessment. Percentile ranks are scores that express the percentage of students who scored as well as or lower than a given student's score (Overton, 2016). A percentile rank of 50 is in the average range of functioning (Table 2-2). For example, Madison earned a percentile rank of 16 on a dyslexia assessment. This means she scored as well as or better than 16% of the children on this assessment. Conversely, 84% of the children on this assessment scored better than Madison. A percentile rank of 16 is in the below average range of functioning. An important point to remember is that percentile ranks express a percentage. It does not mean that the child earned a certain percentage. For example, a percentile rank of 16 does not mean that Madison scored 16% on this standardized assessment.

Table 2-2. Percentile Ranks and Suggested Qualitative Descriptions

PERCENTILE RANK	QUALITATIVE DESCRIPTION
76 to 99.9	Above average
25 to 75	Average
0.1 to 24	Below average
Adapted from Sattler, J. M., & Coalson, D. L. (2015). Percentile ranks and suggested qualitative descriptions for scaled scores on the Wechsler subtests. *Assessment of Children WISC-V and WPPSI-IV.*	

Percentile ranks may be best explained through the eyes of a parent and their toddler's development. Any parent who has taken their toddler for routine checkups may have received some version of the following from the physician "[insert name of toddler] is in the 95th percentile for their height and weight." This means that the toddler scored as well as or better than 95% of the toddlers for height and weight with only 5% of toddlers falling below this level. If the toddler was born premature, the parents will be comforted in knowing that the toddler fell within the above average range for their height and weight.

Age and Grade Equivalency

Age equivalents (AEs) and grade equivalents (GEs) are obtained directly from raw scores and reflect the average score for a particular age or grade level (Pearson Assessments, n.d.; Sattler et al., 2016). They can be used to compare the numbers of correct answers that children of different ages and grades obtained. However, AEs and GEs are often misunderstood and misinterpreted by assessment personnel, parents, and school staff.

For example, Madison is a child who is aged 10 years 2 months, yet on a recent reading assessment she earned an AE of 6–9. This means that Madison responded to as many questions as a typical child who is aged 6 years 9 months on this assessment measure. Taking this example further, Madison obtained a GE of 1.7 (first grader in the seventh month of school). The correct interpretation is that Madison responded to as many questions on the assessment measure as a typical child in the first grade seventh month of school. It does not mean that Madison who is a fourth grader is performing as a first grader. For argument's sake, imagine that Madison earned an AE of 12–3 and a GE of 7.2. This means that Madison responded to as many questions on the assessment measure as a child who is 12 years 3 months old and in the seventh grade second month of school. It does not mean that Madison is achieving as a seventh grader.

Check for Understanding

Percentile ranks and age and grade equivalencies are scores that are often misunderstood and should be used with caution.

The Measures of Central Tendency and the Normal Curve

There exists a mathematical model that can describe all possible traits found in the human population. This model is the normal curve. The normal curve is not something that teachers can physically see or touch, but it can help teachers explain students' performance. To understand how the normal curve works, one must first identify the three measures of central tendency: (1) mean,

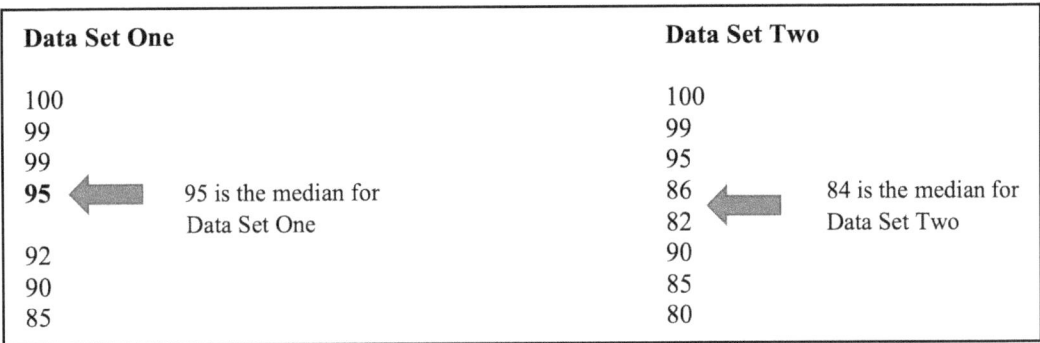

Figure 2-1. Example of calculating the median for an odd and even number set.

Data Set Three	Data Set Four
99	99
89	88
89	88
89	87
75	87
70	72

Figure 2-2. An example of calculating the mode.

(2) median, and (3) mode (Overton, 2016; Wiebe, n.d.). The mean is the arithmetic average of a set of scores. To find the mean, simply add the scores and divide by the number of scores in the set of data. For example, 98 + 88 + 70 = 256. Then divide by the number of scores: 256/3 = 85.

The median is middlemost score in a set of data (Figure 2-1). For an odd numbered data set ($n = 7$) as illustrated in Data Set One, the number that sits directly in the middle is the median (Overton, 2016; Wiebe, n.d.). That is, there are equal numbers above and below the middlemost score. For an even numbered data set ($n = 8$) as illustrated in Data Set Two, the average of the two middle numbers must be calculated to find the median. In this example the two middle numbers are 86 and 82. For Data Set Two, the median is 84.

The mode is the most frequently occurring score in a set of data (Overton, 2016; Wiebe, n.d.) (Figure 2-2). The mode for Data Set Three is 89 since that is the most frequently occurring score in this data set. Data Set Four presents two modes: 88 and 87. This is called a bimodal distribution. Three or more modes represent a multimodal distribution.

APPLYING THE MEASURES OF CENTRAL TENDENCY

Teachers can use the raw scores that students earn on classroom-wide assessments to determine how a specific student is progressing (Overton, 2016). For example, if Madison earned raw scores much lower than her classmates on several reading assessments, this can help the teacher to better understand Madison's abilities and the reading skills she is struggling with. Similarly, if a teacher examines the raw scores from all students who took a class-wide assessment and determines that the raw scores are higher or lower than expected, this can inform the teacher about their teaching practices and aid in the development of specific lessons and activities.

Check for Understanding

The three measures of central tendency are as follows:
Mean—arithmetic average
Median—middlemost score in a data set
Mode—most frequently occurring score in a data set

Normal Distribution

A normal distribution (or curve) is defined as a distribution in which all three measures of central tendency fall exactly at the same point on the curve (Wiebe, n.d.). Figure 2-3 represents a normal distribution where the three measures of central tendency fall at the same point, represented by x.

Standard Deviations and the Normal Curve

The normal curve is also represented by its variability (Wiebe, n.d.). In a normally distributed curve, this variability is defined in segments of the curve equally distant from the midpoint where all three measures of central tendency lie. These segments are known as standard deviations (SD).

The SD of any distribution, which is determined mathematically during the standardization process, will always contain the same share of the population (Wiebe, n.d.). SDs that fall to the left of the midpoint (i.e., mean) are identified by the – sign, and SDs to the right of the mean are identified by the + sign. If the + sign is not represented for the SD that falls to the right of the mean, it is understood that they are positive.

Percentage of Population and the Normal Curve

Ms. Jones, a high school math teacher, says the following to her students on the first day of school: "I know how many of you will make A's, B's, C's, D's, or F's in this class." Understanding the percentage of population and the normal curve is how Ms. Jones is able to make this proclamation to her students.

When considering the population and the normal curve, there are constants. That is, the percentage of population is the same for each standard deviation regardless of whether it is to the left or the right of the mean. Figure 2-4 shows the percentage of population applied to the normal curve.

The percentage of population with scores that fall between +1 SD and the mean is approximately 34%, and the percentage of population that falls between the mean and –1 SD is 34%. Thus, the percentage of population that falls between +1 and –1 SD is 68%. This means that the majority of the population falls between +1 and –1 SD. Therefore, we consider +1 to –1 SD as average performance.

The percentage of population with scores that fall between +1 SD and +2 SD is approximately 13.5% and between –1 SD and –2 SD is also 13.5%. To determine the percent of population between +2 and –2 SD, we must add all four segments of the standard deviations: 34%, 34%, 13.5%, and 13.5%. Thus, the percentage of population between +2 SD and –2 SD is approximately 95%.

The percentage of population with scores that fall between +2 SD and +3 SD is approximately 2.5% and between –2 SD and –3 SD is 2.5% and is why this part of the normal curve is the most extreme. An example of individuals in the school setting who fall between +2 SD and +3 SD are students who fall within the gifted and talented range. Adding 2.5% from both sides to 95%, we have accounted for 99% of the population. Although the normal curve is typically represented up to +3 SD and –3 SD, it continues in both extremes to infinity.

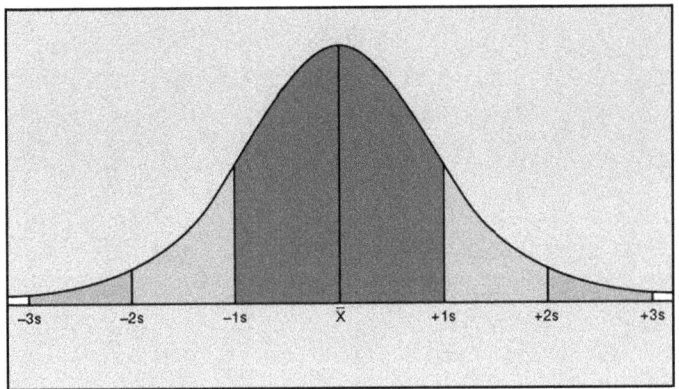

Figure 2-3. Normal distribution of the three measures of central tendency.

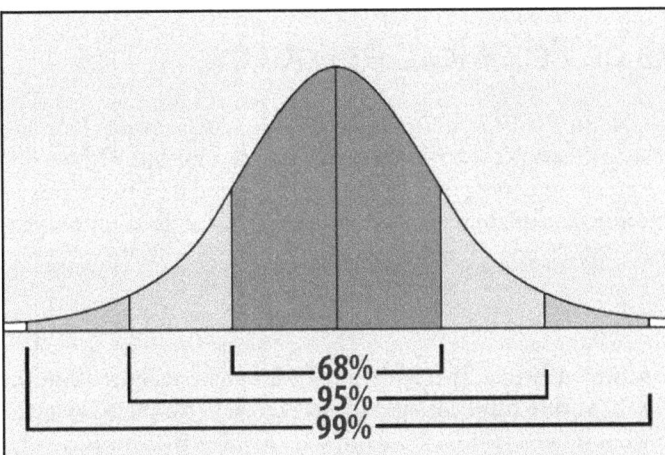

Figure 2-4. Percentage of population applied to the normal curve.

Uses of the Normal Curve

To be able to compare one child's performance to another's, one must know the mean and the standard deviation of the population. Then, one will be able to draw inferences about how the child performs relative to their same age or grade mate peers. Figure 2-5 depicts standard scores applied to the normal curve.

To apply standard scores with a mean of 100 and a standard deviation of 15, simply place 100 at the midpoint (mean) on the normal curve and add or subtract 15 to each side. With +1 to –1 SD being the average range on the normal curve, standard scores that fall between 85 and 115 lie within the average range of functioning. For example, *if Madison earned a standard score of 83 in the area of reading fluency on a dyslexia assessment, this would be interpreted as Madison having below average reading fluency abilities as compared to her same age/grade mate peers.* Similarly, to apply scaled scores with a mean of 10 and a standard deviation of 3, place 10 at the midpoint (mean) on the normal curve and add or subtract 3 to each side. With +1 to –1 SD being the average range on the normal curve, any scaled scores that fall between 7 and 10 would be within the average range of functioning.

CHECK FOR UNDERSTANDING

The normal curve is a theoretical concept that can help explain behaviors in a population. The normal curve is typically applied while interpreting standardized assessment results.

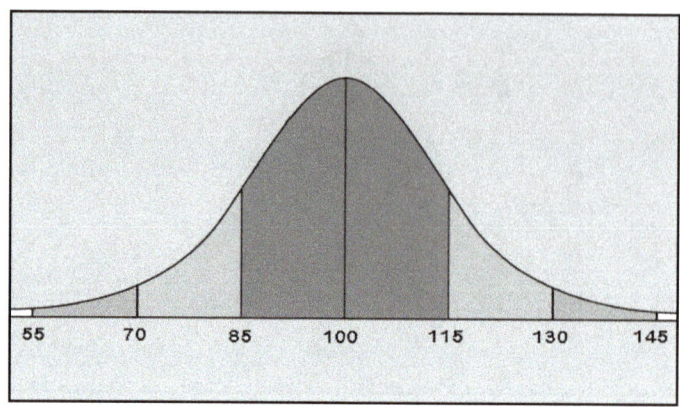

Figure 2-5. Standard scores applied to the normal curve.

TWO TERMS OF TECHNICAL ADEQUACY

It is important that teachers are able to trust the information assessments provide. Teachers rely on assessment data that are consistent and accurate so they can develop meaningful lessons and activities for the students they teach. An understanding of reliability and validity, two terms of technical adequacy, can aid in determining dependability and accuracy and in the decision-making process (Mardell-Czudnowski & Lessen, 1982).

Reliability

Reliability is the consistency of assessment results. That is, the results are consistent over time. In other words, the results are repeatable. To ensure this consistency and repeatability, the assessment must be administered under the same conditions and in the same way. Reliability is measured by the relationship between the assessment administered and another variable. The greater the degree of relationship between the variables, as specified by the correlation coefficient (r), the more reliable the assessment (Overton, 2016).

Correlation

A concept important to reliability is correlation. Correlation is a statistical method used to measure the relationship between two variables (Mukaka, 2012). The two variables may be two administrations of the same test (equivalent form reliability), administration of the same assessment again (test–retest), or administration of the assessment and school achievement.

The correlation coefficient (r) indicates the relationship between the two variables (Overton, 2016). The correlation coefficient is a number between +1.00 and −1.00. A perfect degree of correlation is +1.00 or −1.00. However, perfect correlations are rare. A correlation coefficient of 0 indicates there is no relationship between the variables. The closer the correlation coefficient is to +1.00 or −1.00, the stronger the relationship (Overton, 2016). A correlation coefficient of .70 to .90 (−70 to −90) indicates a high positive (negative correlation). The positive or negative sign does not indicate the strength of the relationship, only the direction of the relationship (Mukaka, 2012). Correlation coefficients of .70 or higher indicate a stronger relationship than correlation coefficients below .70.

> **CHECK FOR UNDERSTANDING**
>
> Correlation coefficients (*r*) indicate the relationships between two variables. An *r* of .70 or higher indicates a stronger relationship than *r* below .70.

FOUR MEASURES OF RELIABILITY

Educators (e.g., teachers, assessment personnel, school administrators) must have confidence the assessment will yield similar results each time it is administered. Included in this discussion are four examples of measuring reliability: interrater, equivalent forms, test–retest, and internal consistency.

Interrater Reliability

The process by which an impartial examiner assesses the phenomenon that has already been evaluated by another examiner is called interrater reliability (Overton, 2016). The test results obtained are then compared to determine how much variability exists between the test scores (Overton, 2016). Specifically, it is the degree to which two or more examiners agree (Lange, 2011). It is important to establish interrater reliability because, by nature, people are subjective, and different people may rate the same experience differently. For example, *Mr. Saunders and Ms. Collins observe Madison orally reading a first-grade reading passage using a consistent error-marking system that they were both trained and proficient in administering. Mr. Saunders and Ms. Collins independently rate Madison's reading errors and then confer with each other on the consistency of their scores.*

Equivalent Forms Reliability

A form of reliability in which different versions of the same assessment are designed to be equivalent to one another is called equivalent forms reliability (Overton, 2016). Simply put, equivalent forms are two versions of the same assessment that measures the same thing (e.g., Form A or Form B). For example, if Mr. Saunders's students are divided into two groups (Group 1 and Group 2), *both groups will take both forms of the assessment.* Group 1 takes Form A, and Group 2 takes Form B. The results from the two groups are compared to one another. If similar results are obtained from both groups, this suggests equivalent reliability (Middleton, 2019a). Another benefit of equivalent forms is that it provides the opportunity to administer both forms of the same assessment in a relatively short time frame, for example, administering at the beginning of the year and end of the year. Having said that, publishers of assessments recommend a specific amount of time that must lapse before administering both forms of the assessment to an individual child (Overton, 2016).

Test–Retest Reliability

The same assessment administered to the same group of individuals at different points in time is called test–retest. It is used when measuring some attribute that is expected to stay the same over time (Middleton, 2019a). Test–retest reliability measures the consistency of test results across time. It is the consistency of scores from repeated test administrations of the same assessment (Salvia et al., 2017). The idea of test–retest reliability is that the attribute being measured is expected to remain consistent over time. If the attribute being measured remains consistent, the readministration of the assessment will yield similar results. The disadvantage of test–retest is the practice effect, meaning students may remember items on the test. The shorter the time period, the greater the impact of the practice effect. The longer the time period, the greater the chance of variation in test scores due to other variables such as interventions, maturity of student, and so on (Overton, 2016).

Internal Consistency

The process of assessing the relationship between multiple items on a single test using one administration of the test is called internal consistency. The advantages of internal consistency include calculating consistency without repeating the test (i.e., test–retest) or involving other researchers (i.e., interrater). Thus, it is a good way to assess reliability when there is only one assessment measure (Middleton, 2019a). There are two methods for calculating internal consistency: split-half reliability, and Kuder–Richardson 20 and coefficient alpha. In split-half reliability, the set of questions is separated into two sets, then the two halves of the test are correlated. Internal consistency can also be calculated statistically using the Kuder–Richardson 20 for items scored only right or wrong or for the coefficient alpha when items are scored pass–fail or when more than one point can be awarded for a response (Salvia et al., 2017).

CHECK FOR UNDERSTANDING

Reliability is the consistency of assessment results. Four measures of reliability include:
- Interrater reliability
- Equivalent forms reliability
- Test–retest reliability
- Internal consistency

CHOOSING RELIABILITY MEASURES

Reliability information can be found in the technical manuals included for all standardized assessment measures. Studying this information can help educational diagnosticians, and/or teachers who have training in administering standardized assessments, make important decisions about which assessment to administer to a specific child. In addition, examiners will want to select a measure that has an adequate degree of reliability with coefficients of .60 or higher and a higher degree of reliability with coefficients of .80 (Overton, 2016). *For example, if Ms. Collins is examining a cognitive processing area such as auditory working memory, a trait that stays relatively consistent over time, she will want to select a measure where reliability has been measured over time. Conversely, if she and Mr. Saunders are interested in observing Madison's oral reading, a behavior that has a greater degree of judgment, they will want to examine the interrater reliability information.*

CHECK FOR UNDERSTANDING

Dr. R. was training to be a pilot. After completing the ground school instruction, she took the written knowledge test as one step of obtaining her private pilot's license. Her score was just below the cutoff point. This disappointed Dr. R., so she met with her flight instructor and spent the entire next month studying and reviewing the material covered in ground school. At the end of the month, she took a different form of the same test. This time she passed with flying colors.

Was Dr. R. reliably evaluated? Yes, she was reliably evaluated. Although Dr. R. took two versions of the same test (one she failed and one she passed), she met with her flight instructor and studied the material in between the testing sessions so that she would be more prepared the second time she took the written exam.

Constructs Related to Reliability

In all standardized assessments, there is a basic assumption that error exists (Overton, 2016). The standard error of measurement (SEM), obtained and true scores, and confidence intervals (CI) represent aspects of reliability.

Standard Error of Measurement

The SEM represents the amount of error in an assessment measure (Salvia et al., 2017). It is used by examiners as a way to measure the precision of assessment measures and it also helps in interpreting results of the assessment. Each assessment measure provides a different SEM. This statistic can be found in the technical manuals of the assessment measure (Venn, 2014).

All assessments contain some measure of variability or error, but some assessment measures contain more error than others (Venn, 2014). That said, error should be considered at all points during the assessment process: administering, scoring, and interpreting the results (Overton, 2016).

Obtained and True Scores

Salient to the SEM is the concept of obtained scores and true scores. An obtained score is the number of points obtained by an examinee on the assessment. These scores can be influenced by several variables such as testing environment, ambiguous items, and a child's emotional state. When these factors are present the examiner cannot assume that the scores obtained are an accurate measure of the child's true abilities (Overton, 2016).

"A true score represents that part of an examinee's observed score uninfluenced by random events" (Harvill, 1991, p. 33). Another way to think of a true score is the score a child would earn if the entire domain of items were evaluated, such as mathematical computations. However, it is impossible to assess an entire domain at any given time. A true score is a hypothetical value and is actually never known (Salvia et al., 2017). Thus, a range of scores based on the obtained score are calculated.

Confidence Intervals

CI use the SEM around the obtained standard score to create a range of scores that increases the confidence that the examinee's true score falls within an identified range. Commonly available CIs are 68%, 90%, and 95%. A CI of 68% means the examiner is 68% confident that the score would fall within a specified range if the assessment were administered under the same conditions. This is also true for 90% and 95% confidence. The higher the degree of confidence, the greater the degree the examiner has that the score will fall within the specified range (Statewide Lead: Evaluation, 2008). *For example, Madison was administered the* Woodcock-Johnson IV Tests of Achievement *(Schrank et al., 2014). On Letter-Word Identification, a subtest that measures basic reading skills, Madison earned a standard score of 66 with 90% confidence that the true score ranges between 62 and 71. A standard score of 66 is in the very low range of functioning and falls 2 SDs below the mean. This means that Madison's basic reading skills are well below her same-age classmates and grade level, necessitating specific and immediate reading interventions.*

Depending on the purpose, examiners should select different CIs. If the purpose is to look for strengths and weaknesses, then a lower CI might be used (i.e., 68%). However, if the purpose is to be used in a high-stakes decision, such as eligibility for special education services, a higher CI (i.e., 90% or 95%) should be selected (Statewide Lead: Evaluation, 2008) since the higher the degree of confidence, the more likely the score will fall within the range if the child is evaluated again. Table 2-3 describes the constructs related to reliability.

TABLE 2-3. CONSTRUCTS RELATED TO RELIABILITY

CONSTRUCT	DESCRIPTION
Correlation coefficient	The greater the degree of relationship between the variables, as specified by the correlation coefficient (r), the more reliable the assessment (Overton, 2016)
Standard error of measurement	Represents the amount of error in an assessment measure (Salvia et al., 2017)
Confidence interval	Uses the standard error of measurement around the obtained standard score to create a range of scores that increases the confidence that the examinee's true score falls within an identified range (Statewide Lead: Evaluation, 2008)

Validity

Validity is the accuracy of the assessment. It is considered the most important of the terms of technical adequacy. Validity represents the degree to which an assessment measures what it claims to measure (Venn, 2014). In other words, does it do what it is supposed to do? The three types of validity are content, criterion-related, and construct.

Content Validity

Content validity refers to how well an assessment measure represents the domain or learning area that is being evaluated. An assessment measure with good content validity will include a representative sample of the behavior in the domain or learning area (Venn, 2014). It must cover all relevant parts of the domain or learning area it is intending to measure (Middleton, 2019b). For example, a reading fluency measure with good content validity will include items that address the broad range of reading fluency skills. Users of the assessment measure can evaluate content validity by reviewing the technical manuals and the quality and relevance of the items that are included (Venn, 2014).

Criterion-Related Validity

Criterion-related validity is the relationship between the results of the assessment measure and results of a comparable measure. There are two main types of criterion-related validity: concurrent validity and predictive validity. Concurrent validity and predictive validity are distinguished by aspects of time (Overton, 2016).

Concurrent Validity

Concurrent validity involves comparing scores from a new assessment measure with scores from a similar measure that includes the same content (Venn, 2014). The assessment measure is administered, and then within a relatively short time frame a similar type of assessment measure is administered (Overton, 2016). Results producing highly positive correlations between the two assessment measures indicate good validity.

Predictive Validity

Predictive validity refers to how effective a test is in predicting future performance (Salvia et al., 2017). Examples of predictive validity include screeners of alphabetic principle to predict a child's ability to read. Other examples include college entrance exams such as the *American College Testing* (ACT) to predict future success in college.

Construct Validity

Construct validity evaluates whether the assessment measure actually measures the trait or characteristic it was intended to measure (Salvia et al., 2017). Examples of constructs include intelligence, vocabulary, expressive and receptive language skills, and mathematical reasoning. Construct validity is more abstract than the other types of validity. A characteristic of construct validity includes a systematic review of the research and is based on accumulation of evidence (Venn, 2014). Some experts claim that construct validity is established as research evidence accumulates (Salvia et al., 2017).

CHECK FOR UNDERSTANDING

Validity is the accuracy of assessment results and is the more important of the two terms of technical adequacy. Validity represents the degree to which an assessment measures what it claims to measure. Three examples of validity include:
- Content validity
- Criterion-related validity, which includes concurrent and predictive validity
- Construct validity

RELIABILITY VERSUS VALIDITY

A standardized assessment may be reliable and produce consistent results time after time, but it does not guarantee that the trait being evaluated is accurate. An assessment may be reliable, but it may not be valid. Therefore, it is critical that standardized assessments undergo rigorous research in both reliability and validity and that they are used for the purposes for which they were intended (Overton, 2016).

SUMMARY

Knowledge of the basic concepts of measurement such as the different types of scores (Table 2-4), reliability and validity, and application of the normal curve helps teachers develop a deeper understanding of the educational performance of the children in their classroom. With this information, teachers are able to target individual academic skills by designing lessons and activities that address a child's unique strengths and weaknesses. Although many teachers do not receive training in standardized assessment procedures, it is still important that they possess a basic understanding of the scores that are obtained and their meaning so that they can work collaboratively with the assessment professional in designing targeted interventions. In conclusion, the goal of this chapter was to explain the basic concepts of measurement and apply these concepts in a case study scenario.

Table 2-4. Summary of Scores

NAME	DESCRIPTION
Raw score	Represents the number of items correct
Scaled score	Derived score—mean of 10 and standard deviation of 3
Standard score	Derived score—mean of 100 and standard deviation of 15
Percentile rank	Score that expresses the percentage of students who scored as well as or lower than a given student's score
Age equivalent	Reflects the average score for a particular age level
Grade equivalent	Reflects the average score for a particular grade level
Obtained score	The number of points obtained by an examinee on the assessment
Standard error of measurement	Represents the amount of error in an assessment measure
True score	The score that a child would earn if the entire domain of items were evaluated
Confidence interval	Uses the standard error of measurement around the obtained standard score to create a range of scores that increases the confidence that the examinee's true score falls within an identified range

Case Study Wrap-Up

Madison was evaluated for a specific learning disability in reading by Ms. Collins using standardized reading assessments that have good evidence of reliability and validity. During the evaluation, Ms. Collins and Mr. Saunders also evaluated Madison's oral reading behavior by using a classroom reading measure consisting of a standard error-marking system that they both were trained on and were proficient in administering. Following are excerpts of the interpretation from the Kaufman Test of Educational Achievement, Third Edition (KTEA-3; Kaufman & Kaufman, 2014), a standardized achievement test, that was administered as part of the evaluation.

The Reading Composite consists of two subtests: Letter and Word Recognition and Reading Comprehension. Madison obtained a standard score of 73, which is within the below average range of functioning. There is a 95% chance that the true score actually ranges between 67 and 79.

<u>Letter and Word Recognition</u>: The student identifies letters and pronounces words of gradually increasing difficulty within an acceptable time (i.e., 3 seconds or less). Most words on this subtest are irregular to ensure that the subtest measures word recognition (reading vocabulary) more than decoding ability. On this subtest Madison obtained a standard score of 73 with 95% confidence that the true score ranges between 67 and 79. A standard score of 73 is in the below average range of functioning. On this index and throughout each of the reading subtests, when Madison did not know a word, she would substitute a word familiar to her for the unknown word. Further, Madison does not appear to have strategies to read unknown words.

<u>Reading Comprehension</u>: The student reads passages of increasing difficulty and answers literal or inferential questions about them. On this subtest Madison obtained a standard score of 69 with 95% confidence the true scores range between 57 and 81. A standard score of 69 is within the low range of performance. Madison was administered Item Set C. Madison was unable to read more than 90% of the words in the first passage given in item Set E, which is the set to be administered for children in Grades 4 to 5. Thus, the examiner engaged the reverse rules twice before Madison was able to read a passage

that was not at her frustration level. Madison read the passages aloud. Her pace of reading was laborious, and her prosody was limited. Madison would try to figure out unknown words by using first letter substitution. When this method did not work, she skipped unfamiliar words.

Madison's scores on the KTEA-3 consistently fell at or below the −2 SD on the bell curve with a percentile rank below the 16th percentile. In addition, Madison's oral reading rate also indicates that she is struggling to read words orally when compared to her classmates. Based on the multiple sources of information collected during the evaluation, which included norm-referenced testing, oral reading assessments, observations, interviews, and classroom work samples, Ms. Collins determined Madison met the eligibility criteria as a child with a specific learning disability in the area of basic reading and reading fluency.

CHAPTER REVIEW

1. Discuss the similarities and differences of standardized assessments and classroom assessments.
2. Using the bell curve, plot the percentage of population, standard scores, and scaled scores for ±1 SD, ±2 SD, and ±3 SD.
3. Mr. Saunders administered Form A of a spelling test to Madison. The next week, Mr. Saunders administered Form B of the same spelling test to Madison. Madison, who did not study for either spelling test, failed Form A but passed Form B. Was Madison reliably evaluated? Why or why not?

REFERENCES

Harvill, L. M. (1991). An NCME instructional module on standard error of measurement. *Educational Measurement: Issues and Practice, 10*(2), 33–41. https://doi.org/10.1111/j.1745-3992.1991.tb00195.x

Kaufman, A. S., & Kaufman, N. L. (2014). *Kaufman Test of Educational Achievement* (3rd ed.). NCS Pearson.

Lange, R. T. (2011). Inter-rater reliability. In J. S. Kreutzer, J. DeLuca, & B. Caplan (Eds.), *Encyclopedia of clinical neuropsychology*. Springer. https://doi.org/10.1007/978-0-387-79948-3_1203

Mardell-Czudnowski, C. D., & Lessen, E. I. (1982). Technical adequacy of assessment instruments: Can we agree? *Diagnostique, 7*(4), 189–202. https://doi.org/10.1177/073724778200700402

Middleton, F. (2019a). *Types of reliability and how to measure them.* https://www.scribbr.com/methodology/types-of-reliability

Middleton, F. (2019b). *The four types of validity.* https://www.scribbr.com/methodology/types-of-validity

Mukaka, M. M. (2012). Statistics corner: A guide to appropriate use of correlation coefficient in medical research. *Malawi Medical Journal: The Journal of Medical Association of Malawi, 24*(3), 69–71. https://www.ncbi.nlm.nih.gov/pmc/articles/PMC3576830/

Overton, T. (2016). *Assessing learners with special needs: An applied approach* (8th ed.). Merrill Pearson.

Pearson Assessments. (n.d.). *Interpretation problems of age and grade equivalents.* https://www.pearsonassessments.com/campaign/interpretation-problems-of-age-and-grade-equivalents.html

Popham, W. J. (1999). Why standardized tests don't measure educational quality. *Educational Leadership, 56*(6), 8–15.

Salvia, J., Ysseldyke, J. E., & Witmer, S. (2017). *Assessment in special and inclusive education* (13th ed.). Cengage Learning.

Sattler, J. M., Dumont, R., & Coalson, D. L. (2015). *Assessment of children: WISC-V and WPPSI-IV.* Percentile Ranks and Suggested Qualitative Descriptions for Scaled Scores on the Wechsler Subtests.

Sattler, J. M., Dumont, R., & Coalson, D. L. (2016). *Assessment of children: WISC-V and WPPSI-IV.* Jerome M. Sattler Publisher. www.sattlerpublisher.com

Schrank, F. A., Mather, N., & McGrew, K. S. (2014). *Woodcock-Johnson IV Tests of Achievement.* Riverside.

Statewide Lead: Evaluation. (2008). *Building the bridge between full individual evaluations (FIEs) and instruction.* TX Education Service Centers, Region 9, 11, 14, 16, & 18.

Venn, J. J. (2014). *Assessing students with special needs* (5th ed.). Pearson.

Wiebe, M. (n.d.). *By the numbers* [PowerPoint slides]. Texas Woman's University.

Legal Issues in Assessment

CHAPTER OBJECTIVES

- Highlight a specific case study involving legal issues in assessment.
- Describe and discuss important court cases involving assessment.
- Define the six principles of the Individuals with Disabilities Education Improvement Act.

KEY TERMS

- **appropriate evaluation:** A student must receive an evaluation in their native language by a trained and knowledgeable person. The evaluation should include a variety of tools and strategies to obtain academic, developmental, and functional information to determine whether or not the student qualifies as having a disability according to the definition of the Individuals with Disabilities Education Act.
- *de facto*: In law and government, *de facto*, or "in fact," is used to describe practices that occur in reality but are not officially recognized by laws. *De facto* generally refers to what occurs in practice.
- *de jure*: The term *de jure*, or "by law," is used to refer to things that occur according to the law.
- *de minimis*: The term *de minimis* is Latin for more than trivial or minor, a very low standard.
- **free appropriate public education (FAPE):** Every student with a disability is entitled to an appropriate public education at no cost to the parents or guardian.
- **Individualized Education Program (IEP):** A written statement based on the *individual* needs of each student with a disability, taking into account the child's present levels of academic achievement and functional performance. The IEP is developed, reviewed, and revised at least one time per year by a team which includes educators, parents, needed experts, and the student.
- **Individuals with Disabilities Education Act (IDEA):** The IDEA is a law designed to ensure all eligible students with disabilities have a free appropriate public education and special education and related services. IDEA provides rights and protections to individuals with disabilities and governs how public agencies and states provide early intervention, special education, and related services to eligible infants, toddlers, children, and youth with disabilities from birth through 21 years of age.
- **least restrictive environment (LRE):** Students with disabilities are required to be educated with their nondisabled peers to the maximum extent appropriate for the student, which is considered their LRE.
- **manifestation determination:** When school officials are seeking a change of placement, suspension, or expulsion in excess of 10 school days, a review of the student's misconduct must take place within 10 days to determine the relationship between the student's misconduct and their disability.
- **parent participation:** The Individuals with Disabilities Education Act clearly indicates schools need to make sure parents have the opportunity to be actively involved in every step of the special education process.
- **procedural safeguards:** Safeguards were established to protect the rights of children with disabilities and their parents or guardians.

KEY ABBREVIATIONS

- FAPE: free appropriate public education
- IDEA: Individuals with Disabilities Education Act
- IEP: Individualized Education Program
- LRE: least restrictive environment

CASE STUDY

Jose is a fifth grader who recently moved to the area and currently attends R. M. Waters Elementary, a Title I school in a rural area. He is able to have conversations with his classmates during lunch but is struggling academically. Jose's teacher, Mrs. Cates, has looked at his academic records to learn more about Jose and his academic abilities. She is interested in learning if he is struggling academically because of his limited English or if he has greater needs that may need to be addressed through an evaluation to determine if he qualifies for special education services.

Children and youth with disabilities have historically received unequal treatment in the public school system (Forte Law Group, n.d.). The unwavering efforts of parents and advocacy groups within the courts and legislatures of the United States paved the way for educational rights of children and youth with disabilities (Yell, 2019). The federal government is designed to protect the rights and liberties of the people and works to attain certain ends for the common good while concurrently sharing power and authority with the states. Although education is governed by the laws of each state, federal involvement has played an important part in the progress and growth of education. The development of the law is cyclical, and through interactions of the different sources of law (constitutional, legislative, regulatory, and case law), we see how special education law evolves.

Actions by the courts (e.g., Pennsylvania Association of Retarded Citizens v. Commonwealth of Pennsylvania [1972]) acknowledged the rights of individuals with disabilities to have special education services under the 14th Amendment to the Constitution (Yell, 2019). To ensure rights of children and youth with disabilities, Congress responds to litigation by passing legislation. Regulations were then disseminated to implement and enforce the law by the Department of Health, Education, and Welfare. Eventually, in response to the federal law, all 50 states passed laws and created regulations at the state level to ensure the delivery of special education to children who qualified. Some litigation has led to more legislation, which has then led to more litigation to interpret the legislation. The purpose of this chapter is to highlight important court cases pertaining to assessment issues and to delineate special education legislation intended to support and protect individuals with disabilities.

Court Cases

In this section, we highlight landmark court cases that paved the way for the rights and protections of children and youth with disabilities. Parents and advocacy groups began their own civil rights movement in providing equal educational opportunities to children and youth with disabilities by using the U.S. federal court system (Forte Law Group, n.d.). The early cases we are discussing reflect how the rights of individuals with disabilities not only emerged but also lead to free appropriate public education (FAPE) and the enactment of federal laws (e.g., Individuals with Disabilities Education Act [IDEA]). Because this book is focused on assessment and special education, it is important to include court cases involving assessment issues for students with disabilities. All the court cases discussed continue to have an impact on students with disabilities and how they are treated in the public school system. Table 3-1 provides information about each court case.

Landmark Court Cases

Brown v. Board of Education (1954, 1955)

Brown v. Board of Education (1954) is considered a landmark case because it was a significant victory for the civil rights movement and resulted in extensive changes in schools' policies and approaches to individuals with disabilities in the school system (Yell, 2019). Originally, *Brown v. Board of Education* was five separate cases heard by the U.S. Supreme Court regarding the issue of segregation in public schools (United States Courts, n.d.). Although the facts of each case were different, the central issue in each case involved the constitutionality of state-sponsored segregation in the public schools. The cases were handled by Chief Justice Thurgood Marshall and the NAACP Legal

TABLE 3-1. COURT CASES AND LEGISLATION

DATE	COURT CASE OR LEGISLATION	DESCRIPTION
1954	Brown v. Board of Education	• Declared segregation in public schools as unconstitutional.
1965	Elementary and Secondary Education Act	• Federal funding was given to states to help educate students and was designed to fight poverty.
1967	Hobson v. Hansen	• Ruled a tracking system used to determine a student's academic ability should be eliminated from the school because it was unconstitutional and violated equal protection laws under the 14th Amendment. The tracking system was found to be based on status and race rather than ability.
1970	Education of the Handicapped Act	• Combined and increased federal grant programs. • Provided funding to institutions of higher education. • Provided funds to develop regional resource centers.
1970	Diana v. State Board of Education	• Ruled that students should be assessed for special education eligibility in their primary language. States developed and standardized IQ tests in other languages.
1972	PARC v. Commonwealth of Pennsylvania	• Citing Brown, the state of Pennsylvania was required to provide students with mental retardation a FAPE.
1972	Mills v. Board of Education of the District of Columbia	• Citing Brown, the D.C. Board of Education could not prohibit students with disabilities from receiving an education.
1975	Education for All Handicapped Children Act	• Provided funding to states who agreed to educate students with disabilities as required in EAHCA. • Established rights of students with disabilities to a FAPE in the student's LRE. • Outlined procedural safeguards. • Required schools to develop an appropriate IEP.
1979	Larry P. v. Riles	• School district was prohibited from using IQ tests to identify or place Black students in special classes for the educable mentally retarded.
1981	Luke S. & Han S. v. Nix et al.	• The state was not evaluating students for special education services within the 60-day time limit. The State Department of Education ruled the state had to make a plan to be in compliance within 3 years.

(continued)

TABLE 3-1 (CONTINUED). COURT CASES AND LEGISLATION

DATE	COURT CASE OR LEGISLATION	DESCRIPTION
1982	*Board of Education of the Hendrick Hudson Central School District v. Rowley*	• The Court found the "basic floor of opportunity" provided by EHA entails access to specialized instruction and related services individually created to give educational benefit to the student. The *Rowley* decision explained that children and youth with disabilities are allowed "access" to an education that provided "educational benefit," and a school district is not required to "maximize" every student with a disability's potential.
1988	*Honig v. Doe*	• The Court ruled a student could not be removed from their school if their inappropriate behaviors were a result of the student's disability. This is considered a landmark decision because of what is now known as the "10-day rule." The review is known as manifestation determination.
1988	*Timothy W. v. Rochester, New Hampshire, School District*	• The judges cited the passage of EAHCA (1975) stating the law had clear intentions in that all children, including "handicapped children," are provided a public education unconditionally and without exception.
1990	Individuals with Disabilities Education Act	• EAHCA was renamed IDEA. • Autism and traumatic brain injury were added to the list of disability categories. • Added an individualized transition plan in a student's IEP at the age of 16 or older requirement. • Changed the language of the law to "person first" and changed "handicap" to "disability."
1997	Individuals with Disabilities Education Act Amendments	• Added new disciplinary provisions and new IEP contents. • Changed the IEP team. • Restructured the organization of the law. • Added a requirement for states to provide mediation to parents before a due process hearing.
2004	Individuals with Disabilities Education Improvement Act	• Eliminated the use of the "wait to fail" discrepancy model to determine eligibility for a learning disability. • Encouraged the use of response to intervention when determining if a student has a learning disability. • Defined a highly qualified special education teacher and required special education teachers be certified in special education. • Removed the requirement of short-term objectives in a student's IEP, except for students with severe disabilities.
2017	*Endrew F. v. Douglas County School District*	• Required a new standard for FAPE when determining educational benefit. IEPs must be designed to provide measurable benefit given the student's capabilities.

Defense and Education Fund. The U.S. District Court that heard the cases acknowledged some of the plaintiffs' claims but ruled in favor of the school boards; in turn, the plaintiffs appealed to the U.S. Supreme Court.

When the cases went before the Supreme Court in 1952, all five cases were consolidated under the name *Brown v. Board of Education* (United States Courts, n.d.). Thurgood Marshall argued the cases, and although he raised several legal issues on appeal, the most common issue was that having separate school systems for White and Black students was fundamentally unequal, thus in violation of the "equal protection clause" under the 14th Amendment to the U.S. Constitution. Additionally, Marshall argued segregated schools were inclined to make Black children feel lesser than White children, which he argued should not be legally allowed.

The Supreme Court justices were divided over the issues raised by Marshall, and while most wanted to declare segregation unconstitutional in the public schools, they had differing reasons for doing so and were unable to come to a solution by the end of the Court's 1952–1953 term. The Court decided to rehear the case in December 1953, and Chief Justice Warren was able to bring all the justices together to support a unanimous decision. On May 14, 1954, they declared segregation in public schools unconstitutional, stating separate educational settings are inherently unequal, and the field of public education has no place for the doctrine of separate but equal. The Supreme Court did not immediately direct schools with how to proceed with desegregation, but after hearing more cases regarding desegregation, the justices handed down a plan on May 31, 1955, for how the public schools needed to proceed with "all deliberate speed."

Brown v. Board of Education became the catalyst for all efforts to ensure educational rights for individuals with disabilities (Yell, 2019). If segregation by race is now considered a denial of education opportunity, then total exclusion of children and youth with disabilities is also a denial of equal educational opportunity. There were a series of court cases brought on behalf of individuals with disabilities by advocates, families, and those with disabilities based on *Brown* where they challenged and pursued redress for similar inequities.

Pennsylvania Association for Retarded Children v. Commonwealth of Pennsylvania (1972) and Mills v. Board of Education of the District of Columbia (1972)

Pennsylvania Association for Retarded Children (PARC) and *Mills* are considered seminal Federal District Court cases and landmark decisions applying the concept of equal opportunity for children and youth with disabilities based on the *Brown* decision (Yell, 2019). In both cases, action was brought against state policies and statutes excluding students with disabilities.

In January 1971, a class action suit was brought against the Commonwealth of Pennsylvania by the PARC and parents of 13 individual "retarded" children on behalf of all "mentally retarded" individuals between the ages of 6 and 21 years who were being excluded from publicly supported education (JUSTIA US Law, 2022). The suit named 13 individual school districts throughout the Commonwealth. The plaintiffs argued that the state was ignoring or delaying its constitutional obligations to provide a public education for the students, thus violating the state statute as well as the rights of the students under the 14th Amendment of the U.S. Constitution for equal protection.

Four critical points were established. First, although the children had mental retardation, they were capable of benefiting from a program of education and training (Yell, 2019). Second, education for children cannot be defined only as the delivery of academic experiences. Third, the state could not deny students with mental retardation access to a free public education because the Commonwealth of Pennsylvania had assumed responsibility for providing a free public education to all children. And fourth, it was determined that the sooner students with mental retardation were provided an education, the greater the amount of learning that could be predicted. *PARC* was resolved with a consent agreement approved by the District Court for the Eastern District of Pennsylvania (Forte Law Group, n.d.). The consent agreement specified not only that all children with mental retardation between the ages of 6 and 21 years must be provided a free public education but also that the program must be most like programs provided to students without disabilities (Yell, 2019).

Mills v. Board of Education (1972) occurred soon after the *PARC* decision (Yell, 2019). The class-action suit against the District of Columbia's Board of Education was filed on behalf of all out-of-school students with disabilities in the Federal District Court for the District of Columbia, stating students were inappropriately excluded from school without due process of law. Parents and guardians of seven children with various disabilities brought the action. The seven children were certified as a class and thereby represented more than 18,000 students who were denied or excluded from a public education in Washington, D.C. Citing the *Brown* case, the court held that excluding students with disabilities was also unconstitutional and mandated the board provide all students with disabilities a publicly supported education. The district was also ordered to provide due process safeguards and outlined due process procedures for labeling, placement, and exclusion of children with disabilities. The safeguards are the framework for the due process element of the Education for All Handicapped Children Act (EAHCA) and include:

- The right to a hearing with representation, a record, and an impartial hearing officer
- The right to appeal
- The right to access records
- The requirement of written notice at all stages of the process

Honig v. Doe (1988)

Honig v. Doe (1988) involved two students with disabilities in the San Francisco Unified School District (SFUSD; Steketee, 2022). John Doe, a 17-year-old who qualified under EAHCA (now IDEA) as a student with an emotional disturbance, had difficulty controlling his anger and impulses. In November 1980, he choked a student who was "taunting" him and kicked out a window as he was being taken to the principal's office. Although he was initially suspended for 5 days, the SFUSD Student Placement Committee contacted John Doe's mother and recommended he be expelled, stating his suspension would continue until the expulsion process was complete. Doe filed suit under the EAHCA, alleging their disciplinary actions were in violation of the so-called "stay-put" provision of the act and his rights were violated by the educators when he was indefinitely suspended. Under the provision, students with disabilities must stay in their current educational placement during any review proceedings unless otherwise agreed upon by the family and educational officials. The superintendent, Bill Honig, was named as the respondent in the suit. Doe's request for a preliminary injunction, ordering the school officials allow him to return to his existing placement pending review of his Individualized Educational Program (IEP), was granted by the Federal District Court.

"Jack Smith" was the second student in the case who also qualified under EAHCA as a student with an emotional disturbance (Steketee, 2022). Typically, Smith reacted to stress by becoming aggressive and verbally hostile, which escalated when he was in middle school. In November 1980, much like John Doe, Smith was suspended for 5 days, but the SFUSD Student Placement Committee recommended Smith be expelled, and the suspension continued until the proceedings were complete. Although Smith began to be homeschooled, after hearing about Doe's case, Smith opposed the actions of the school and joined in Doe's suit. It was determined by the District Court that SFUSD officials could not suspend any students with disabilities for more than 5 days when their misconduct was a result of their disability. The Court ordered the state to directly provide services to students if the local educational agency failed to do so. The Ninth Circuit Court of Appeals confirmed the orders with a slight modification allowing suspensions of more than 10 days.

Honig sought review by the U.S. Supreme Court, and on November 9, 1987, the cause was argued before the Court. Although it decided the case was moot regarding Doe because he was 21 years old and was no longer eligible under EAHCA, Smith still met eligibility under EAHCA. The Supreme Court largely upheld the Ninth Circuit decision but ruled suspensions of more than 10 days were not permissible (Steketee, 2022).

The *Honig* case is considered a landmark decision because of what is now known as the 10-day rule (Forte Law Group, n.d.). Additionally, the Court ruled a student could not be removed from their school if the inappropriate behaviors were a result of the student's disability. Now, under IDEA (2004), a student can be expelled for up to 10 days for disciplinary infractions, and for behaviors involving drugs or weapons, students can be expelled for up to 45 days. However, if the school is seeking an alternative placement, suspension, or expulsion of the student more than 10 days, an IEP meeting must take place to review the contributing relationship between the student's disability and behaviors. This type of IEP meeting is now known as a manifestation determination review.

> **CHECK FOR UNDERSTANDING**
>
> Many of the preceding cases are considered landmark cases because they paved the way for students with disabilities to be included in school. The cases also paved the way for the legislation we have today to ensure students with disabilities have equal rights to a FAPE in their LRE.

COURT CASES INVOLVING ASSESSMENT ISSUES

Hobson v. Hansen (1967)

Prior to the case of *Hobson v. Hansen* (1967) was *Brown v. Board of Education* (1954), which ruled it is unconstitutional to segregate a school based on race (Boss, n.d.). The case allowed for the integration of students of color in schools and led to many school reforms. However, some schools began ability grouping, or tracking, which allowed them to avoid desegregation through within-school segregation. In 1956, the District of Columbia school system adopted a track system where students were grouped into separate tracks based on their ability (JUSTIA US Law, 2020a). The three tracks for elementary through junior high school (middle school) students included basic or special academics ("mentally disabled" students), general (average to above average students), and honors (gifted students). A fourth track for high school students included the regular track (college preparation) for the above average students. Each track consisted of educational content ranging from very basic to very advanced. Carl Hansen, the superintendent of the District of Columbia school system, said the purpose of the track system was to give students the opportunity to achieve to their maximum academic potential.

A civil rights activist, Julius Hobson, filed a class action lawsuit against the District of Columbia Board of Education and superintendent Carl Hansen (Boss, n.d.). Hobson contended the track system discriminated against students based on their race and socioeconomic status because they were being disproportionately assigned to the lower ability tracks, hence denied equal educational opportunities. The court ruled in favor of Hobson.

Circuit Judge J. Skelly Wright ruled in favor of Hobson, citing *Bolling v. Sharpe* (1954), which is considered a companion case to *Brown v. Board of Education* (JUSTIA US Law, 2020a). Specifically, *de jure* segregation was established as being unconstitutional in *Bolling* where the Supreme Court found the District of Columbia's racially segregated public school system violated the Fifth Amendment due process clause. In *Hobson v. Hansen,* Judge Wright addressed questions of *de facto* segregation in the District of Columbia public schools based on trends where legal desegregation survived. Judge Wright ruled the tracking system should be eliminated from the school because it was unconstitutional and violated equal protection laws under the 14th Amendment. He found the track system was not based on ability, but rather status and race, because the tests were culturally biased and standardized on a White, middle-class sample. Furthermore, it was determined that the educational opportunities for students in the lower tracks were inferior and significantly different. However, in and of itself, ability grouping was not found to be unconstitutional, and the intention of Hansen and the Board of Education could not be proven. In 1969, Hansen and a member of the Board of Education filed an appeal, but it was denied (Boss, n.d.).

Diana v. State Board of Education (1970)

The *Hobson v. Hansen* (1967) case led up to the case of *Diana v. California State Board of Education* (1970; Boss, n.d.). *Diana v. California State Board of Education* (1970) involved Diana and eight other Spanish-speaking students being assessed in English for intellectual disability and inappropriately placed in special education (Special Education Rights & Responsibilities [SERR], 2020b). Prior to the case, English was the only language used to assess students for an intellectual disability (Lilljevall, n.d.). The assessment questions were heavily dependent on verbal responses. Additionally, test questions were found to be culturally biased; students not raised in a White middle-class family had a difficult time being successful when answering assessment questions, leading schools to inaccurately place students in special education. All nine students were given an English-only IQ test to determine placement in special education. The case challenged the English-only IQ test and wanted the students to be retested in their primary language to determine special education placement eligibility.

The case was filed in 1969 and settled out of court in 1970 (SERR, 2020b) in favor of Diana (Lilljevall, n.d.). All the students were reassessed in their primary language. For the state of California, the court ruled all future students must be assessed for special education in their primary language or a nonverbal assessment needed to be used. The settlement also required the California Board of Education to monitor schools for and correct racial imbalances, annually collect data, and use Latino representatives from the community during audit in school districts (SERR, 2020b). The ruling also applied to other "Mexican American" students already placed in special education as a student with an intellectual disability (Lilljevall, n.d.). Students were required to be reassessed in their primary language or given a nonverbal assessment.

At the time of the case, Latinos were overrepresented in classes for students with intellectual disabilities. Specifically, in 1967, Latinos represented 26% of the total statewide population of students with intellectual disabilities yet only represented 14% of the statewide school-age population (SERR, 2020b). Following the *Diana* ruling, the California Department of Education was required to comply with the court order to ensure Spanish-speaking students were proportionately represented (Lilljevall, n.d.). Because students must be assessed in their primary language, states developed and standardized IQ tests that could be administered in other languages. *Diana* ensured no child would be placed in special education due only to their limited English (SERR, 2020b).

From our case study example, it is important to remember the Diana case and not let Jose's limited English be the determining factor in him qualifying for special education services. Additionally, if Mrs. Cates and the multidisciplinary team determine Jose needs to be evaluated for special education, Jose needs to be assessed in his native language of Spanish.

Larry P. v. Riles (1979)

The *Hobson v. Hansen* (1967) case also led up to the case of *Larry P. v. Riles* (1979; Boss, n.d.). The case of *Larry P. v. Riles* was filed in 1971 when five African American students in San Francisco Unified School District were placed in special education and put in classes for "educable mentally retarded" (EMR; SERR, 2020a). The plaintiffs argued that the standardized individual intelligence (IQ) tests in California used for placement decisions were racially biased and discriminatory and allegedly resulted in the misplacement of Black students in special education (JUSTIA US Law, 2020b). Furthermore, placement in EMR classes, they contended, not only created a stigma but provided inadequate education and failed to develop skills needed to be successful members of society. According to the case, 25% of the population enrolled in EMR classes were Black, yet Black children only represented 10% of the general student population in California. The *Hobson v. Hansen* (1967) case, being the first to examine standardized test validity, became the mechanism driving the use of IQ test scores. For some schools the IQ test scores were "proof" that African Americans were inferior to White Americans, causing some schools to continue segregation (Scheller, n. d.).

The court ruled in favor of the plaintiffs, and the school district was prohibited from using IQ tests to identify or place Black students in special classes for the educable mentally retarded (JUSTIA US Law, 2020b). The court stated the district's use of standardized IQ tests was in violation of Title VI of the Civil Rights Act of 1964, the Rehabilitation Act of 1973, and the EAHCA of 1975 because the tests were racially and culturally biased, discriminatorily impacting Black children and resulting in a large overrepresentation of Black children in the special EMR classes. Additionally, the court ruled the defendants' conduct violated state and federal constitutional guarantees for equal protection of the laws. The school district appealed the ruling, but the Court upheld the ruling in 1984 (SERR, 2020a). The Court expanded its ruling in the case by prohibiting the use of IQ testing for all Black students referred for special education services.

The *Larry P.* ruling banning IQ tests being used for Black children was challenged in the Federal District Court case of *Crawford v. Honig*, which provoked the reexamination of the rights of multicultural students in special education (SERR, 2020a). Consequently, the *Crawford* ruling found three Black children were in fact allowed to take the IQ test because their parents wanted them to take the test. However, after the Ninth Circuit Court of Appeals confirmed the *Crawford* ruling, California Department of Education issued a legal advisory in October 1994 that continued the directive prohibiting IQ testing.

Luke S. and Han S. v. Nix et al. (1981)

Since the landmark legislation of Public Law 94–142, there was a boom in special education programs throughout school districts across the country. However, not all school districts were in a position to adequately meet the additional mandate to locate and evaluate all children suspected of having a disability (Taylor et al., 1986). In the state of Louisiana, all evaluations were required to be completed within a 60-day time period. The plaintiffs, *Luke S. and Hans S.*, were two 7-year-old children who failed and were repeating first grade. Each child had been referred for an individual evaluation to determine if they were eligible for special education services. Additionally, formal written parent approval to conduct an evaluation was requested and received by the school district about 6 months before the suit was filed and an evaluation had not been conducted.

In the *Luke S. and Hans S. vs. Nix et al.* (1981) class action suit, "findings of fact" estimated about 1,000 children had been referred for a special education evaluation, but evaluations were not being conducted within the 60-day time limit specified in the state regulations (Taylor et al., 1986). Later, estimates by the State Department of Education and Special Consultant in the case were closer to 10,000 referrals not meeting the 60-day time limit for special education evaluation. The court ruled in favor of the plaintiffs and informed the state of Louisiana that better prereferral assessment should be conducted prior to a special education referral being made.

The state and plaintiffs negotiated and agreed on a plan requiring an increasing level of compliance across a 3-year period of time (Taylor et al., 1986). Specifically, by June 30, 1982, the state defendants had to ensure 70% to 80% of all children referred for evaluation during the 1981–1982 fiscal year were evaluated in a timely manner. Additionally, all children referred prior to the beginning of the 1981–1982 fiscal year would be evaluated. By June 30, 1983, 90% of all children referred for evaluation during the 1982–1983 fiscal year were evaluated in a timely manner. By June 30, 1984, and thereafter, 97% to 100% of all children referred for special education evaluation are evaluated within the 60-day time limit. The state defendants were also required to take all actions reasonably necessary to comply with the aforementioned requirements and objectives. The state defendants were required to make more than $1 million available to the school systems to bring on qualified appraisal personnel to complete the evaluations in a timely manner during the 1981–1982 fiscal year to decrease the backlog of children waiting for an evaluation. Additionally, it was established that the ratio for school psychologists needed to increase to prevent a future backlog.

In reality, the *Luke S. and Han S.* lawsuit was against both special education and general education, and cooperation between the two needed to occur for the successful conclusion of the case (Taylor et al., 1986). The ease with which general education staff could refer children for special education evaluation was a large contributing factor to the immense backlog of referrals, which caused the system to be overwhelmed with inappropriate referrals. At the time, referral for special education was the first step rather than the last for students struggling with learning or behavior in the classroom. The complete redesign of the referral-to-placement system occurred because of the lawsuit and forced general education screening and intervention prior to special education referral. Assessment was mandated which focused on the student's problems in the classroom and with the existing curriculum. The lawsuit caught the attention of all those involved in education in the state of Louisiana, creating the powerful motive for needed change in correcting an outdated process. On July 15, 1985, it was announced that the suit was over, and the State of Louisiana successfully met all requirements and there was no longer a waiting list for evaluations.

Board of Education of the Hendrick Hudson Central School District v. Rowley (1982)

Amy Rowley was a Deaf student who performed better than most of her peers and easily advanced from grade to grade (JUSTIA US Supreme Court, 2022). Although she performed well in the least restrictive environment (LRE) of a general education classroom with a special hearing aid provided by school authorities, Amy's parents requested the school provide a qualified sign language interpreter for all academic classes, stating that under the Education of the Handicapped Act (EHA; now IDEA), measures such as this were deemed "appropriate." They believed she was only able to understand about 60% of the information presented in class. However, the school district felt the services provided to Amy, including the hearing aids and tutor, met the requirements of EHA by providing her a FAPE in her LRE. The Rowleys believed the minimal services offered did not allow Amy to reach her full potential.

The Rowleys lost at due process and review levels and then appealed to the U.S. District Court, where they won (Forte Law Group, n.d.). The school district appealed the decision, but the U.S. Court of Appeals for the Second Circuit affirmed the District Court's decision. The U.S. District Court found that although Amy was doing well in her classes, she was not performing as well academically as if she did not have her "handicap," and because of the disparity between her achievement and potential, Amy was not being provided a FAPE (JUSTIA US Supreme Court, 2022).

After the school district appealed to the U.S. Court of Appeals for the Second Circuit confirmed the U.S. District Court's decision, the school district appealed to the U.S. Supreme Court (Forte Law Group, n.d.). On March 23, 1982, the Court heard the argument and were determining what was meant by EHA requirements to a free "appropriate" public education. On June 28, 1982, after reviewing the legislative history of EHA, the Court held the intent of the law was provide more public education opportunities to children with disabilities on "appropriate" terms than to guarantee any specific level of education. They found the "basic floor of opportunity" provided by EHA entails access to specialized instruction and related services individually created to give educational benefit to the student. The *Rowley* decision explained that children and youth with disabilities are allowed "access" to an education that provided "educational benefit," and a school district is not required to "maximize" every student with a disability's potential.

Timothy W. v. Rochester, New Hampshire, School District (1988)

Timothy W. was born 2 months prematurely and had severe respiratory problems. Shortly after he was born he experienced an intracranial hemorrhage, seizures, subdural effusions, hydrocephalus, and meningitis that resulted in him being "multiply handicapped" and "profoundly mentally retarded," suffering from "complex developmental disabilities, spastic quadriplegia, cerebral palsy, seizure disorder, and cortical blindness" (JUSTIA US Law, 2021). His mother tried to obtain appropriate services for him. Although he did receive some services from Rochester Child Development Center, he did not receive educational programming when he became of school age from the Rochester School District.

In February 1980, Rochester School District met to determine if Timothy was considered educationally handicapped under state and federal laws (JUSTIA US Law, 2021). Although testimony was heard, the district adjourned without making a decision. However, on March 7, 1980, the district decided Timothy was not educationally handicapped, determining he was not entitled to an education because his handicap was so severe, he was not "capable of benefiting" from an education. The New Hampshire Department of Education reviewed the Rochester School District's special education program in May 1982, where the district was found to be noncompliant, stating that the district was not allowed to use "capable of benefiting" as a measure for eligibility. Action was not taken in response to the finding until June 1983 when the district met to discuss the case. Although it was determined he responded to bells and his mother's voice, the district continued to refuse any educational programming or services for Timothy other than physical therapy.

The school district's placement team met in January 1984 in response to a letter from Timothy's lawyer. It was recommended by the placement team for Timothy to be placed at the Child Development Center and receive educational services (JUSTIA US Law, 2021). However, the district stated they needed additional information and requested Timothy be given a CAT scan, but his mother refused. In April 1984, a complaint was filed on Timothy's behalf with the New Hampshire Department of Education requesting he be immediately placed in an educational program. In October 1984, the Department of Education issued an order requiring Timothy be placed in an educational program within 5 days, but the school district refused. The school district filed an appeal, and on November 8, 1984, a meeting was held by the Rochester School Board to review Timothy's case, which determined he was not eligible for special education. However, on November 17, 1984, Timothy filed a complaint in the U.S. District Court stating the Rochester School District violated Timothy's rights under the EAHCA, Section 504 of the Rehabilitation Act of 1973, the New Hampshire state law, and the equal protection and due process clauses of the United States and New Hampshire Constitutions. The case was heard on January 3, 1985, where the District Court denied Timothy's motion. Court filings continued to occur for several more years as the district refused to provide special education services.

Although Rochester School District prevailed in the lower courts, where they agreed Timothy was not capable of benefiting from an education and was thus not entitled to one, the U. S. Court of Appeals for the First Circuit in Boston reversed the decision. The judges in the case stated that the passage of EAHCA had clear intentions in that all children, including "handicapped children," are provided a public education unconditionally and without exception (JUSTIA US Law, 2021). The judges continued to say that the law embodies a universal right and is not based on any type of assurances the child will benefit from the special education and services prior to being considered eligible to receive an education. The judges found the District Court's holding to be a direct contradiction of the act's legislative history and statutory language.

Endrew F. v. Douglas County School District (2017)

Endrew F., referred to as Drew, was diagnosed with autism at age 2 and was later diagnosed with attention-deficit/hyperactivity disorder. Drew attended Douglas County schools in Colorado from preschool through fourth grade, where he was provided special education and relation services as specified in his IEP (Yell & Bateman, 2017). Fourth grade was a difficult year for Drew. His parents rejected his IEP, stating that he was not making meaningful progress in fourth grade and felt the IEP for fifth grade was essentially the same as it was in fourth grade. Therefore, Drew's parents placed him in a school designed for students with autism. While at Firefly Autism House, Drew made academic, social, and behavioral progress.

Drew's parents filed a due process hearing where they argued that Douglas Country School District had not provided Drew with a FAPE and therefore requested reimbursement for tuition and related expenses for Drew's placement in private school (Yell & Bateman, 2017). The hearing officer in the case found the district provided Drew with some academic benefit, and therefore a FAPE, by relying on the *Board of Education of the Hendrick Hudson Central School District v. Rowley* (1982) case, where a standard was established as a guide for hearing officers and courts when determining whether a child was receiving a FAPE. Specifically, a two-part process was established through the *Rowley* case to determine if a FAPE was provided. Part one of the *Rowley* test involves determining whether the student's IEP was developed in accordance with the law's procedural requirements, and part two is designed to determine whether the IEP was reasonably calculated to enable the child to receive educational benefit.

Drew's parents filed suit in the U.S. District Court, which affirmed the hearing officer's decision. Specifically, the court found Drew had made at least minimal progress, which was all IDEA required (Yell & Bateman, 2017). Drew's parents then appealed to the U.S. Appeals Court for the Tenth Circuit. According to Drew's parents, the school district committed procedural violations. First, the district failed to provide Drew's parents with progress reports as required by IDEA. Although the Circuit Court noted Drew's IEP lacked progress monitoring data or progress reporting, the court did not believe those errors had an influence on Drew's progress, and therefore did not constitute a procedural violation denying a FAPE. Second, Drew's parents believed the district failed to properly assess Drew's behavior problems and put in an appropriate plan to address the problems. Although the court recognized Drew's problem behaviors impacted his ability to learn in the classroom, school personnel had considered his behavior problems and had not committed a procedural violation. Additionally, Drew's parents believed the school district committed substantive violations because all Drew's IEPs were materially the same and he made no progress toward his goals, and they believed Drew's IEP did not address his escalating behavior problems. The Circuit Court found that Douglas County School District was not responsible for tuition reimbursement. While he was thriving at the Firefly Autism House, he did make some educational progress when attending the school district and found the district provided FAPE because IDEA only requires educational benefit provided be "merely more than *de minimis*" for students in special education; therefore, they denied Drew's parents tuition reimbursement.

Drew's parents appealed to the U.S. Supreme Court. The question brought to the Court was, "What is the level of educational benefit that school districts must confer on children with disabilities to provide them with the free appropriate public education guaranteed by the Individuals with Disabilities Education Act?" (SCOTUSblog, 2017). The U.S. Supreme Court announced they would hear the case on September 29, 2017, and on January 11, 2017, the Court heard oral arguments. In a unanimous ruling, delivered by Chief Justice John Roberts, the Court held that "to meet its substantive obligation under the IDEA, a school must offer an IEP reasonably calculated to enable a child to make progress appropriate in light of the child's circumstances" (JUSTIA US Supreme Court, 2021). Justice Roberts indicated an IEP is an exercise that is fact intensive and school personnel and the student's parents should be collaborating when developing and implementing a special education program to ensure academic and functional advancement (Yell & Bateman, 2017). Justice Roberts also said the focus of an IEP should be on the unique and individual needs of the student and be developed with full consideration of the student's present levels of academic achievement and functional performance (PLAAFP), their disability, and their potential for growth. The Court ruled that a FAPE is designed to meet the individual needs of the student through the IEP. According to the Court, the IEP must be reasonable and designed by considering education progress. Additionally, the standard developed by the justices was decidedly more demanding than the "merely more than *de minimis*" test. The Court found "merely more than *de minimis*" progress from one year to the next for a student cannot be said that they have actually been offered an education and receiving instruction that aims so low would be equal to sitting idly, and the IDEA demands more. The *Endrew F.* decision requires a new standard for FAPE in determining educational benefit. IEPs can no longer be designed to confer just some educational benefit, but rather, a student's IEP must be designed to provide measurable benefit given the student's capabilities.

> **CHECK FOR UNDERSTANDING**
>
> One court case is often used to inform another court case. Litigation has come a long way in determining rights of students with disabilities. We have gone from not only ensuring students with disabilities are included in school but also ensuring students with disabilities are taught to the highest standard possible so students are receiving educational benefit when they are in school.

FEDERAL INVOLVEMENT

The first noteworthy federal involvement in educating students with disabilities occurred in the late 1950s and early 1970s. The federal legislative efforts were intended to improve the education of students with disabilities. In the following sections we highlight major pieces of legislation designed to fund and support the educational needs of students with disabilities.

The Elementary and Secondary Education Act of 1965

In 1965, President Lyndon Johnson passed and signed the Elementary and Secondary Education Act (ESEA; Yell, 2019), which was designed to fight the war on poverty. The law was the first to provide direct funding to states to help in educating specific groups of students. The purpose of ESEA was to provide states with federal money to improve educational opportunities for disadvantaged children, including individuals with disabilities who attended schools for the deaf, blind, and retarded.

The Education of the Handicapped Act of 1970

The EHA of 1970 replaced ESEA and became the basic framework for most of the legislation to come (Yell, 2019). The purpose of EHA was to combine and increase previous federal grant programs. EHA was also intended to support funding pilot projects at the local and state levels to expand, improve, or initiate programs and projects for students with disabilities. Funding was also provided to institutions of higher education to create programs for training teachers of students with disabilities. The law provided funds to develop regional resource centers to provide technical assistance for local and state school districts. EHA was the first freestanding law in special education that required students with disabilities be educated. The law also required students with disabilities receive special education and related services needed to progress.

The Education for All Handicapped Children Act of 1975

Prior to 1975, students with disabilities had limited access to educational opportunities. First, many students with disabilities were completely excluded from public schools (Yell, 2019). Second, more than three million students with disabilities who were admitted into public school were not receiving an education appropriate for their needs. On November 29, 1975, to address these problems, President Gerald Ford signed into law the EAHCA. Also known as P.L. 94-142, EAHCA was the most substantial increase in the federal government's role in special education because it combined an educational bill of rights with the agreement of federal financial incentives. Participating states were required to provide a FAPE for all students with disabilities between the ages of 3 and 18 by September 1, 1978, and all students up to age 21 by September 1, 1980 (EAHCA, 1975). Additionally, EAHCA mandated qualified children and youth with disabilities had the right to:

- Nondiscriminatory procedures for testing, evaluation, and placement
- An education in the student's LRE
- Procedural due process which also includes parental involvement
- A free education
- An appropriate education based on an IEP created by a group of individuals, including the student's parents

The EAHCA outlined educational rights for students with disabilities while also providing federal funding to states (Yell, 2019). The funding would go from the federal government to the state educational agencies (SEAs) and then to the local education agencies (LEAs). States were required to submit a plan for meeting the federal requirements to receive funding. Local school districts had to provide programs to meet the state requirements. It is important to note federal funding was an addition to state and local dollars and could not be used to replace these funds. All states complied with the requirements of the EAHCA by 1985.

The main issue driving the law to be passed was access to education for students with disabilities. Prior to the law, students with disabilities were either excluded from education altogether, were segregated from their nondisabled peers, or were placed in programs not appropriate for their needs (Yell, 2019). The EAHCA successfully improved these problems, and today, students with disabilities can be assured the right to access education.

The Individuals with Disabilities Education Act of 1990

The EAHCA was renamed the Individuals with Disabilities Education Act (IDEA) in the 1990 amendments. The amendments of IDEA (1990) made numerous changes. The term "handicap" was changed to the term "disability" throughout the law. "Person-first" language was also used throughout the law. For example, rather than saying "disabled student," the law used "student with a disability" to emphasize that a person should precede the category of disability. Autism and traumatic brain injury were added as disability categories to IDEA 1990. To qualify for special education services, a child must fall under one of the 13 disabilities categories (Table 3-2), and as a result of the disability, have a need for special education in order to progress in school. Additionally, IDEA (1990) added and clarified types of related services, rehabilitation services, and assistive technology. For students 16 years of age or older, individualized transition planning was now required to be included in the student's IEP.

The purpose of the IDEA (1990) was to ensure all students with disabilities are provided a FAPE where special education and related services are designed to meet students' unique needs and prepare them for continued education, employment, and independent living. The IDEA intended to ensure rights are protected for students with disabilities and their families. State agencies, local agencies, educational service agencies, and federal agencies are to assist in providing for the education of all children and youth with disabilities through the IDEA.

The IDEA was amended in 1997 to improve the effectiveness of special education for students with disabilities. The IDEA (1990) was successful in ensuring students access to a FAPE and improving educational results for individuals with disabilities (Yell, 2019). However, school systems had low expectations of students with disabilities, and there was not enough focus on translating research into practice. Additionally, there was too much emphasis on legal requirements and paperwork at

Table 3-2. Disability Categories Under IDEA

- Autism
- Intellectual disability
- Multiple disabilities
- Specific learning disabilities (including dyslexia, dyscalculia, dysgraphia, and other learning differences)
- Emotional disturbance
- Traumatic brain injury
- Other health impairment
- Visual impairment including blindness
- Speech or language impairment
- Hearing impairment
- Deafness
- Deaf-blindness
- Orthopedic impairment

the expense of teaching and learning. To change this, Congress adopted amendments in 1997 with the goal of improving educational achievement of individuals with disabilities.

In 2004, the law was reauthorized as the Individuals with Disabilities Education Improvement Act. Children are covered under IDEA (2004) from birth through the age of 21 or high school graduation, whichever comes first. Early intervention services are provided up to age 3, and special education services are provided for children in public school. There were other significant changes made to amendments of IDEA. The law defines a highly qualified teacher and requires special education teachers be certified in special education (Yell, 2019). Instructional strategies must be scientifically research based. Additionally, there are changes to the identification of students with learning disabilities. Rather than a "wait to fail" discrepancy model, schools are encouraged to use the model of response to intervention to determine if a student has a learning disability.

Check for Understanding

The Education of the Handicapped Act (EHA) of 1970 became the basic framework for most of the legislation to follow, including the Education for All Handicapped Children Act (EAHCA), also known as P.L. 94-142, which included the biggest increase in the role of the federal government in supporting students with disabilities. The EAHCA was renamed the Individuals with Disabilities Education Act (IDEA), which leads to where we are now. The IDEA's last updates occurred in 2004 and included a name change to the Individuals with Disabilities Education Improvement Act, but it is still commonly known as IDEA and is the basis of the law we are required to follow today.

Six Principles of the Individuals with Disabilities Education Improvement Act

The IDEA is founded on six principles to ensure the rights of eligible children with disabilities to benefit from public education with the use of specially designed instruction, supports, and services to best meet the student's individualized needs. The six principles are outlined as follows.

Free Appropriate Public Education

According to the IDEA (2004), every eligible child with a disability is entitled to a FAPE, which is the cornerstone of the IDEA. For a student to receive a FAPE, special education and related services must meet the unique needs of the child and prepare the student for continued education, employment upon graduation, as well as independent living. Educational services must be provided at no additional cost to parents and meet standards created by the state department of education. The primary mechanism for providing a FAPE is a specially designed IEP based on the child's needs by taking into account their PLAAFP. According to the law, students are eligible to receive services from preschool through high school (ages 3 to 21) and are required to continue for students who have been suspended or expelled (Access for Special Kids [ASK], 2020).

Special education programs are intended for students to make progress in general education curriculum (ASK, 2020). Students must be provided the opportunity to meet challenging goals with more than a minimal benefit and no requirement for maximizing student potential—for example, providing a vehicle that is serviceable rather than a fully-loaded brand vehicle. Under FAPE, special education programs also include related supports and services and provide for participation in other school and extracurricular activities. Under FAPE, students need to be provided extended year services when necessary.

Appropriate Evaluation

A requirement of the IDEA (2004) is that a student must receive an evaluation before special education services are provided, which is done to determine whether the student qualifies as a child with a disability, according to the definition of the IDEA. Additionally, the evaluation should determine the educational needs of the student. Parents must give permission for the student to be evaluated prior to the evaluation and before services are provided. Once parents have given permission, an evaluation must be conducted within 60 calendar days. The evaluation should not be based on one type of measure or assessment and given in the child's native language. A range of strategies and tools should be used by trained and knowledgeable personnel to collect academic, developmental, and functional information in all areas of a suspected disability.

A comprehensive re-evaluation must be conducted a minimum of every 3 years unless parents and educators agree a re-evaluation is not necessary (IDEA, 2004). Although re-evaluation can occur more often if needed, it cannot occur more than once a year. A re-evaluation can occur prior to 3 years if circumstances warrant new information or if a parent requests it.

A parent has the right to request an independent evaluation, at the expense of the public, if there is disagreement with the results of the school's evaluation (IDEA, 2004). Parents may obtain an independent evaluation any time at their own expense. Although the school multidisciplinary team must consider recommendations made by outside sources, the team does not necessarily have to follow the recommendations.

When considering our case study example, Jose's parents need to provide consent, but any forms need to be in their native language. Additionally, any evaluation given must be in Jose's native language.

Individualized Education Program

The foundation of the IDEA is the right of each eligible child with a disability to receive a FAPE (U.S. Department of Education, n.d.). According to the law, special education and related services must be designed to meet the child's unique needs and prepare them for continued education, employment, and independent living (IDEA, 2004). The main mechanism for providing FAPE is through developmentally appropriately IEP based on the individual needs of the child. The key term is *individualized*. The IEP is a written statement for a child with a disability and is designed based on the child's PLAAFP. Another aspect the IEP must account for is the impact of the student's disability on their involvement and progress in general education curriculum.

The IEP must include goals that are measurable, aligned with grade-level content standards, and allow for the student to make meaningful progress in functional performance and the general education curriculum (IDEA, 2004). Taking into account the student's PLAAFP, IEP goals are written for where the student's academic and functional skills should be at the end of the school year.

An IEP is developed, reviewed, and revised a minimum of one time per year by a team including parents, educators, and other individuals who are needed (e.g., speech therapist, diagnostician, physical therapist) to develop the student's special education program (IDEA, 2004). The student should be involved in the process as well to whatever capacity they are able. The student and parents should be meaningfully involved in the development of the program and placement decisions as well as when revisions are needed. It is important to note that special education is not a place. Educational program decisions are made first, and placement (i.e., educational setting) is determined second. A student's IEP must be developed, reviewed, and revised in agreement with requirements outlined in the law.

Least Restrictive Environment

The requirement of providing the LRE has existed since the EAHCA and is a fundamental component of educating students with disabilities (Yell, 2019). IDEA (2004) requires students with disabilities be educated with their peers without disabilities to the maximum extent appropriate including public schools, private schools who accept federal funding, or other care facilities. A lack of funding is not an appropriate justification for a more restrictive placement.

To ensure a child is being educated in the LRE, placement outside the general education classroom must be justified by the disability-related individualized needs of the student (IDEA, 2004). Moreover, the student should be able to get required services in the general education classroom or other integrated settings. It is important to note that, when appropriate, the student must have meaningful access to their same-aged peers without disabilities. Additionally, accommodations must be made during involvement in extracurricular activities, clubs, school trips, music, physical education, art, or any other activities. States are required to provide a full range of placement options to meet the needs of children who require specialized treatment programs.

Parent Participation

According to the IDEA (2004), research has shown education of students with disabilities is more effective when parents have meaningful opportunities to participate. Although parents are not required to participate, the IDEA is very explicit regarding what schools need to do to make certain parents have the opportunity to be actively involved in each step of the special education process. Moreover, the student should also be meaningfully involved in the process whenever appropriate. Meaningful involvement in the special education process includes developing, reviewing, and revising the IEP; deciding FAPE educational placement; being a part of the team deciding if the student is a child with a disability and meets eligibility criteria for special education and related services; determining appropriate data collection during the evaluation; reviewing data; and planning for transition services no later than the age of 14. If parents are unable to attend the IEP meetings, the school must provide options for other methods of participation, including video or conference calls.

When considering our case study with Mrs. Cates and Jose, it will be important for the committee to ensure Jose's parents are given information in their native language. An interpreter will need to be present for any phone conversation and/or meeting being held. Additionally, all written material needs to be in Jose's family's native language. Although Jose's parents are not fluent in English, the team must ensure Jose's family has all information and can fully participate in the decision-making process.

Procedural Safeguards

Procedural safeguards were included when Congress enacted Public Law 94-142 as the EAHCA (Wrightslaw, 2020). The safeguards were established to protect the rights of children with disabilities and their parents. Congress maintained and made additions to the procedural safeguards following subsequent reauthorizations of the law. According to IDEA (2004), procedural safeguards include parents' right to (1) have written notice when there are proposed changes, or refusal to change, identification, evaluation, or placement of a child; (2) participate in all meetings; (3) examine all educational records; and (4) attain an independent educational evaluation (IEE) of the child. Procedural safeguards also include confidentiality and legally binding agreements when attempting to resolve disputes through medication, a resolution session, and due process hearings.

> **CHECK FOR UNDERSTANDING**
>
> Under IDEA, students receive an appropriate evaluation to determine eligibility of special education services. An IEP is created to ensure students with disabilities are receiving instruction in their LRE. It is important for parents to be included when making decisions for their child.

SUMMARY

This chapter provided a brief overview of the historic development of special education and assessment in special education through case law and legislation. The history of special education law is considered a movement to ensure equal access to education and to ensure quality of educational programming for students in special education (Yell, 2019). Achieving equal educational opportunity for children and youth with disabilities has been onerous, but much progress has been made in the early 21st century. There is still work to be done to ensure all children and youth with disabilities receive a meaningful education.

CASE STUDY WRAP-UP

Mrs. Cates looked at Jose's previous school records and saw a pattern of him struggling throughout his school, even when he was receiving education in Spanish. With that information, and data she collected in the classroom, she spoke with the special education team. The multidisciplinary team decided to contact Jose's family and discuss options with them. After following all best practices to ensure Jose's needs are appropriately met, it was determined that Jose qualifies for special education services as a student with a learning disability. Jose was then able to get the services he needed to be successful in school.

CHAPTER REVIEW

1. Looking at the various cases, describe how things have changed and how one landmark case can build on another landmark case.
2. Find a current court case using one of the landmark cases discussed in this chapter. Describe the current court case. Discuss how the landmark case was used in the case.
3. Compare and contrast the *Endrew* case and the *Rowley* case by creating a Venn diagram.
4. Create a flowchart (with time frames included as necessary) based on the six principles of the Individuals with Disabilities Education Improvement Act to determine what school personnel need to do in determining eligibility.

REFERENCES

Access for Special Kids. (2020). *Six principles of IDEA: The Individuals with Disabilities Education Act.* https://www.askresource.org/resources/six-principles-of-idea

Board of Education of Hendrick Hudson Central School District v. Rowley, 458 U.S. 176 (1982).

Bolling v. Sharpe, 347 U.S. 497 (1954).

Boss, A. (n.d.). Legal briefs: Hobson v. Hansen. *School Psychologist Resource.* https://sites.google.com/site/schoolpsychquickreference/legal-briefs/hobson-v-hansen

Brown v. Board of Education of Topeka, 347 U.S. 483 (1954).

Diana v. State Board of Education, Civil Action No. C-70-37 (N. D. Cal. 1970).

Endrew F. v. Douglas County School District, Re–1, 137 S. Ct. 988 (2017).

Education of All Handicapped Children Act, Public Law 94-142, 94th Congress (1975).

Forte Law Group. (n.d.). *History of special education: Important landmark cases.* https://www.fortelawgroup.com/history-special-education-important-landmark-cases

Hobson v. Hansen, 269 F. Supp. 401 (D.D.C. 1967).

Honig v. Doe, 484 U.S. 305 (1988).

Individuals with Disabilities Education Act, Public Law 101-476, 101st Congress (1990).

Individuals with Disabilities Education Act, Public Law 105-17, 105th Congress (1997).

Individuals with Disabilities Education Improvement Act, Public Law 108-446, 108th Congress (2004).

JUSTIA US Law. (2020a). *Hobson v. Hansen, 269 F. Supp. 401 (D.D.C. 1967).* https://law.justia.com/cases/federal/district-courts/FSupp/269/401/1800940

JUSTIA US Law. (2020b). *Larry P. v. Riles, 495 F. Supp. 926 (N.D. Cal. 1979).* https://law.justia.com/cases/federal/district-courts/FSupp/495/926/2007878

JUSTIA US Law. (2021). *Timothy W., Etc., Plaintiff, Appellant, v. Rochester, New Hampshire, School District, Defendant, Appellee, 875 F.2d 954 (1st Cir. 1989).* https://law.justia.com/cases/federal/appellate-courts/F2/875/954/179023

JUSTIA US Law. (2022). *Pennsylvania Ass'n, Ret'd Child. V. Commonwealth of Pa., 343 F. Supp. 279 (E.D. Pa. 1972).* https://law.justia.com/cases/federal/district-courts/FSupp/343/279/1691591

JUSTIA US Supreme Court. (2021). *Endrew F. v. Douglas County School District RE-1, 580 U.S. (2017).* https://supreme.justia.com/cases/federal/us/580/15-827

JUSTIA US Supreme Court. (2022). *Board of Educ. V. Rowley, 458 U.S. 176 (1982).* https://supreme.justia.com/cases/federal/us/458/176

Larry P. v. Riles, 495 F. Supp. 926 (N.D. Cal. 1979).

Lilljevall, B. (n.d.). Legal briefs: Diana v. CA State Board of Education. *School Psychologist Resources.* https://sites.google.com/site/schoolpsychquickreference/legal-briefs/diana-v-ca-state-board-of-education

Luke S. and Hans S. vs. Nix et al., United States District Court, ColukeEastern District of Louisiana, Civil Action No. 81-3331, August 1981.

Mills v. Board of Education of District of Columbia, 348 F. Supp. 866 (1972).

Pennsylvania Association for Retarded Citizens v. Pennsylvania, 334 F. Supp. 1257 (E.D. Pa. 1972).

Scheller, D. (n.d.). Legal briefs: Larry P. v. Riles. *School Psychologist Resources.* https://sites.google.com/site/schoolpsychquickreference/legal-briefs/larry-p-v-riles

SCOTUSblog. (2017). *Petition for a writ of certiorari.* https://www.scotusblog.com/wp-content/uploads/2016/05/15-827-Petition-for-Certiorari.pdf

Special Education Rights & Responsibilities. (2020a). *What is the Larry P. v. Riles case? How did it originate?* https://serr.disabilityrightsca.org/serr-manual/chapter-2-information-on-evaluations-assessments/2-45-what-is-the-larry-p-v-riles-case-how-did-it-originate

Special Education Rights & Responsibilities. (2020b). *What was the Diana v. State Board of Education case? What impact does the Diana case have on Spanish-speaking students?* https://serr.disabilityrightsca.org/serr-manual/chapter-2-information-on-evaluations-assessments/2-48-what-was-the-diana-v-state-board-of-education-case-what-impact-does-the-diana-case-have-on-spanish-speaking-students

Steketee, A. M. (2022). *Honig v. Doe. Encyclopedia Britannica.* https://www.britannica.com/topic/Honig-v-Doe

Taylor, J. M., Tucker, J. A., & Galagan, J. E. (1986). The *Luke S.* class action suit: A lesson in system change. *Exceptional Children, 52*(4), 376–382.

Timothy W., Etc. v. Rochester, New Hampshire School District, 875 F.2d 924 (1989).

U.S. Department of Education. (n.d.). *IDEA: Individuals with Disabilities Education Act.* https://sites.ed.gov/idea/topic-areas

United States Courts. (n.d.). *History—Brown v. Board of Education.* https://www.uscourts.gov/educational-resources/educational-activities/history-brown-v-board-education-re-enactment

Wrightslaw. (2020). *Procedural safeguards & parent notice.* https://www.wrightslaw.com/info/safgd.index.htm

Yell, M. L. (2019). *The law and special education* (5th ed.). Pearson.

Yell, M. L., & Bateman, D. F. (2017). *Endrew F. v. Douglas County School District (2017)*: FAPE and the U.S. Supreme Court. *TEACHING Exceptional Children, 50*(1), 7–15. https://doi.org/10.1177/0040059917721116

Norm-Referenced Assessment

CHAPTER OBJECTIVES

- Define norm-referenced assessment.
- Differentiate group and individual norm-referenced assessments.
- Evaluate strengths and weaknesses of norm-referenced assessment.
- Identify norm-referenced group assessments commonly administered to aid in instructional planning and placement decisions.
- Identify norm-referenced individual assessments commonly administered to aid in instructional planning and placement decisions.
- Define high-stakes testing.

KEY TERMS

- **field testing:** A draft version of a test is given to a small group of individuals allowing the test developer to analyze components including the test items, the format of the presentation, and the administration procedures used.
- **group assessment:** Group assessments are administered in groups to measure how a child's intellectual performance compares with that of other children in the same age group.
- **high-stakes testing:** A high-stakes test is any test used to make important decisions about students, educators, schools, or districts, most commonly for the purpose of accountability.
- **individual assessment:** Assessments administered individually to measure how a child's intellectual performance compares with that of other children in the same age group.
- **item pool:** A collection of test items which are thought to represent a domain or content area.
- **norm-referenced assessment:** Assessment that measures a student's performance in comparison to the performance of the same-age student on the same assessment.
- **norms:** Samples of test takers who are representative of the population for whom the test is intended.
- **protocol:** Booklet in which a test examiner records correct and incorrect responses.
- **rapport:** A positive relationship between two individuals.

KEY ABBREVIATIONS

- ABAS-3: *Adaptive Behavior Assessment System, Third Edition*
- CogAT: *Cognitive Abilities Test*
- KTEA-3: *Kaufman Test of Educational Achievement, Third Edition*
- OLSAT: *Otis-Lennon School Ability Test*
- WISC-V: *Wechsler Intelligence Scale for Children, Fifth Edition*
- WJ IV COG: *Woodcock-Johnson IV Tests of Cognitive Abilities*

CASE STUDY

Prior to the beginning of his second year of teaching, Mr. Dollins is reviewing the cumulative files for his incoming fifth-grade students. As he peruses the folders, he notices some students have participated in a group standardized assessment used to measure intellectual functioning. Mr. Dollins received some training in his teacher preparation program regarding standardized assessments but does not feel he has a good grasp on the use of the assessments for educational purposes. He is particularly concerned when he comes across a very low score for his student Marcus. Marcus scored in the lowest percentile on the group assessment listed in the folder. Additionally, Mr. Dollins notices several sets of minutes from the response to intervention team regarding Marcus's progress in the areas of reading and mathematics. Marcus has received Tier 3 interventions for the past 2 years with the reading and math interventionist with minimal progress. Mr. Dollins wants all his students to be successful in his classroom and wants to ensure a good start as Marcus begins his fifth-grade year. Mr. Dollins decides to reach out to the campus assessment coordinator to learn more about norm-referenced assessment to assist his students and to develop appropriate educational plans.

What Is Norm-Referenced Assessment?

Norm-referenced assessments, also referred to as standardized tests, are used to compare one student's performance to others in a predetermined peer group (McLoughlin et al., 2018). These assessments are administered under strict uniform conditions and interpreted in a consistent manner. Norm-referenced assessments may be either group or individually administered. Norm-referenced assessments can provide information about delays or acceleration in development compared to typically developing peers and are often used for purposes of eligibility for educational services including special education, Section 504, or gifted and talented programs.

Norm-referenced tests report whether test takers performed better or worse than a hypothetical average student (Overton, 2015). For example, on a statewide achievement test, Jackson's score places him in the 98th percentile in his school, but only at the 55th percentile in the state. Although Jackson's score was extremely high when compared with students in his school, it is well below average compared to the larger pool of students. In the United States, both public and private schools use norm-referenced assessments. Often these assessments are used to assess a student's strengths and weaknesses in cognitive and academic areas. Additionally, students may be administered norm-referenced assessments to determine if schools are meeting state and federal guidelines.

Norms are obtained by administering the test to a large representative sample and tend to have high estimates of reliability and validity (McLoughlin et al., 2018). The nationally representative sample is often a sample of several thousand students in the same grade. Norm groups may also be narrowed by age, socioeconomic status, race/ethnicity, and language status. Typical scores from a norm-referenced assessment include standard scores, scaled scores, and percentile ranks. Schools and parents often use these scores to make educational decisions about a child's education. When selecting and implementing norm-referenced assessments, it is important to ensure the norms represent the characteristics of the normative sample and determine whether students with disabilities were included in the norm sample.

How Are Norm-Referenced Tests Constructed?

The first step in developing a norm-referenced test centers on defining the theoretical basis for the test (Overton, 2015). Test developers may wish to develop a test that can assess a language ability, motor ability, cognitive ability, or educational domain. Once the theoretical basis has been determined, the test developer must develop an item pool. An item pool is simply a collection of test items that are thought to represent a domain or content area. Sources for items for the pool may be gathered from curriculum guides, published educational materials, or research. Following the selection of the item pool, the items will then be arranged according to their difficulty.

Field testing is the next step in test development. At this stage, the draft version of the test is given to a small group of individuals (McLoughlin et al., 2018). This allows the test developer to analyze components including the test items, the format of the presentation, and to revise the administration procedures used. Following the field tests, the test developer is able to make changes to the original version and develops the version of the test that is to be standardized. The test is then normed on a sample population of students.

After the tests are administered to the sample group, the test developers will then gather the data from the administration and analyze the data. These data are used to establish test validity, reliability, and norms. The final step in the test development process is to make corrections and changes to the test and then develop standardized assessment manuals and to work with a publisher to create the protocols and the actual test kit.

Basics of Standardized Test Administration Procedures

Test administration procedures are developed to reduce measurement error and to increase the likelihood of a fair, valid, and reliable assessment (McLoughlin et al., 2018; Overton, 2015). Any test administration should be completed in a manner set forth by the test developer and should only be administered by trained personnel. When the test is administered to a student, the conditions under which it was normed must be replicated as closely as possible. Any deviation may result in invalidation of scores.

When administering the test, the examiner must ensure they are adequately prepared to administer the test. Some measures, such as intelligence tests, require extensive preparation. It is the professional responsibility of the evaluator to administer only those tests they are trained for (McLoughlin et al., 2018).

The next step in basic administration is to prepare the environment for testing, which includes finding an appropriate room, making sure the ventilation and lighting are adequate, and confirming that the room is free from distractions. Adequate and comfortable seating should be available, and the testing table should be the appropriate height and size to allow for a surface large enough for materials.

After the evaluator has prepared the testing environment, it is time to prepare the student for the testing session. The examiner should take time to build rapport with the student. Often examiners begin the testing session with conversation, discussing something of interest to the student, such as what they do in their leisure time, favorite school subject, or any sports the student plays. Next, the evaluator will need to explain the purpose of the testing. A lengthy explanation is not needed, and most assessment instruments will provide a statement labeled "Introducing the Test," which the examiner will read to the student.

After rapport is established, the examiner will begin the testing session. It is important to adhere to all test manual guidelines. The manual informs the evaluator and provides instructions and test items to be read or actions to be taken during the testing session. Throughout the testing session, the examiner needs to encourage the examinee by using comments such as "you are really working hard" or "good job"; however, the examiner needs to make sure comments are not revealing whether the answer is correct or incorrect. As the student answers questions, the examiner carefully marks responses in the test protocol. Additionally, the evaluator needs to make observations during the testing session and record those observations.

As needed, the examiner should provide breaks during the testing session to ward off any fatigue or frustration. The testing session ends when all activities have been completed or the time allotted has expired. At the conclusion of the testing session, the examiner should thank the student for their cooperation and explain the next steps that will be taken in the process. The remainder of this chapter highlights norm-referenced assessment instruments often used in the school setting.

Check for Understanding

Basics of test administration are as follows:
- Prepare the environment for testing.
- Build rapport with the student.
- Adhere to testing manual guidelines.
- Encourage the examinee.
- Keep observations notes in the protocol.
- Provide breaks as needed.
- Thank student for participating in testing session.

GROUP ASSESSMENTS

Group assessments are increasingly used within school systems for placement in gifted and talented programs and to make instructional decisions based on a student's performance over time (Powell, 2019). While these assessments may be used in general education classrooms, they should not be used in special education classrooms for the purpose of identification for services. These tests are often pencil-and-paper–administered tests presented by a teacher who may not have experience in testing. While group assessments are easy to administer, caution must be exercised in the interpretation of the scores. Because these tests are not individually administered, students may not ask questions for clarification, and a variety of factors could impact performance. Group assessments are often preferred by schools because they can be administered to a very large group simultaneously with an examiner who does not need to be trained in assessment. The disadvantages of using group assessments include lack of ability for the examiner to maintain student interest and the lack of depth often associated with group assessments.

Three group assessments most often administered in schools include the *Cognitive Abilities Test* (CogAT; Lohman, 2011), the *Otis-Lennon School Ability Test* (OLSAT; Otis & Lennon, 2003), and the *Iowa Assessments* (Welch & Dunbar, 2011).

Cognitive Abilities Test (CogAT)

The CogAT is a group-administered multiple choice assessment designed for K–12 schools (Lohman, 2011). It is designed to measure verbal, quantitative, and nonverbal reasoning within a 90- to 120-minute time frame and is available for grades K–12 in either an online or paper format. The CogAT ensures equity for all learners, and directions are offered in many languages, including English, Spanish, Arabic, Mandarin, Russian, Somali, and Vietnamese. The verbal section measures a child's ability to understand words and to use them to make inferences and judgments. Subtests that comprise the verbal domain include Picture Analogies, Sentence Completion, and Picture Classification. The quantitative section is used to measure a child's basic understanding of quantitative concepts. Subtests include Number Analogies, Number Series, and Number Puzzles. The nonverbal section of the CogAT measures reasoning using pictures and geometric shapes. Subtests for the nonverbal section of the CogAT include Figure Matrices, Figure Classification, and Paper Folding. Scores that make up the CogAT include a raw score, universal scale score, standard age score, and percentile rank. Accommodations allowed for the CogAT include off-level testing, repeated directions, large print, extended time, and the ability to read aloud (Lohman, 2011). Results from the assessment may be used by school personnel to tailor instruction to a student's needs. Guides are available to assist teachers in differentiating instruction based on test performance. The guides can be used to assist teachers in adapting instructional goals, methods, and materials to best meet the unique learning needs of each student. Results of the CogAT are also used as part of one measure for consideration for placement in a school's gifted and talented program.

TEST AT A GLANCE

Cognitive Abilities Test (CogAT)
- Type of assessment: Norm-referenced
- Type of administration: Group
- Administration time: 90 to 120 minutes
- Age/grade level: K–12
- Scores: Raw score, universal scale score, standard age score, and percentile rank

Otis-Lennon School Ability Test (OLSAT)

Another assessment that schools employ for group assessment of cognitive abilities is the OLSAT (Otis & Lennon, 2003). This multiple-choice assessment measures verbal, quantitative, and spatial reasoning abilities and yields both a verbal and nonverbal score, which are used to derive a total score known as the School Ability Index (SAI). The OLSAT can be administered in approximately 60 to 75 minutes. The verbal sections of the assessment contain verbal comprehension (following directions, identifying antonyms, sentence arrangement, and completion) and verbal reasoning (logical selection, verbal analogies, verbal classification, and inferences) questions and is designed to measure a child's ability to understand the relationship between words, build sentences, and understand definitions. The nonverbal section is comprised of a variety of pictorial reasoning (picture classification, picture analogies, and picture series), figural reasoning (figural classification, figural analogies, and picture series), and quantitative reasoning (number series, numeric inference, and number matrices) questions and measures the ability to comprehend and continue progressions and to understand similarities and differences (Otis & Lennon, 2003). A school may use the OLSAT to measure individual year-to-year progress, to develop intervention plans to meet the needs of a student's academic needs, or to assess gifted and talented candidates.

TEST AT A GLANCE

Otis-Lennon School Ability Test (OLSAT)
- Type of assessment: Norm-referenced
- Type of administration: Group
- Administration time: 60 to 75 minutes
- Age/grade level: K–12
- Scores: School Ability Index, percentile rank, and stanine

Iowa Assessments

A final group-administered assessment that is popular with school districts is the *Iowa Assessments*. The *Iowa Assessments* is a group-administered achievement test comprised of 10 core academic sections including reading, writing, mathematics, science, social studies, vocabulary, spelling, capitalization, punctuation, and computation (Welch & Dunbar, 2011). The tests are tailored for K–8 and may be used to monitor yearly progress. The test yields scores including a raw score, percent correct, grade equivalent, developmental standard score, and percentile rank. School districts may use the *Iowa Assessments* to improve instruction and learning for students and to evaluate the overall the effectiveness of instruction.

TEST AT A GLANCE

Iowa Assessments
- Type of assessment: Norm-referenced
- Type of administration: Group
- Administration time: 60 to 75 minutes
- Age/grade level: K–12
- Scores: Raw score, percent correct, grade equivalent, developmental standard score, and percentile rank

Individually Administered Assessment

An individually administered assessment is given to one individual at a time (McLoughlin et al., 2018). Many of the scales on an individually administered test require oral response from the examinee and may require the examinee to manipulate materials. Additionally, the administration of an individual assessment provides the opportunity for the examiner to observe the examinee in a standardized situation in order to explain how the individual's behavior may impact the results of the assessment. For the purposes of identification of a disability, individually administered assessments are preferred. Some advantages of an individually administered test include the ability of the examiner to interact with the examinee, allowing the examiner to get the "full picture" of the examinee's performance, and some individual tests do not rely heavily on an examinee's reading ability. Disadvantages include the need for a highly trained examiner and time required for administration.

There are several types of individually administered assessments that may be given in a school setting. This chapter highlights four popular assessments used in the K–12 setting including the *Wechsler Intelligence Scale for Children, Fifth Edition* (WISC-V; Wechsler, 2014), *Woodcock-Johnson IV Tests of Cognitive Abilities* (WJ IV COG; Schrank et al., 2014), *Kaufman Test of Educational Achievement, Third Edition* (KTEA-3; Kaufman & Kaufman, 2014), and the *Adaptive Behavior Assessment System, Third Edition* (ABAS-3; Harrison & Oakland, 2015).

Wechsler Intelligence Scale for Children, Fifth Edition (WISC-V)

Often used widely in school settings to measure a student's cognitive abilities, the WISC-V is an individually administered assessment that assess cognitive processing ability of children ages 6 years, 0 months to 16 years, 11 months (Wechsler, 2014). It takes approximately 45 to 65 minutes to administer. Examiners require training in administration and interpretation of clinical instruments to administer this assessment. The WISC-V yields a Full-Scale IQ and five primary index scores including Verbal Comprehension Index, Visual Spatial Index, Fluid Reasoning, Working Memory Index, and Processing Speed Index. The WISC-V can be used as part of an assessment battery to identify giftedness, learning disabilities, and cognitive strengths and weaknesses to assist in developing an appropriate educational plan for a student.

The WISC-V is comprised of various subtests (see Table 4-1 for descriptions) that are used to determine the Full-Scale Intelligence Quotient (FSIQ; Wechsler, 2014). The FSIQ is a term used to describe a person's complete cognitive capacity and is divided into classifications based on a composite range of scores. Table 4-2 highlights the various descriptive categories.

Test at a Glance

Wechsler Intelligence Scale for Children, Fifth Edition (WISC-V)
- Type of assessment: Norm-referenced
- Type of administration: Individual
- Administration time: 45 to 65 minutes
- Age/grade level: 6-0 to 16-11
- Scores: FSIQ and five primary index scores including Verbal Comprehension Index, Visual Spatial Index, Fluid Reasoning, Working Memory Index, and Processing Speed Index

TABLE 4-1. WECHSLER INTELLIGENCE SCALE FOR CHILDREN, FIFTH EDITION SUBTEST DESCRIPTIONS

SUBTEST	DESCRIPTION
Vocabulary	Examinee provides word definition.
Similarities	Examinee compares how two items are related.
Information	Examinee answers knowledge questions.
Comprehension	Examinee answers questions about social situations.
Block Design	Examinee replicates a model with blocks.
Visual Puzzles	Examinee selects visual images to create a puzzle.
Matrix Reasoning	Examinee finds patterns among images.
Figure Weights	Examinee selects a photo to balance weight on a scale.
Picture Concepts	Examinee identifies a photo with common characteristics.
Arithmetic	Examinee mentally solves math problems.
Digit Span	Examinee orally repeats a series of numbers presented by examiner.
Picture Span	Examinee identifies picture presented after a time delay.
Letter Number Sequencing	Examinee repeats letters and numbers in sequence after presentation by examiner.
Coding	Examinee copies symbols to match a code.
Symbol Search	Examinee scans items seeking specific symbol to match prompt.
Cancellation	Examinee crosses out specific photos in an array.

TABLE 4-2. WECHSLER INTELLIGENCE SCALE FOR CHILDREN, FIFTH EDITION FULL-SCALE INTELLIGENCE QUOTIENT DESCRIPTIVE CLASSIFICATIONS

COMPOSITE SCORE RANGE	CLASSIFICATION
130 and above	Extremely High
120-129	Very High
110-119	High Average
90-109	Average
80-89	Low Average
70-79	Very Low
69 and below	Extremely Low

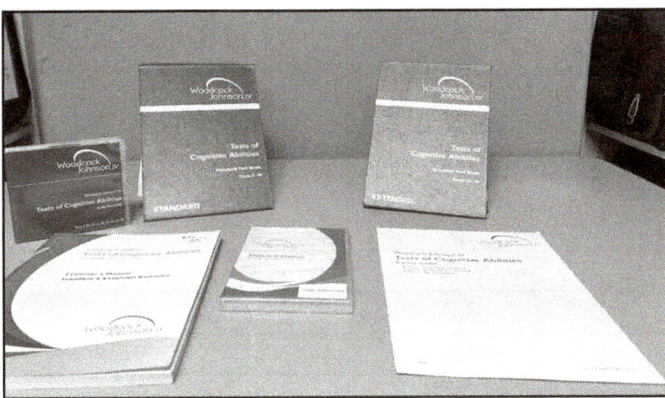

Figure 4-1. *Woodcock-Johnson IV Tests of Cognitive Abilities.* (Reproduced with permission from Riverside Insights.)

Woodcock-Johnson IV Tests of Cognitive Abilities (WJ IV COG)

The WJ IV COG is a battery that evaluates strengths and weaknesses among cognitive abilities (Mather & Wendling, 2014). The WJ IV COG includes 18 subtests measuring broad abilities including Comprehension-Knowledge, Fluid Reasoning, Long-Term Retrieval, Visual Processing, Auditory Processing, Cognitive Processing Speed, Short-Term Working Memory, and Quantitative Knowledge. Definitions of the measured abilities are based on the Cattell-Horn-Carroll (CHC) theory of cognitive abilities (Figure 4-1). The WJ IV COG can provide guidance in educational and clinical settings. In schools, the WJ IV COG is useful in diagnosing the nature and type of learning disabilities and can used to develop Individualized Education Programs related to specific accommodations and adjustments to the curriculum.

Eighteen subtests comprise the WJ IV COG. Table 4-3 provides an overview of each subtest description. The scores of the first seven subtests are used to generate a General Intellectual Ability (GIA) score. This score is considered the best overall predictor of school achievement related to cognitive ability (Mather & Wendling, 2014). The WJ IV COG provides a profile of an individual's strengths and weaknesses and provides information to aid in diagnosis. For example, if a student has a deficit in fluid reasoning, it may help determine the best approach a teacher can use to aid a student in mathematics. The results of the WJ IV COG may be useful in diagnosing learning disabilities and can be used to justify accommodations for an individual.

Examiners may wish to provide verbal labels when presenting WJ IV COG testing scores to parents or teachers. Table 4-4 provides a classification of standard scores as a guideline. Professional judgment is prudent when applying verbal labels to describe a range of scores (Mather & Wendling, 2014).

Scores yielded from the WJ IV COG include standard scores, percentiles, age and grade equivalents, and a Relative Proficiency Index (RPI), which is related to the examinee's predicted quality of performance (Mather & Wendling, 2014). For example, an RPI of 70/90 means the examinee would be predicted to demonstrate 70% proficiency with similar tasks that average individuals in the comparison group perform at 90%. Scores are reported using an online platform that provides the examinee with a score report as shown in Figure 4-2.

TABLE 4-3. WOODCOCK-JOHNSON IV TESTS OF COGNITIVE ABILITIES SUBTEST DESCRIPTIONS

SUBTEST	DESCRIPTION
Oral Vocabulary	Examinee listens to a word and provides response for an antonym or a synonym.
Number Series	Examinee must determine missing digit.
Verbal Attention	Examinee answers questions regarding sequence.
Letter-Pattern Matching	Examinee locates identical letter patterns.
Phonological Processing	Examinee provides a specific phonemic element.
Story Recall	Examinee listens to a story and retells the story.
Visualization	Examinee examines shapes to create puzzle.
General Information	Examinee answers general knowledge questions.
Concept Formation	Examinee reviews stimulus set to find the rule.
Numbers Reversed	Examinee recalls a span of numbers in reverse order.
Number-Pattern Matching	Examinee locates two identical numbers in a row.
Nonword Repetition	Examinee repeats nonsense words as presented.
Visual-Auditory Learning	Examinee learns and recalls rebuses.
Picture Recognition	Examinee recalls pictures in a field of distractions.
Analysis-Synthesis	Examinee draws conclusions based on symbols.
Object-Number Sequencing	Examinee reorders information presented from audio.
Pair Cancellation	Examinee locates and marks repeated patterns.
Memory for Words	Examinee repeats list of unrelated words in the correct sequence.

TABLE 4-4. WOODCOCK-JOHNSON IV TESTS OF COGNITIVE ABILITIES CLASSIFICATION OF STANDARD SCORES

STANDARD SCORE RANGE	CLASSIFICATION
130 and higher	Very Superior
121-130	Superior
111-120	High Average
90-110	Average
80-89	Low Average
70-79	Low
69 and below	Very Low

CLUSTER/Test	W	AE	GE	RPI	WDiff	Proficiency	SS (68% Band)
GEN INTELLECTUAL ABIL	487	8-4	2.9	81/90	-7	limited to avg	90 (86-95)
Gf-Gc COMPOSITE	499	10-4	4.9	95/90	6	average	109 (106-112)
COMP-KNOWLEDGE (Gc)	498	10-0	4.6	93/90	4	average	104 (100-108)
FLUID REASONING (Gf)	500	10-7	5.2	96/90	9	avg to advanced	110 (106-114)
S-TERM WORK MEM (Gwm)	481	7-7	2.2	70/90	-12	limited to avg	87 (82-92)
AUDITORY PROCESS (Ga)	487	7-3	1.8	74/90	-10	limited to avg	86 (81-90)
L-TERM RETRIEVAL (Glr)	487	7-2	1.7	79/90	-8	limited to avg	86 (82-90)
VISUAL PROCESSING (Gv)	500	11-2	5.8	94/90	5	average	108 (103-114)
NUMBER FACILITY	462	7-3	1.8	34/90	-26	limited	80 (73-88)
PERCEPTUAL SPEED	452	7-0	1.6	11/90	-39	very limited	76 (69-84)
VOCABULARY[a]	497	9-8	4.3	92/90	2	average	103 (98-108)
COGNITIVE EFFICIENCY	471	7-0	1.6	36/90	-25	limited	79 (72-86)

[a] Cluster obtained, in part, from the WJ IV Tests of Oral Language.

	W	AE	GE	RPI	WDiff	Proficiency	SS (68% Band)
Oral Vocabulary	496	9-5	4.0	91/90	1	average	101 (95-108)
Number Series	505	11-5	6.0	98/90	17	advanced	116 (110-121)
Verbal Attention	480	7-7	2.1	68/90	-13	limited to avg	88 (82-93)
Letter-Pattern Matching	461	6-9	1.4	12/90	-38	very limited	77 (67-86)
Phonological Processing	485	7-1	1.7	70/90	-12	limited to avg	84 (78-89)
Story Recall	476	6-0	K.6	60/90	-16	limited	74 (68-80)
Visualization	498	10-6	5.1	93/90	4	average	106 (100-111)
General Information	500	10-7	5.2	95/90	7	avg to advanced	107 (101-112)
Concept Formation	496	9-7	4.1	92/90	2	average	102 (97-106)
Numbers Reversed	481	7-7	2.2	71/90	-12	limited to avg	90 (83-96)
Number-Pattern Matching	442	7-1	1.7	10/90	-40	very limited	81 (72-89)
Nonword Repetition	488	7-5	2.0	78/90	-8	limited to avg	92 (87-96)
Visual-Auditory Learning	497	9-6	4.1	90/90	0	average	101 (97-105)
Picture Recognition	503	12-8	7.2	94/90	6	average	108 (100-115)

Woodcock-Johnson IV Tests of Oral Language (Norms based on age 9-3)

CLUSTER/Test	W	AE	GE	RPI	WDiff	Proficiency	SS (68% Band)
ORAL LANGUAGE	499	10-1	4.7	93/90	4	average	105 (100-111)
BROAD ORAL LANGUAGE	495	9-4	3.9	90/90	0	average	100 (96-105)
ORAL EXPRESSION	498	9-8	4.2	92/90	2	average	103 (98-107)

Figure 4-2. *Woodcock-Johnson IV Tests of Cognitive Abilities* Online Scoring Report sample. (Reproduced with permission from Riverside Insights.)

TEST AT A GLANCE

Woodcock-Johnson IV Tests of Cognitive Abilities (WJ IV COG)
- Type of assessment: Norm-referenced
- Type of administration: Individual
- Administration time: 35 to 90 minutes
- Age/grade level: 2 to 95+ years
- Scores: General Intellectual Ability, raw scores, standard scores, Relative Proficiency Index

In addition to individually administered cognitive assessments, educational achievement assessments are also administered in a one-to-one format. Academic achievement assessments are used to contribute information to instructional decisions. Like cognitive assessments, academic assessments are designed for a wide span of grades, often PK–12. Student responses in educational achievement assessments may be oral, written, or use gestures. One widely used academic assessment is the KTEA-3.

Kaufman Test of Educational Achievement, Third Edition (KTEA-3)

The KTEA-3 is an individually administered assessment of academic achievement for students in grades PK–12, or ages 4 to 25 years (Kaufman & Kaufman, 2014). The KTEA-3 has two forms (A and B) and covers a wide range of achievement and language domains. Additionally, the KTEA-3 provides the ability for the examiner to conduct error analysis. Examiners can administer a single subtest or any combination of subtests to assess achievement in all eight areas of specific learning disability areas as defined in the Individuals with Disabilities Education Improvement Act of 2004 including oral expression, listening comprehension, basic reading skills, reading comprehension, reading fluency skills, written expression, mathematics calculation, and mathematics problem solving. The KTEA-3 is useful in facilitating decisions regarding education placement, instructional levels, and accommodations and can provide information about the effectiveness of specific academic interventions used in response to intervention (Kaufman & Kaufman, 2014). Response to intervention will be discussed in detail in Chapter 6.

TABLE 4-5. KAUFMAN TEST OF EDUCATIONAL ACHIEVEMENT, THIRD EDITION SUBTEST DESCRIPTIONS

SUBTEST	DESCRIPTION
Letter/Word Recognition	Examinee identifies letters and words.
Nonsense Word Decoding	Examinee pronounces made-up words.
Reading Comprehension	Examinee reads passages and answers comprehension questions.
Reading Vocabulary	Examinee reads a word in sentence and selects word with same meaning.
Word Recognition Fluency	Examinee reads as many words a possible within a specified time limit.
Decoding Fluency	Examinee reads as many made-up words as possible within a specified time limit.
Silent Reading Fluency	Examinee has 2 minutes to silently read questions and circle yes or no to each one.
Math Concepts and Applications	Examinee solves math problems.
Math Computation	Examinee solves calculation problems.
Math Fluency	Examinee writes answers to problems within a specified time limit.
Written Expression	Examinee completes a story by writing letters, words, sentences, and an essay.
Spelling	Examinee writes dictated letters or words.
Writing Fluency	Examinee writes simple sentences within a specified time limit.
Listening Comprehension	Examinee listens to sentences/passages and responds to comprehension questions.
Oral Expression	Examinee describes photographs of increasing complexity.
Associational Fluency	Examinee provides words in a 60-second time limit.
Phonological Processing	Examinee orally responds to items that require them to manipulate sounds.
Object Naming Facility	Examinee names pictured objects as quickly as possible.
Letter Naming Facility	Examinee names letters as quickly as possible.

The KTEA-3 is comprised of 19 subtests that yield composite scores for Reading, Reading Fluency, Mathematics, Writing, Oral Language, and Language Processing. Table 4-5 provides descriptions of each subtest that comprises the KTEA-3.

The KTEA-3 provides an examiner with scores including raw scores, standard scores, percentile ranks, growth scale values, and age/grade equivalents. A unique feature of the KTEA-3 is its error analysis capabilities (Kaufman & Kaufman, 2014). This feature allows the examiner to examine a student's specific academic weaknesses and to develop interventions to address the issues noted in the testing session.

TEST AT A GLANCE

Kaufman Test of Educational Achievement, Third Edition (KTEA-3)
- Type of assessment: Norm-referenced
- Type of administration: Individual
- Administration time: 15 to 85 minutes
- Age/grade level: 4 to 25 years
- Scores: Raw scores, standard scores, percentile ranks, growth scale values, and age/grade equivalents

Adaptive Behavior Assessment System, Third Edition (ABAS-3)

The ABAS-3 is an individually administered assessment that is used to measure adaptive skills and is often used to evaluate individuals with developmental delays, sensory or physical impairments, intellectual disabilities, autism spectrum disorder, and learning disabilities. The assessment may be used with individuals birth through 89 years, 11 months. In administering the instrument, a "variety of respondents (e.g., parents, teacher, family members, supervisors, self) complete a rating form that, when scored and interpreted by the professional user, provides information about an individual's adaptive behavior relative to a national, normative sample of peers" (Harrison & Oakland, 2015, p. 1). The ABAS-3 measures skills including communication, functional academics, self-direction, leisure, social, community use, home/school living, health and safety, self-care, motor, and work. Scores yielded from the ABAS-3 include a General Adaptive Composite (GAC), Conceptual Domain, Social Domain, and Practical Domain. ABAS-3 results can be used to assist in diagnosing and classifying various developmental and behavioral disorders.

TEST AT A GLANCE

Adaptive Behavior Assessment System, Third Edition (ABAS-3)
- Type of assessment: Norm-referenced
- Type of administration: Individual
- Administration time: 20 minutes
- Age/grade level: Birth to 89 years, 11 months
- Scores: Raw scores, standard scores, percentile ranks, General Adaptive Composite

Table 4-6. Norm-Referenced Assessments

ASSESSMENT INSTRUMENT	TYPE	PURPOSE
California Achievement Test	Group	Measures basic achievement skills in the areas of reading, language arts, and math.
Cognitive Abilities Test	Group	Assesses general abstract reasoning.
Comprehensive Tests of Nonverbal Intelligence, Second Edition	Individual	Measures general intelligence of children and adults.
Differential Abilities Scale, Second Edition	Individual	Measures a child's processing abilities.
Iowa Assessments	Group	Measures achievement in math, reading, and writing.
Kaufman Assessment Battery for Children, Second Edition	Individual	Assesses cognitive and processing abilities.
Kaufman Test of Educational Achievement, Third Edition	Individual	Measures skills in reading, math, writing, and oral language.
Otis-Lennon School Ability Test	Group	Measures verbal and nonverbal abilities.
Raven Progressive Matrices	Group	Nonverbal test which measures abstract reasoning.
Slosson Intelligence Test, Fourth Edition	Individual	Verbal measure of cognitive ability.
Stanford-Binet, Fifth Edition	Individual	Measure of cognitive processing abilities.
Test of Nonverbal Intelligence, Fourth Edition	Individual	Language-free measure of cognitive ability.
Universal Nonverbal Intelligence Test	Individual	Comprehensive assessment of nonverbal intelligence.
Wechsler Intelligence Scale for Adults, Fourth Edition	Individual	Measure of intellectual ability for adults.

Table 4-6 provides an overview of the different types of group and individual assessments that may be used by school personnel. Effective educators "need to understand the different types of assessment tools available to them, and how to use those tools and the information generated from them to help the educational team design, implement, evaluate, and revise programs that meet the individual needs of students" (McLeskey et al., 2017, p. 44).

HIGH-STAKES TESTING

One of the newest categories of standardized tests in the United States is the state standards-based test based on specific state standards (Powell, 2019), often referred to as high-stakes testing. These tests are high stakes because there may be consequences associated with poor test results. These consequences may entail action such as retention or promotion of students to the next grade level or the inability of students to graduate from high school (Gonzalez et al., 2017). High-stakes testing policies have caused a "trickle-down effect in which politicians put pressure to increase standardized test scores on school boards and superintendents, superintendents put pressure on principals, principals on teachers, and teachers on students" (Croft et al., 2015, p. 73). The high-stakes testing movement can be traced back to the publication of *A Nation at Risk*. This report triggered a wave of educational reforms in the 1980s and 1990s. In 2001, the No Child Left Behind Act mandated public-school students in Grades 3 through 8 be tested in reading and math and students in high school be tested once in those same curricular areas.

While often portrayed as norm-referenced, high-stakes tests are not based on specific norms. High-stakes assessments are not norm-referenced because comparison is not possible since the tests have not been administered to a cross-section of students; rather they would be considered criterion-referenced (Au, 2013). These assessments are tied to a state-based standard and do not provide educative feedback for instructional planning. The results of high-stakes testing are often misused. In attempt to raise test scores, schools may inadvertently be narrowing the curriculum, eliminating enrichment classes and recess, and increasing "drill and kill" instruction and "teaching to the test." Research on the effects of high-stakes testing on curriculum indicates that high-stakes testing results in certain subject matter, such as science and social studies, being given less attention than mathematics and language arts (Abrams et al., 2003; Winstead, 2011).

Proponents of high-stakes testing often stress that high-stakes testing can improve education as a whole because of the effect it has on raising standards and ensuring all students have access to a high-quality education and that standardized testing has a positive impact on student achievement. Huddleston (2014) opined "some teachers have found tests useful for identifying students' strengths and weaknesses and attaining additional resources for students" (p. 6). Starr and Spellings (2014) claim that high-stakes testing allows for the tracking of academic progress of American students. The authors tout high-stakes testing by claiming that "during the NCLB era, student achievement in reading and math improved for African American, Hispanic, and white students alike, and achievement gaps among these groups narrowed" (p. 73).

Conversely, others would assert high-stakes testing has produced students who lack creativity, problem-solving skills, critical thinking, and effective communication (Wernert, 2013). Madus and Clarke (2001) conclude there is no room for originality when high-stakes testing is inflexible and teachers are not allowed to deviate from the curriculum. The authors noted, "Teachers in high-minority classrooms significantly more often reported teaching test-taking skills, teaching topics known to be on the test, increasing emphasis on tested topics, beginning preparation more than one month before the test, and including topics not otherwise taught" (p. 10). Additionally, there is a gap in educational opportunity in the U.S. public school system, and low-income and students of color often face inequalities when compared to peers from high-income areas (Thompson & Allen, 2012).

Since the inception of formal education, education has been results-oriented rather than knowledge-oriented (Gay, 2010). To date, peer-reviewed literature supporting high-stakes testing is not common. While high-stakes testing remains active in public schools, a majority of research indicates that high-stakes testing is not advantageous to education.

> **CHECK FOR UNDERSTANDING**
>
> A high-stakes test is any test used to make important decisions about students, educators, schools, or districts, most commonly for the purpose of accountability.

SUMMARY

Norm-referenced assessments compare a student's performance to that of students in the same norm group. Norm-referenced assessments may be administered individually or, in some instances, can be administered in a group setting. Data from norm-referenced assessments may be used for special education eligibility, for gifted and talented program considerations, and to develop appropriate instructional interventions for students (Overton, 2015). Norm-referenced assessments are commonly administered by individuals trained in testing and measurement, and strict adherence to testing environment, administration, and scoring must be followed. There are numerous standardized assessments used by schools today, and the potential for bias is present. To ameliorate possible bias, testers should carefully select testing instruments based on the cultural, linguistic, and socioeconomic status of students they assess.

CASE STUDY WRAP-UP

Following his meeting with the campus assessment coordinator, Mr. Dollins has a better understanding of norm-referenced assessment. Based on his conversations with the coordinator, Mr. Dollins realizes that norm-referenced assessment is standardized and that scores are often used to compare the individual performance of students. He further understands the strengths and weaknesses of using group and individual assessments and that the results of the assessments are used for instructional planning and placement decisions. Further, Mr. Dollins realizes that the high-stakes testing occurring in the district is not norm-referenced as he once thought. Mr. Dollins has decided to visit more with the coordinator to share his concerns related to his student Marcus and to determine if further assessment is warranted.

CHAPTER REVIEW

1. Discuss the differences between group and individually administered assessments.
2. Why are high-stakes tests not a norm-referenced assessment?
3. What are some strengths associated with norm-referenced assessments?

REFERENCES

Abrams, L., Pedulla, J., & Madaus, G. (2003). View from the classroom: Teachers' opinions of statewide testing. *Theory into Practice, 42*, 18-29. https://doi.org/10.1207s/1543042tip4201_4

Au, W. (2013). Hiding behind high-stakes testing: Meritocracy, objectivity, and inequality in U.S. education. *The International Education Journal: Comparative Perspectives, 12*(2), 7-19. https://doi.org/10.1093.acrefore/9780190264093.013.1123

Croft, S. J., Roberts, M. A., & Stenhouse, V. L. (2015). The perfect storm of education reform: High-stakes testing and teacher evaluation. *Social Justice, 42*(1), 70-92.

Gay, G. (2010). *Culturally responsive teaching: Theory, research and practice* (2nd ed.). Norton.

Gonzalez, A., Peters, M. L., Orange, A., & Grigsby, B. (2017). The influence of high stakes testing on teacher self-efficacy and job-related stress. *Cambridge Journal of Education, 47*(4), 513-531. https://doi.org/10.1080/0305764x.2016.1214237

Harrison, P. L., & Oakland, T. (2015). *Adaptive behavior assessment system* (3rd ed.). [Manual]. Western Psychological Services.

Huddleston, A. P. (2014). Achievement at whose expense? A literature review of test-based grade retention policies in US schools. *Education Policy Analysis Archives/Archivos Analíticos de Políticas Educativas, 22*, 1-31. https://doi.org/10.104507/epaa.v22n18.2014

Individuals with Disabilities Education Improvement Act, Public Law 108-446, 108th Congress (2004).

Kaufman, A. F., & Kaufman, N. L. (2014). *Kaufman Test of Educational Achievement* (3rd ed.). NCS Pearson.

Lohman, D. F. (2011). *Cognitive Abilities Test, Form 7*. Riverside.

Madus, G. F., & Clarke, M. (2001). The adverse impact of high-stakes testing on minority students: Evidence from 100 years of test data. In G. Orfield & M. Kornhaber (Eds.), *Raising standards or raising barriers? Inequality and high-stakes testing in public education*. The Century Foundation.

Mather, N., & Wendling, B. J. (2014). *Examiner's manual: Woodcock-Johnson IV Tests of Cognitive Abilities*. Riverside.

McLeskey, J., Barringer, M-D., Billingsley, B., Brownell, M., Jackson, D., Kennedy, M., Lewis, T., Maheady, L., Rodriguez, J., Scheeler, M. C., Winn, J., & Ziegler, D. (2017). *High-leverage practices in special education*. Council for Exceptional Children & CEEDAR Center.

McLoughlin, J. A., Lewis, R. B., & Kritikos, E. P. (2018). *Assessing students with special needs* (8th ed.). Pearson.

No Child Left Behind Act, Public Law 107-110, 107th Congress (2001).

Otis, A. S., & Lennon, R. T. (2003). *Otis-Lennon School Ability Test* (8th ed.). NCS Pearson.

Overton, T. (2015). *Assessing learners with special needs: An applied approach* (8th ed.). Pearson.

Powell, S. D. (2019). *Your introduction to education* (4th ed.). Pearson Education.

Schrank, F. A., Mather, N., & McGrew, K. S. (2014). *Woodcock-Johnson IV Tests of Cognitive Abilities*. Riverside.

Starr, J., & Spellings, M. (2014). Examining high-stakes testing: Education Next talks with Joshua P. Starr and Margaret Spellings. *Education Next, 14*(1), 70-77.

Thompson, G. L., & Allen, T. G. (2012). Four effects of high-stakes testing movement on African American K–12 students. *The Journal of Negro Education, 81*(3), 218-227. https://doi.org/10.7709/jnegroeducation.81.0.0218

Wechsler, D. (2014). *Wechsler Intelligence Scale for Children* (5th ed.). Pearson.

Welch, C., & Dunbar, S. (2011). *The Iowa Assessments*. Riverside Insights.

Wernert, S. (2013). *No Child Left Behind comes to college: The implications of limiting early age play on incoming college students*. http://www.nacada.ksu.edu

Winstead, L. (2011). The impact of NCLB and accountability on social studies: Teacher experiences and perceptions about teaching social studies. *The Social Studies, 102*, 221-227. https://doi.org/10.1080/00377996.2011.571567

KEY TERMS

- **authentic assessment:** A form of performance [...] children.
- **exit slips:** Examples of formative assessments [...] tion they learned during the lesson.
- **formative assessments (FAs):** Daily assessment [...] dents' learning.
- **graphic organizers (GOs):** Provides students [...] information to pre-existing information.
- **performance-based assessments:** Assessment [...] strate their learning or knowledge (presentatio [...]
- **portfolio assessments (PAs):** Assessments tha [...] a story of learning and/or effort.
- **response cards:** Offer students an opportunit [...] without the use of spoken language. Typical r [...] can hold up to display responses to questions [...]
- **rubric:** A type of matrix that specifies a set of [...] of an assignment, paper, project, or presentatio [...]
- **summative assessments (SAs):** High-stakes a [...] son or learning cycle. These assessments are h [...] almost always recorded.
- **Think-Pair-Share (TPS):** A cooperative learn [...] gether to answer a question or discuss a specifi [...]

KEY ABBREVIATIONS

- ESSA: Every Student Succeeds Act
- FA: formative assessment
- GO: graphic organizer
- HLP: high-leverage practice
- NCLB: No Child Left Behind
- PA: portfolio assessment
- SA: summative assessment
- SEA: state education association
- TPS: Think-Pair-Share

ASSESSMENTS

[...]ly assessment strategies teachers implement to gauge [...] assessment for learning" (Gardner, 2010). FAs are in[...]. FAs are routinely and consistently conducted in the [...]uch as interactions between the student and teacher, [...]e on one (Ruiz-Primo & Furtak, 2007). Moreover, FAs [...] assessment techniques.

FAs are "those activities undertaken by teachers and [...] provide information to be used as feedback to modify [...] as Heritage (2007) appropriately noted, FAs feature a [...]dents' learning. FA should begin immediately during [...]nce, FAs can take a wide variety of formats from more [...]ques such as conversations with students about their [...], FAs are vehicles that provide teachers and students [...]rning (Heritage, 2007).

[...]base that supports their impact on learning (Marzano, [...]nger than summative assessments (SAs; e.g., end of [...]h FAs indicates stronger effect sizes whereas SAs are

UNDERSTANDING

[...]e informal in nature, design, and implementation. [...]ction.

[...]tion to make decisions is critical in helping teachers [...]variety of assessment strategies are necessary in pro-[...], teachers, parents, students, and other stakeholders [...]y be a variety of FA techniques used by teachers, com-[...]quent occurrence, and positive and constructive feed-

CASE S[...]

Ms. Carter is a first-year teacher at the Best E[...]icipation by students. Examples of active participation teacher preparation program from a reputable unive[...]g how their learning is progressing, and planning for her students' learning. Although she hates to admit [...]ed goals between teachers and students, positive rela-between formative and summative assessments and [...]ement is through self-assessment. Self-assessment is a gling with classroom assessment procedures, she does[...]gn a score for each standard created by the teacher for standards. To that end, Ms. Carter has been meeting [...] the standards clearly articulated and shared with stu-identify formative and summative assessments that s[...]t provides teachers a vehicle for communicating their [...]n opportunity to self-assess their progress (Jonsson,

TABLE 5-1. THREE COMMON FEATURES OF FORMATIVE ASSESSMENTS	
FEATURE	**CHARACTERISTIC**
Student involvement	Active participants
Frequent	Ongoing/daily
Feedback	Intentional/descriptive

2014). One of the primary uses of self-assessment is to provide a point of contrast to the teacher's perspective (Marzano, 2006). Another method to increase student involvement is through 1-minute reflection activities. One-minute reflections can be implemented in a variety of ways (see exit slip discussion later in the chapter). Typically, the teacher provides students with a writing prompt, such as, "What is the muddiest point from today's lesson?" or stated in another way, "What is the one concept you still do not understand?" These specific prompts encourage students to describe what they were most confused about (Marzano, 2006).

Frequent

FAs' main purpose is to drive instruction. Specifically, FA is an ongoing activity and occurs before and during the lesson. Because FAs are continual sources of information about students' understanding and because they occur frequently as part of the daily instruction, teachers can make changes to instruction immediately instead of waiting until the end of the grading cycle—thus driving instruction (Dixson & Worrell, 2016). Moreover, when teachers use FA for learning, there are no formal grades reported in the gradebook and no final marks on the paper (Chappuis & Chappuis, 2008).

Feedback

Perhaps the single most important feature of FA is feedback. The Council for Exceptional Children (CEC) has identified 22 high-leverage practices (HLPs) that can support special education teacher candidates as they learn effective teaching practices for their classrooms (McLeskey et al., 2017). Although HLPs are geared toward the preparation of special educators, all pre-service educators can benefit from these practices. HLPs 8 and 22 address the critical role of feedback—"Provide positive and constructive feedback to guide students' learning and behavior" (McLeskey et al., 2017, pp. 21, 25). Since feedback was designated as a critical feature of instruction and behavioral outcomes, it is listed under both the Instruction domain (HLP 22) and the Social/Emotional/Behavioral practices domain (HLP 8).

"The purpose of feedback is to guide student learning and behavior and increase student motivation, engagement, and independence, leading to improved student learning and behavior" (McLeskey et al., 2017, pp. 21, 25). As an impactful teacher practice, positive and constructive feedback can result in positive learning and behavior outcomes for school-aged children (Ackerman & Horn, 2021; Hattie & Timperley, 2007). Descriptive feedback is intentional, identifies areas of strength, targets areas that need work, and recommends a series of action students can take to narrow the gap between where they are now and where they ought to be all without providing grades. Moreover, it models the kind of internal thinking students need to engage in when they self-assess their own learning (Chappuis & Chappuis, 2008).

TABLE 5-2. EXAMPLES OF THE DIFFERENT TYPES OF FORMATIVE ASSESSMENTS

TYPE	EXAMPLE
Oral evidence	Think-Pair-Share
Written evidence	Exit slips
Graphic evidence	Graphic organizers
Practical evidence	Observations of student learning behaviors
Nonverbal evidence	Response cards

Different Types

FAs use classroom learning activities that provide evidence of students' understanding. Just as there are numerous classroom activities, so too are there many different types of FAs: (1) oral evidence, (2) written evidence, (3) graphic evidence, (4) practical evidence, and (5) nonverbal evidence (Ruiz-Primo, 2011). Table 5-2 provides examples of the different types of FAs.

Mr. Baker and Ms. Carter determine a variety of FAs are required to appropriately gauge her students' level of learning. They create an assessment plan and decide to implement FAs depending on the lesson and classroom activities from each of the preceding areas.

Think-Pair-Share (Oral Evidence)

TPS is a cooperative learning strategy which requires students to work together to answer a question or discuss a specific topic (Reading Rockets, n.d.-a). TPS involves the following three steps: (1) each student silently thinks about the topic presented, (2) each student pairs with another student to discuss the topic or answer the question, and (3) pairs share their conversations with the rest of the class. Kaddoura's (2013) study of 91 nursing students suggested the use of TPS led to increased critical thinking skills in a health assessment course. Moreover, Kaddoura's findings align with Robertson (2006), who asserts the precepts of TPS (i.e., engaging students in their learning, thinking, and discussing) is an active teaching-learning strategy. In particular, the TPS strategy is a useful technique to increase student participation in academic conversations, focus attention, and share ideas with others. When used as an FA, teachers are able to observe students' level of engagement, quality of conversations between students, and which students readily share information about the topic.

When using the TPS strategy with her class on the stages of a thunderstorm, Ms. Carter directed her students to think about two to three ideas. During this step, Ms. Carter encouraged students to think about their ideas in their minds and to jot down or draw the ideas on a piece of paper. Next, Ms. Carter invited students to pair with their "elbow-partner" and discuss their ideas. Finally, she directed each group to select one idea they thought was the most important to share with the class. While the students were engaged in the TPS strategy, Ms. Carter rotated from group to group, listened to conversations, and observed the interactions (or lack thereof) between the students. In addition to observing, she carefully jotted down notes to review later.

CHECK FOR UNDERSTANDING

TPS strategy steps:
1. Each student silently thinks about the topic presented (*Think*).
2. Each student pairs with another student to discuss the topic or answer the question (*Pair*).
3. Pairs share their conversations with the rest of the class (*Share*).

Figure 5-1. Understanding exit slip example.

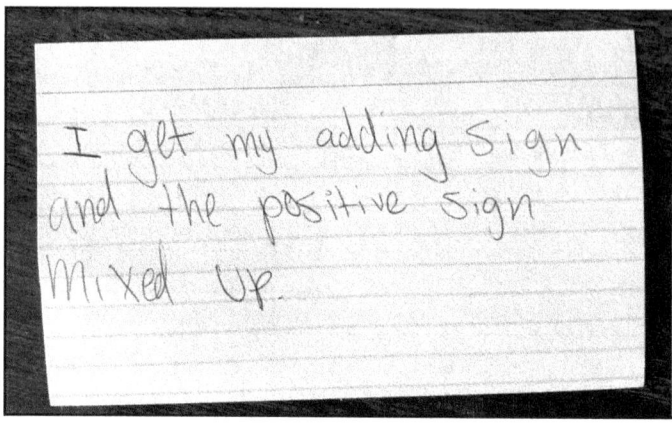

Exit Slips (Written Evidence)

Exit slips are a useful strategy to help students reflect on information they learned during the lesson and to express their ideas about the new information. Typically, exit slips require students to respond in writing to a prompt given by the teacher and give their written reflections to the teacher upon exiting the room. Moreover, the exit slip strategy is a great tool for incorporating writing in a variety of content areas (Allen & Striegel, n.d.). According to Albers (2006), exit slips offer information about thoughts and ideas students have learned and offer insights about questions they may still have. In addition, their questions drive instruction for the next class.

Exit slip prompts may be categorized into three different subcategories: thinking, understanding, and feeling. The first type of prompt is thinking. The purpose of thinking prompts is to provide guidance for the teacher on future topics (Knight, 2013). Moreover, thinking prompts offer students agency over their learning. Prompts such as "I would like to learn about . . ." is an example of a thinking prompt. This type of prompt provides an outlet for proposing future topics and creates a sense of ownership over students' learning while also providing the teacher with ideas for lesson planning.

The second type of prompt is understanding. Examples of understanding prompts include: "Write down or draw one thing that was very clear to you from today's lesson" and "Write down or draw one thing from today's lesson that is still unclear to you." Prompts for understanding provide clarity on what the student learned and, importantly, which concepts they are still struggling with (Figure 5-1; Fisher & Frey, 2004).

The third type of prompt is related to the student's feelings about a topic and can be categorized as other exit prompts (Reading Rockets, n.d.-b). These prompts typically encourage the student to check in with their feelings about the lesson. The following prompt is designed so all students can participate, even those who struggle with expressing their ideas on paper. For example, "Draw a smiley, frowny, or neutral face for how you feel about . . ." Another way to make feelings prompts more accessible for students who are reluctant writers is to invite one- or two-word responses—for example, "I feel . . . when I am asked to do . . ."

When selecting a prompt, teachers should choose the type of prompt carefully and purposefully. In addition, using a variety of prompts will help teachers gain a deeper understanding of a student's strengths and weaknesses and will illuminate the student's feelings toward the lesson, topic, or concept (Albers, 2006). This is especially critical when working with students who are struggling to learn. Table 5-3 provides examples of prompts for the three categories of exit slips.

TABLE 5-3. THREE TYPES OF EXIT SLIPS WITH PROMPT EXAMPLES

EXIT SLIP	PROMPT
Thinking	What was one thing from today's lesson I wished I learned but I didn't? Why?
	I would like to learn about… Why?
Understanding	What did I understand clearly from today's lesson?
	What was the one concept that I still do not understand?
Feeling	I feel… about today's lesson.
	Draw a smiley, frowny, or neutral face for how you feel about…

Graphic Organizers (Graphic Evidence)

The primary purpose of graphic organizers (GOs) is to make abstract concepts or ideas and relationships clear (Baxendell, 2003). GOs provide students with a visual road map as they connect new information to pre-existing knowledge (Dye, 2000). In particular, GOs help students connect existing knowledge with new concepts (Singleton & Filce, 2015).

By presenting a framework for students to create visual representations of the most important information in the text, GOs reduce cognitive demands which are often placed on students (Singleton & Filce, 2015). Reducing cognitive demands is especially critical for upper elementary and secondary-age students as academic content becomes more challenging with the increases in grade level.

When choosing a GO to use in a lesson, it is important for teachers to identify the type and purpose of the GO and to select a GO that will work best in organizing information (Singleton & Filce, 2015). In addition, academic areas will have GOs specific to their discipline. Common examples of GOs that may be used across the different content areas include spider maps, sequencing charts, and Venn diagrams.

Spider maps help students investigate a topic or organize their thoughts about a topic (Singleton & Filce, 2015). Spider maps are easy for students to create. Information is organized around a central topic, typically presented in a bubble. Details about the topic extend outward to bubbles that contain the details about the topic (Figure 5-2).

The next type of GO is sequencing charts. These types of charts depict a linear sequence of events (Singleton & Filce, 2015). Examples include "how to" (e.g., how to write a paragraph; Figure 5-3) and demonstrating the steps in solving multistep word problems.

The third type of GO commonly used across content areas is Venn diagrams. Venn diagrams (Figure 5-4) help students compare and contrast two or more concepts and provide an excellent visual display of the similarities and differences between these concepts (Baxendell, 2003).

Observations of Student Learning Behaviors (Practical Evidence)

Observations of students performing a specific task or instructional activity are an excellent way that teachers can apply practical evidence as a form of FA to gauge their students' progress. Even though observations are sometimes overlooked as a trustworthy source of information, data collected from the classroom and other settings can provide important information about a student's academic abilities and the way the student approaches a task (McLeskey et al., 2017). For example, when a student reads aloud, the teacher can assess the student's oral reading rate and conduct error analysis of the child's reading. This helps the teacher pinpoint the specific types of errors the student commits. Once the teacher identifies the errors, they can then tailor the classroom instruction to help correct these errors. *In our case study scenario, Ms. Carter uses observations of oral reading to help her identify her students' reading errors. Ms. Carter determines that some of her students are substituting known words in their vocabulary for unknown words, such as "car" for "automobile." With this*

Figure 5-2. Spider map example: Life.

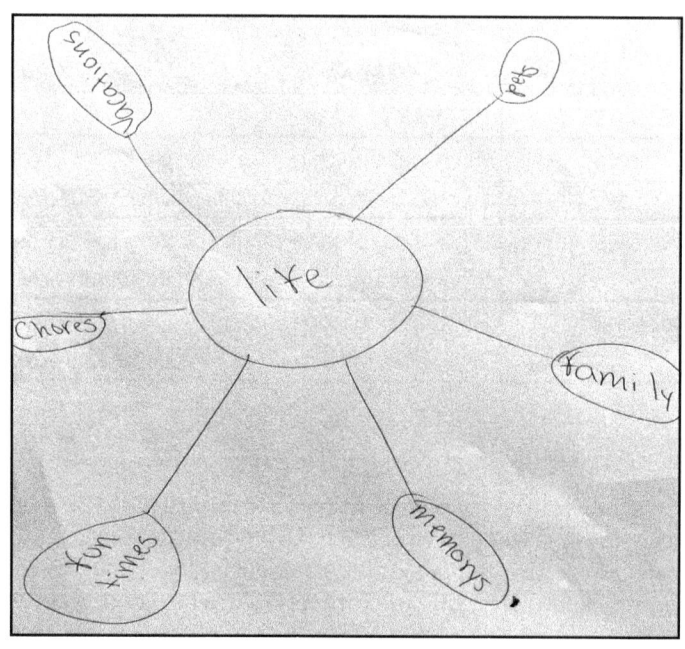

Figure 5-3. Sequencing chart: How to write a paragraph.

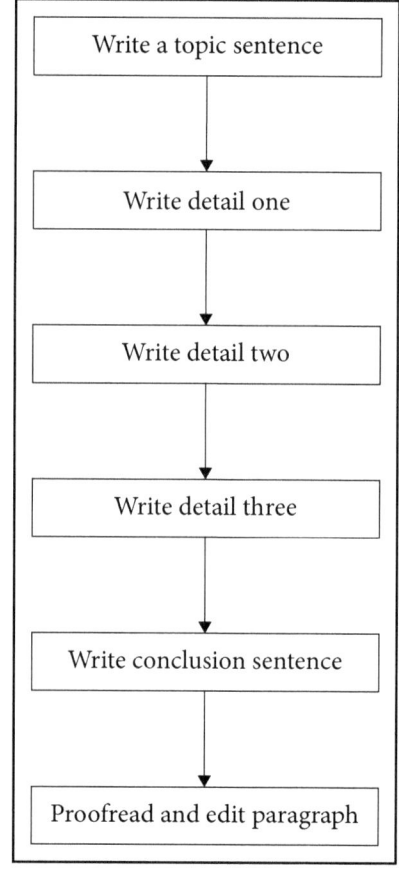

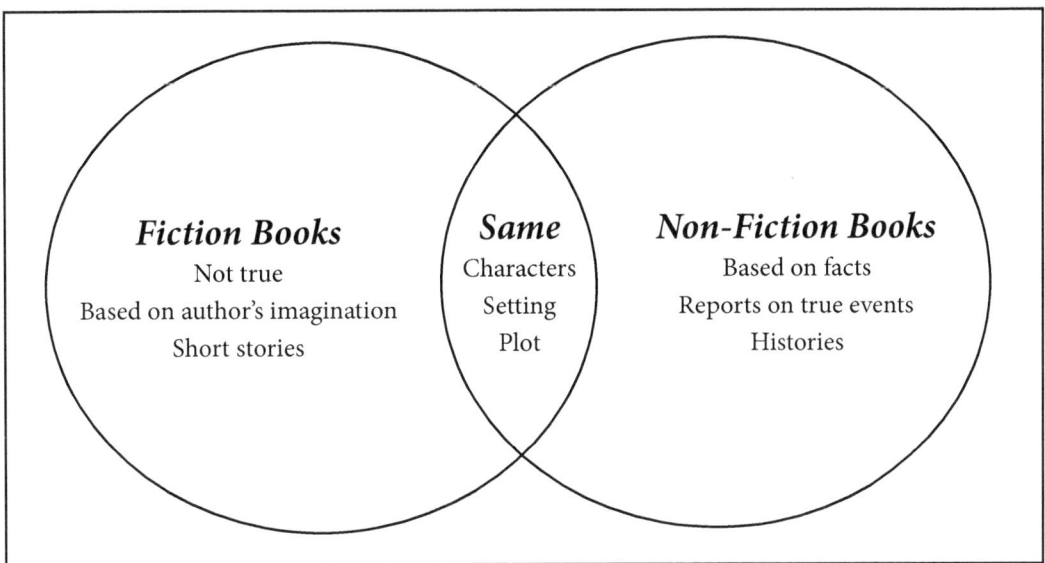

Figure 5-4. Venn diagram: Similarities and differences of fiction and non-fiction books.

information, Ms. Carter designs lessons that focuses on oral reading fluency and vocabulary development. Observation data also include the teacher paying specific attention to how the student approaches a task. For example, when asked to complete a calculation problem, Ms. Carter might notice one of her students works the problem from left to right instead of right to left. When Ms. Carter notices this behavior, she provides immediate feedback to the student and re-teaches the correct way to approach a multiple-digit calculation problem. In sum, there are many observable behaviors that a teacher can witness while a child is completing a task or responding to a question.

Response Cards (Nonverbal Evidence)

Nonverbal evidence provides an opportunity for students to demonstrate what they know about a topic without the use of spoken language while promoting higher rates of active participation for students (Ruiz-Primo, 2011). An example of nonverbal evidence is response cards. Although response cards come in many forms, typical response cards are dry erase boards each student holds up to display responses to questions or problems that are posed by the teacher (Randolph, 2007). One of the benefits of using response cards is that teachers can support students with a wide range of disabilities, including those with intellectual disabilities, by collecting more frequent measures of FA data (Clarke et al., 2016). Moreover, Randolph (2007) concluded that with the use of response cards students obtained higher rates of test and quiz scores, increased their participation, and exhibited less off-task behaviors when compared to hand-raising.

To set the stage for an upcoming lesson on multidigit multiplication, Ms. Carter uses response cards to conduct a review and to help her gauge her students' pre-existing knowledge of single-digit multiplication. Ms. Carter begins with a review of multiplication and asks her students to write on their response cards the sign that means multiplication. She also poses basic multiplication problems such as 4 × 2 for students to respond to. In this way, Ms. Carter is using response cards to actively involve all her students, and she is able to easily determine which students need re-teaching of basic multiplication facts before moving on to the lesson on multi-digit multiplication.

Summary

FAs are the daily assessment strategies teachers use to gauge students' learning with the primary purpose of driving instruction (Heritage, 2007). These types of assessments encompass a wide variety of formats: TPS conversations (oral evidence), exit slips (written evidence), observations of students' learning behaviors (practical evidence), GOs (graphic evidence), and response cards (nonverbal evidence). The main features of FA are that it (1) involves active student participation, (2) occurs frequently as part of daily instruction (i.e., ongoing), and (3) includes descriptive and intentional feedback. Another prominent characteristic of FAs is that they are informal. As such, there is the lack of emphases of grades in the gradebook. When teachers use FA for learning, there are no formal grades reported in the gradebook and no final marks on the paper (Chappuis & Chappuis, 2008).

> **CHECK FOR UNDERSTANDING**
>
> Common examples of FAs include TPS, exit slips, GOs, observations of students' learning behaviors, and response cards.

SUMMATIVE ASSESSMENTS

In contrast to FAs, SAs occur at the end of the lesson or learning cycle, are less frequent, and are cumulative, and grades are almost always recorded (Dixson & Worrell, 2016). Rather than providing immediate feedback to students and teachers, which is one of the primary features of FAs, SAs are used to get a final determination of how much learning has occurred (Gardner, 2010). Moreover, SAs occur far too late in the lesson cycle to provide information to the teacher and students to make adjustments to learning (Garrison & Ehringhaus, n.d.), and if students meet the learning outcomes, typically no more formal learning occurs after they are evaluated except in the case of cumulative exams (Dixson & Worrell, 2016). Table 5-4 illustrates SA examples.

Exams—State Assessments

Although there are many different types of exams that serve as SAs, perhaps the most recognizable and consequential are state assessments that resulted in part from the No Child Left Behind Act (NCLB; 2001), which has since been reauthorized as the Every Student Succeeds Act (ESSA; 2015). Under ESSA, states have an increased role in holding schools accountable for student achievement. ESSA requires states to test students in reading and math once a year for Grades 3 through 8 and once in high school. States are also required to test students in science once a year in Grades 3 through 5, 6 through 8, and 10 through 12. Students with disabilities and who are on 504 Plans are eligible to receive accommodations on state assessments, but only 1% of the total number of students being assessed can be given alternate assessments (ASCD, 2015; The Understood Team, n.d.). In addition to frequent state testing requirements, ESSA maintained many of the accountability measures from NCLB.

TABLE 5-4. SUMMATIVE ASSESSMENT EXAMPLES BY TYPE

TYPES OF SUMMATIVE ASSESSMENT	EXAMPLES
Exams	Spelling tests
	Unit tests
	Final exams
	End of course exams
	State assessments
	District benchmark exams
	College entrance exams
Performance-based assessments	Presentations
	Performances
	Projects
	Papers
Portfolio assessments	Portfolios of learning/e-portfolios

Over the past 2 decades, the prominent philosophy of state education associations (SEAs) and school districts is the singular goal of developing, implementing, and using tests to hold students accountable to K–12 standards (Edgerton, 2019). This push has resulted in state assessments being high-stakes ventures for students, families, teachers, and school districts. Brown (2010) reported pre-service candidates enrolled in a teacher education program recognized the high-stakes testing system in Texas drove public school teachers' instruction and students' learning. Even as early as 2000, Barksdale-Ladd and Thomas (2000) asserted teacher decision making about what is best for children appears to have been dismissed.

Although there remains a strong accountability culture in schools, SEAs are now beginning to use the data from state assessments in more targeted ways, resulting in more district-level capacity building (e.g., professional development) and less focus on compliance (Edgerton, 2019). To help promote more robust assessment measures, ESSA provided states with opportunities to expand their accountability systems specifically by assessing students from multiple measures. Thus, states may develop and implement assessment measures beyond test scores to evaluate school quality and student success. However, only a small number of states ($n = 15$) have opted to do this. In fact, most states ($n = 35$) continue to focus on more traditional models of assessment, indicating a strong preference for test scores and graduation rates. Moreover, most states continue to focus more on student success as opposed to school quality, perpetuating the emphasis on individual student growth. While there continues to be an emphasis on state testing and student success, the small number of states that focus on multiple measures are the leaders in the movement to develop the next generation of school accountability and to consider a broader range of factors that contribute to school success (Portz, 2021).

CHECK FOR UNDERSTANDING

Under the Every Student Succeeds Act (2015), states have an increased role in holding schools accountable for student achievement, which has reinforced a culture of high-stakes testing.

Performance-Based Assessments

Performance-based assessments include activities where students demonstrate their learning or knowledge (National Research Council, 2001). Performance-based assessments focus on student performance and offer an alternative to more traditional types of assessment activities (e.g., objective tests, essays). Specifically, performance-based assessments provide observable evidence of what students know and can do (Dorn, 2003). Importantly, these types of assessments originate from the curriculum and are aligned with the class learning objectives.

A form of performance-based assessments often used with very young children is authentic assessment. This type of assessment "refers to the systematic recording of developmental observations overtime about the naturally occurring behaviors of young children in daily routines by familiar and knowledgeable caregivers in the child's life" (Bagnato & Ho, 2006, p. 29). Authentic assessments are based on performance, "not contrived activities," integrating assessment and curriculum (Bagnato & Ho, 2006, p. 27). For school-aged children, examples of performance-based assessments might include a teacher evaluating student's presentations, speeches, book reports, and so on. *Using our case study example, Ms. Carter assessed her students' knowledge of the United States capitals through individual student presentations of the map of the United States. Because these presentations served as a cumulative evaluation of her students' knowledge of the United States' capitals, they provide an example of an SA that is performance-based.*

> **CHECK FOR UNDERSTANDING**
>
> Performance-based assessments focus on student performance, which offers an alternative to more traditional types of assessment activities. Importantly, these types of assessments originate from the curriculum and are aligned with the class learning objectives. Examples include presentations, speeches, and book reports.

Portfolio Assessments

Another type of SA is portfolio assessments (PAs). Portfolios represent a collection of student work that tells a story of learning and/or effort (National Research Council, 2001). Because portfolios are an alternative to more traditional assessment practices, teachers can document growth over time when new artifacts are added (Swicegood, 1994).

An important characteristic of creating a portfolio is the students are responsible for selecting pieces of their work to demonstrate progression of learning (National Research Council, 2001). While students assume an increased ownership of their learning by selecting samples to include in their portfolios, collaborative relationships that occur between teachers and students can help in sharing the responsibility for learning (Swicegood, 1994). The following list describes PA purposes that have been adapted from Swicegood (1994):

- To provide a concrete display of student's work or student's development
- To obtain multiple sources of assessment information over time
- To provide a concrete display of the range of learning activities or experiences
- To provide a means for teacher and student to reflect on learning goals
- To encourage dialogue and collaborative conversations among educators and between student and teacher

PAs include critical decisions on the part of the teacher. When students are required to demonstrate their knowledge via performance-based assessments or portfolio-based assessments, the standards or criteria for inclusion must be clearly identified and discussed prior to the demonstration, presentation, performance, or the selection process (Jonsson, 2014). One tool that can help demystify the grading criteria is the use of rubrics when evaluating portfolios and performance-based assessments.

CHECK FOR UNDERSTANDING

- Portfolios represent a collection of student work that tells a story of learning and/or effort (National Research Council, 2001).
- Because portfolios are an alternative to more traditional assessment practices, teachers can document growth over time when new artifacts are added (Swicegood, 1994).
- An important characteristic of creating a portfolio is that students are responsible for selecting pieces of their work to demonstrate progression of learning (National Research Council, 2001).

Summary

SAs are one of the many tools that teachers can use to evaluate students' learning. SAs occur at the end of the lesson and are less frequent, and grades are typically recorded (Dixson & Worrell, 2016). Because SAs occur far too late in the lesson cycle, they do not provide real-time information about students' learning. Thus, teachers and students do not receive the feedback they need to adjust learning (Garrison & Ehringhaus, n.d.). Therefore, SAs are not the ideal tool for driving instruction. Rather, they serve as a final determination of students' understanding (Gardner, 2010). Nevertheless, when used in conjunction with FAs and frequent feedback, SAs provide valuable information for the classroom teacher.

CHECK FOR UNDERSTANDING

SAs occur at the end of the lesson cycle, are less frequent, and are cumulative, and grades are almost always recorded. Examples include exams, performance-based assessments, and portfolios.

RUBRICS

Rubrics are scoring guides to evaluate quality of students' work and can be a helpful tool that enhance instruction (Popham, 1997). More specifically, rubrics are a type of matrix specifying a set of criteria students can use to guide the creation of an assignment, paper, project, or presentation (Allen & Tanner, 2006). Rubrics are often used to evaluate SAs such as open-ended written responses on exams, performance-based assessments, and portfolios.

General Design Principles

An important characteristic of creating a rubric is the consideration of the teacher's values and expectations for the assignment. As such, the creation of a rubric first requires the teacher to examine their values and expectations for student learning outcomes (Allen & Tanner, 2006). Once this occurs, a teacher is ready to begin creating or selecting a pre-existing rubric.

When designing rubrics, the first step is to develop a list of qualities the student should demonstrate proficiency in when completing the learning activity. This can be accomplished by reflecting on two critical questions—"What do I want students to know and be able to do?" and "How will I know when they know it and can do it well?" (Allen & Tanner, 2006, p. 198). Another way to create rubrics is to find existing rubrics for similar tasks and review the criteria to see if they are a good fit. Popham (1997) suggests teachers design rubrics containing three to five criteria (i.e., standards), and these criteria represent the key attribute of the skill being evaluated. In addition, Moskal (2000) suggests that when creating a rubric, the teacher should avoid the use of words that are subjective such as "good" or "excellent" as these terms are too general, do not guide the learner in meeting the standards, and must be defined. Finally, with respect to length of a rubric, Popham (1997) asserts rubrics should not exceed two pages in length.

Why Use Rubrics

When used as part of the instructional process, rubrics can help clarify the grading criteria (Moskal, 2000), thus making them more explicit. When students understand the grading criteria, they have a clearer sense of the expectations for high levels of performance and what they need to do to reach these expectations. From a teacher's perspective, even though the time creating the rubric may be significant, rubrics help streamline the grading process. The more specific the criteria on the rubric, the feedback required to justify and explain a grade is significantly reduced, thus decreasing the subjectiveness of the grade awarded for each criterion (Allen & Tanner, 2006). Rubrics also provide specific feedback to students on how they can improve their performance (Moskal, 2000) and encourage students to reflect on their learning and to monitor their progress toward the standards (Allen & Tanner, 2006).

When communicating the expectations on rubrics, teachers should make the rubric accessible to students by explaining the criteria on the rubric, which can be completed by reviewing each standard on the rubric (Jonsson, 2014) and by showing a variety of examples from previous students' performance. Although the next step may seem obvious, teachers should provide a copy of the rubric to students and review the criteria before students begin the assignment. Table 5-5 provides an example of a rubric developed for an exit slip prompt.

SUMMARY

FAs and SAs are important assessment strategies that teachers can use to help understand how the children in their classrooms are learning. The goal of FA is to provide teachers with real-time information during the lesson about students' learning. This allows teachers the opportunity to gauge learning and intervene before it is too late. On the other hand, SA measures what children have already learned. That said, SA typically occurs at the end of the lesson. When deciding which assessment strategy to use, teachers should consider the purpose of the assignment and how and when they measure student learning.

TABLE 5-5. EXAMPLE OF A RUBRIC—"ONE THING I LEARNED"

	5	3	0
Summary	I wrote a 5- to 6-sentence summary of one thing I learned from the lesson.	I wrote a 3- to 5-sentence summary of one thing I learned from the lesson.	I wrote less than 3 sentences on one thing I learned from the lesson.
Sentences	I wrote complete sentences of differing lengths with 0 errors in punctuation.	I wrote complete sentences that are the same length with 1 error in punctuation.	I wrote sentences that are not complete and have more than 1 error in punctuation.
Proofreading	My summary has 0 grammatical and/or spelling errors.	My summary has 1 to 2 grammatical and/or spelling errors.	My summary has more than 2 grammatical and/or spelling errors.

CASE STUDY WRAP-UP

Although there are many types of FA that help gauge students' learning, Ms. Carter decided to use only a few (e.g., response cards, exit slips, TPS) so that she could better manage their use. In addition to FA, Ms. Carter evaluated her students' learning at the end of the grading period by using SA (e.g., traditional exams and student presentations). To evaluate the presentations, Ms. Carter used a rubric that she and Mr. Baker designed. Because she used a variety of assessment techniques, Ms. Carter was better able to drive instruction by understanding her students' learning in real time.

CHAPTER REVIEW

1. Identify one to two formative assessments for a lesson you will teach. Document each assessment in your lesson plan.
2. Identify one to two graphic organizers for the subject areas that you plan to teach.
3. Create a three- to five-standard rubric for a learning activity.
4. Interview a teacher and discuss the different types of assessments they use in their classroom. Discuss why they selected the ones they use. Identify if the assessments are formative and/or summative.

REFERENCES

Ackerman, K., & Horn, C. (2021). The positive implications of intentional feedback. *Journal of Special Education Preparation, 1*(1), 16-24. https://doi.org/10.33043/JOSEP.1.1.16-24

Albers, P. (2006). Imagining the possibilities in multimodal curriculum design. *English Education, 38*(2), 75-101.

Allen Simon, C., & Striegel, P. (n.d.). Strategy guide: Exit slips. *National Council of Teachers of English.* http://www.readwritethink.org/professional-development/strategy-guides/exit-slips-30760.html

Allen, A., & Tanner, K. (2006). Rubrics: Tools for making learning goals and evaluation criteria explicit for both teachers and learners. *CBE—Life Sciences Education 5*, 197-203. https://doi.org/10.1187/cbe.06–06-0168

ASCD Government Relations. (2015). Elementary and secondary education act: Comparison of the No Child Left Behind Act to the Every Student Succeeds act. *ASCD*, 1–8. https://files.ascd.org/staticfiles/ascd/pdf/siteASCD/policy/ESEA_NCLB_ComparisonChart_2015.pdf

Bagnato, S. J., & Ho, H. Y. (2006). High-stakes testing with preschool children: Violation of professional standards for evidence-based practice in early childhood intervention. *KEDI International Journal of Educational Policy, 3*(1), 22-43.

Barksdale-Ladd, M. A., & Thomas, K. F. (2000). What's at stake in high-stakes testing: Teachers and parents speak out. *Journal of Teacher Education, 51*(5), 384-397. https://doi-org.ezproxy.uttyler.edu/10.1177/0022487100051005006

Baxendell, B. W. (2003). Consistent, coherent, creative: The 3 C's of graphic organizers. *TEACHING Exceptional Children, 35*(3), 46-53.

Black, P., & Wiliam, D. (2010). Inside the black box: Raising standards through classroom assessment. *Phi Delta Kappan, 92*(1), 81-90. https://doi.org/10.1177/003172171009200119

Brown, C. P. (2010). Children of reform: The impact of high-stakes education reform on preservice teachers. *Journal of Teacher Education, 61*(5), 477-491. https://doi.org/10.1177/0022487109352905

Chappuis, S., & Chappuis, J. (2008). The best value in formative assessments. *Educational Leadership, 65*, 14-19.

Clarke, L. S., Haydon, T., Bauer, A., & Epperly, A. C. (2016). Inclusion of students with an intellectual disability in the general education classroom with the use of response cards. *Preventing School Failure, 60*(1), 35-42. https://doi:10.1080/1045988X.2014.966801

Crooks, T. J. (1988). The impact of classroom evaluation practices on students. *Review of Educational Research, 58*(4), 438-481. https://doi.org/10.3102/00346543058004438

Dixson, D. D., & Worrell, F. C. (2016). Formative and summative assessment in the classroom. *Theory into Practice, 55*(2), 153-159. https://doi.org/10.1080/00405841.2016.1148989

Dorn, C. M. (2003). Models for assessing art performance (MAAP): A K-12 project. *Studies in Art Education, 44*(4), 350-371.

Duckor, B. (2014). Formative assessments in seven good moves. *Educational Leadership, 71*(6), 28-32.

Dye, G. A. (2000). Graphic organizers to the rescue. Helping students link-and remember-information. *TEACHING Exceptional Children, 32*(3), 72-76. https://doi-org.ezproxy.uttyler.edu/10.1177/004005990003200311

Edgerton, A. K. (2019). The essence of ESSA: More control at the district level? *Phi Delta Kappan, 101*(2), 14-17. https://doi.org/10.1177/0031721719879148

Every Student Succeeds Act, S.1177, 114th Congress (2015). https://www.congress.gov/bill/114th-congress/senate-bill/1177

Fisher, D., & Frey, N. (2004). *Improving adolescent literacy: Strategies at work.* Pearson Prentice Hall.

Gardner, J. (2010). Developing teacher assessments: An introduction. In J. Gardner, W. Harlen, L. Hayward, G. Stobart, & M. Montgomery (Eds.), *Developing teacher assessment* (pp. 1-11). Open University Press.

Garrison, C., & Ehringhaus, M. (n.d.). *Formative and summative assessments in the classroom.* https://www.amle.org/formative-and-summative-assessments-in-the-classroom

Graham-Day, K. J., Fishley, K. M., Konrad, M., Peters, M. T., & Ressa, V. A. (2014). Formative instructional practices: How core content teachers can borrow ideas from IDEA. *Intervention in School and Clinic, 50*(2), 69-75. http://doi.org/10.1177/1053451214536041

Hattie, J., & Timperley, H. (2007). The power of feedback. *Review of Educational Research, 77*, 81-112. https://doi.org/10.3102/003465430298487

Heritage, M. (2007). Formative assessment: What do teachers need to know and do? *Phi Delta Kappan, 89*(2), 140-145.

Jonsson, A. (2014). Rubrics as a way of providing transparency in assessment. *Assessment & Evaluation in Higher Education, 39*(7), 840-852. http://doi.org/10.1080/02602938.2013.875117

Kaddoura, M. (2013). Think pair share: A teaching learning strategy to enhance students' critical thinking. *Educational Research Quarterly, 36*(4), 3-24.

Knight, J. (2013). *High-impact instruction: A framework for great teaching.* Corwin Press.

Marzano, R. J. (2006). Classroom assessment and grading that work. *Association for Supervision & Curriculum Development*, 1-11.

McLeskey, J., Barringer, M-D., Billingsley, B., Brownell, M., Jackson, D., Kennedy, M., Lewis, T., Maheady, L., Rodriquez, J., Scheeler, M. C., Winn, J., & Ziegler, D. (2017). *High-leverage practices in special education.* Council for Exceptional Children & CEEDAR Center.

Moskal, B. (2000). Scoring rubrics: What, when and how? *Practical Assessment, Research, and Evaluation, 7*, Article 3. https://doi.org/10.7275/a5vq-7q66

National Research Council. (2001). *Classroom assessment and the National Science Education Standards.* National Academies Press. http://www.nap.edu/catalog/9847/classroom-assessment-and-the-national-scienceeducation-standards

No Child Left Behind Act of 2001, Public Law 107-110 (2002). https://www.wrightslaw.com/info/nclb.law.overview.htm

Popham, W. J. (1997). What's wrong—and what's right—with rubrics. *Educational Leadership, 55*(2), 72-75. http://www.ascd.org/publications/educational-leadership/oct97/vol55/num02/What%27s-Wrong%E2%80%94and-What%27s-Right%E2%80%94with-Rubrics.aspx

Portz, J. (2021). Beyond test scores: "School quality or student success" in state ESSA plans. *Teacher College Record, 123*(6), 1-36. https://doi.org/10.1177/016146812112300603

Randolph, J. J. (2007). Meta-analysis of the research on response cards: Effects on test achievement, quiz achievement, participation, and off-task behavior. *Journal of Positive Behavior Interventions, 9*(2), 113–128. https://doi.org/10.1177/10983007070090020201

Reading Rockets. (n.d.-a). *Think-Pair-Share*. https://www.readingrockets.org/strategies/think-pair-share

Reading Rockets. (n.d.-b). *Exit slips*. https://www.readingrockets.org/strategies/exit_slips

Robertson, K. (2006). *Increase student interaction with "Think-Pair-Shares" and "Circle Chats."* ¡Colorín Colorado! http://www.colorincolorado.org/article/13346

Ruiz-Primo, M. A. (2011). Informal formative assessment: The role of instructional dialogues in assessing students' learning. *Studies in Educational Evaluation, 37*, 15-24. https://doi.org/10.1016/j.stueduc.2011.04.003

Ruiz-Primo, M. A., & Furtak, E. M. (2007). Exploring teachers' informal formative assessment practices and students' understanding in the context of scientific inquiry. *Journal of Research in Science Teaching, 44*(1), 57-84.

Singleton, S. M., & Filce, H. G. (2015). Graphic organizers for secondary students with learning disabilities. *TEACHING Exceptional Children, 48*(2), 110-117. https://doi.org/10.1177/0040059915605799

Swicegood, P. (1994). Portfolio-based assessment practices. *Intervention in School and Clinics, 30*(1), 6-15. https://doi.org/10.1177/0040059915605799

The Understood Team. (n.d.). *The difference between the Every Student Succeeds Act and No Child Left Behind*. https://www.understood.org/articles/en/the-difference-between-the-every-student-succeeds-act-and-no-child-left-behind

Progress Monitoring and Response to Intervention

CHAPTER OBJECTIVES

- Define progress monitoring and response to intervention.
- Describe curriculum-based measurement and mastery measurement in the classroom, progress monitoring, and response to intervention.
- Provide examples of progress monitoring, response to intervention, and curriculum-based measurement to help make a connection on how to apply it in the classroom.

KEY TERMS

- **baseline:** The student's current level of performance prior to an intervention being implemented. Three probes are administered to establish baseline.
- **curriculum-based measurement (CBM):** A general outcome measure used to assess a student's progress across the entire curriculum, and measures are administered frequently.
- **data-based decision making (DBDM):** The process of collecting and interpreting data to make instructional decisions and adjustments.
- **mastery measurement (MM):** Used to determine a student's understanding and mastery of a specific target skill. It is used to evaluate a student's level of performance.
- **median:** The midpoint between the three data points collected from the baseline probes.
- **progress monitoring:** A type of formative assessment used to regularly evaluate student learning.
- **response to intervention (RTI):** A multi-tiered framework for providing instruction to students through progressively intensive and individualized interventions.

KEY ABBREVIATIONS

- CBM: curriculum-based measurement
- DBDM: data-based decision making
- MM: mastery measurement
- RTI: response to intervention

CASE STUDY

Parker is an energetic third-grade student at Three Lakes Elementary School. Parker did well in kindergarten and first grade, but in second grade, things began to change. In the past Parker liked school, but according to his mother, he began to resist going to school. His mother, a kindergarten teacher at the school, noticed Parker was not progressing in reading like she thought he should be and wondered if that was what was causing him to not want to go to school. She asked his teacher, Mrs. Miller, for a conference. Mrs. Miller explained to Parker's mother that Parker's performance was average during the beginning of the year assessments, but she was also noticing changes in Parker. During guided reading groups, he was very quiet and often relied on his group members to answer questions. Mrs. Miller decided to pull Parker individually to get a better idea of what his reading level was.

Assessment is an essential part of any educational system. States use assessment data for evaluating the effectiveness of school districts in their state. School districts use assessment data to monitor progress of their school systems and the success of instructional programs (Stecker et al., 2008). Teachers use assessment data to determine students' academic strengths and weaknesses. Data-based decision making (DBDM) allows educators to collect and interpret data to make instructional decisions (Filderman & Toste, 2018). The DBDM process is intended to address consistent academic difficulties. Teachers can regularly use data to examine the continued interaction between academic instruction and student learning (Furey & Loftus-Rattan, 2022). Federal reforms in education through the passage of No Child Left Behind Act (NCLB; 2001) stress the importance of setting high standards for all students and increasing accountability expected of educators in meeting high standards for student achievement (Stecker et al., 2008). High standards include teachers' use of evidence-based curricular materials and instructional strategies to increase student achievement regardless of students' ethnic background, language, or disability status. In order for teachers to promote high levels of achievement among all students, assessment tools are needed to guide educators' instructional decision making because student progress monitoring is an important way to alert teachers when data show specific students are not making progress at acceptable rates.

In special education, student progress is monitored regularly, and the Individualized Education Program (IEP) is used to ensure appropriate growth is occurring toward measurable and meaningful academic goals. Although teachers are required to monitor progress of all their students, there has been an increased emphasis on accountability through NCLB (2001) and the Individuals with Disabilities Education Improvement Act (IDEA; 2004) to ensure students show improvements in academic outcomes. The federal mandates require educators to monitor student progress and use data when making instructional decisions (Lingo et al., 2011). Additionally, in a multi-tiered system of support framework (i.e., response to intervention [RTI]), students who are performing below grade-level expectations are identified, specific academic interventions are implemented, and the student's progress is regularly monitored. Research suggests that students with disabilities have better outcomes when their instructional gaps are identified, progress is monitored relative to those gaps, and specific intensive interventions are provided (Cornelius & Johnson-Harris, 2017).

PAST AND PRESENT ASSESSMENT PRACTICES

Standardized, norm-referenced achievement tests have traditionally given schools scores summarizing the overall success of their educational program. Additionally, classroom teachers rely on teacher- or curriculum developer–created assessments to evaluate student performance (Stecker et al., 2008). Recently, standards-based reform efforts have driven the use of benchmark assessments at several times during the year to determine if students are on track toward meeting the expectations of their district or state as demonstrated by students' performance on high-stakes end-of-year tests. Although these various types of assessments have merit, they have limitations including being time consuming, failing to reflect content actually taught, or only showing mastery of a particular skill rather than a student's overall proficiency in an academic area. One challenge of benchmark testing is their infrequency, which makes it difficult to rate student progress. For example, a student's scores may show them below the cutoff and needing intervention. However, the benchmark test may not show that the student is growing at a similar rate as their peers but started at a lower performance level. A student like this will have different instructional needs than a student who is targeted as needing intervention and whose performance changes very little over time. On the other hand, a student who is seen as high performing may be able to meet or even exceed benchmark scores but does not show continued academic growth. A teacher might incorrectly assume the student is achieving at a satisfactory rate because they reached the established benchmark. Subsequently, without consistent rates of student improvement, assessment information is limited when it only includes a level of a score.

There are life-long implications for students when determining eligibility for special education services. There are serious consequences for students who are not provided interventions that are appropriate before a full evaluation is conducted (Hallahan et al., 2019). Prereferral interventions can help prevent a student from being inaccurately placed in special education. The way students are found to be eligible for special education services has drastically changed since the passage of the IDEA (2004), particularly for students with a learning disability. Although there are variations schools follow in the prereferral process, many states now follow the systematic method of RTI. An additional option for determining special education eligibility was included by Congress where varying levels of support must be added in general education before a student is referred to special education.

Within the multi-tiered framework of RTI, teachers use progress monitoring data to target and track students who are not performing satisfactorily to determine academic growth using evidence-based instructional strategies and interventions (Stecker et al., 2008). Progress monitoring is an increasingly important assessment method most teachers readily use. It is important for progress monitoring tools to be educationally meaningful, not monopolize too much instructional time, and be sensitive to student change. One well-established form of progress monitoring is curriculum-based measurement (CBM; Cornelius & Johnson-Harris, 2017). The purpose of this chapter is to walk the reader through RTI and how progress monitoring fits within RTI. We examine in detail what progress monitoring is and highlight CBM and mastery measurement (MM).

CHECK FOR UNDERSTANDING

Assessment is an essential component to ensure students are making progress. RTI is *not* an assessment tool. Rather it is a framework. Within RTI, students' progress is monitored through the use of assessment tools such as CBM and MM.

RESPONSE TO INTERVENTION

RTI is a multi-tiered model for providing instruction and support to students through progressively intensive and individualized interventions (IRIS Center, 2021b). RTI is intended to ensure all students have access to engaging and high-quality instruction with universal screening for all students in the general education classroom (RTI Action Network, 2021). When thinking about the idea of RTI, we are determining if a student's change, or lack of change, in academic performance is due to instruction (Hallahan et al., 2019). Students first receive quality instruction in their general education classroom before a formal evaluation for special education services can occur. Data are collected by the teachers to determine if the student is benefiting from instruction, and only after it has been determined the student is not responding to quality, evidence-based instruction by a general education teacher that a formal evaluation for special education services occurs. Although RTI is typically associated with students with learning disabilities and academic learning, it has implications for students with other disabilities such as intellectual disabilities, autism, emotional and behavioral disorders, and giftedness.

For RTI to work effectively, there are important components that need to be implemented with fidelity. All students must receive high-quality, researched-based instruction in their general education classroom (RTI Action Network, 2021). Student assessment should be ongoing through universal screening and progress monitoring. The assessment data provide information on a student's rate of learning and level of achievement. Data are compared within the classroom and individually to determine which students need to be monitored more closely or if intervention is required. Student progress is frequently monitored throughout the RTI process to determine student achievement and gauge curriculum effectiveness. Instructional decisions are made based on multiple data points taken in context over time to examine the needs of the students. Instruction is efficiently differentiated for all students through a multi-tiered approach with each tier increasing in intensity of research-based instruction to meet the needs of the student. Parents should be informed of their child's progress, the instruction and intervention used, the school personnel providing instruction, and their child's academic or behavioral goals.

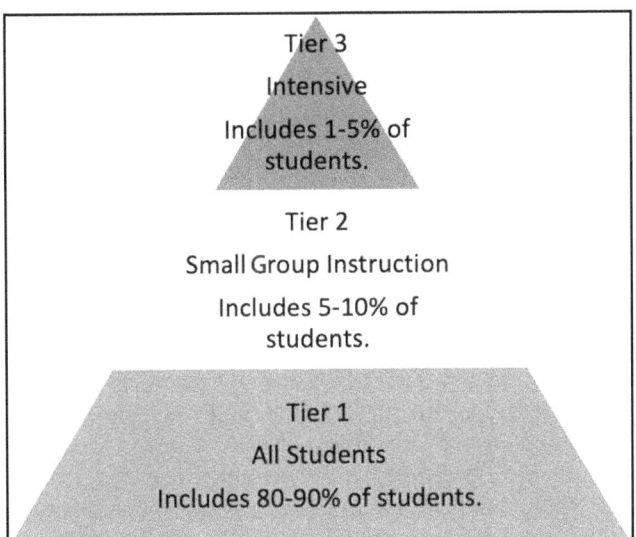

Figure 6-1. Three-tiered response to intervention model.

Response to Intervention Implementation

The RTI framework is based on a multi-tiered model of prevention. Figure 6-1 provides an example of the tiered framework. Although there is not a single researched and widely practiced RTI process model, typically speaking, the process is defined as a three-step or three-tier model of school supports that use evidence-based academic and/or behavioral interventions (RTI Action Network, 2021). All students benefit from high-quality, evidence-based instruction (Hallahan et al., 2019). Learners who are struggling receive interventions at increasing levels of intensity with the intention of accelerating the rate of the student's learning (RTI Action Network, 2021). Interventions can be delivered by a variety of school personnel, such as general education or special education teachers and specialists. Progress is monitored closely to assess the performance of individual students and the rate of their learning. Educational decisions regarding the length and intensity of interventions provided are based on the individual student's response. The three-tier model is described subsequently.

Tier 1

All students receive high-quality Tier 1 instruction. Within Tier 1, all students receive scientifically based instruction from qualified personnel, which is intended to ensure difficulties students face are not due to inadequate instruction (RTI Action Network, 2021). Typically speaking, 80% to 90% of students in a classroom stay in Tier 1 where they receive instruction. Students are periodically screened to establish an academic baseline and identify the students who are struggling and in need of additional support. Universal screening and/or results from district-wide or state tests help identify students considered "at risk" to receive supplemental instruction in the regular classroom during the school day. Although the length of time for this step can vary, generally it should not exceed 8 weeks. Student progress is monitored closely using a validated screening system (e.g., CBM). Typically, students who show significant progress at the end of the period return to their regular classroom program, and students who do not show adequate progress move to Tier 2.

Tier 2

Students who are not making adequate progress in Tier 1 within the regular classroom move to Tier 2 where they receive targeted interventions to match their needs based on their levels of performance and rates of progress (RTI Action Network, 2021). Typically, only 5% to 10% of students progress to Tier 2. The intensity of interventions varies across group size, the level of training of professionals providing instruction, and the frequency and duration of the intervention. In addition to receiving instruction in the general curriculum, students receive targeted intervention and services in small group settings. Generally, students receive small group instruction three to four times per week from a teacher or a highly trained assistant using a research-validated program or intervention in the areas of difficulty (Hallahan et al., 2019). Typically, interventions in early grades (kindergarten through third grade) are in the areas of reading and math. Although students are required to be in Tier 2 for a longer period of time, generally speaking, the time period should not exceed a grading period. Students who continue to show little progress while receiving Tier 2 interventions are then considered for additional intensive interventions and move to Tier 3.

Tier 3

Students who are not making progress with targeted Tier 2 interventions move to Tier 3 for intensive interventions and a comprehensive evaluation, which can include 1% to 5% of the students in the class. At Tier 3, students should receive intensive interventions that are individualized and targeted at the student's skill deficits (RTI Action Network, 2021). If the student does not achieve the level of progress needed in response to the targeted and intensive interventions, they are then referred for a comprehensive evaluation. At this time, the student is considered for eligibility for special education services according to the IDEA (2004). Data collected at all tiers are included in the documentation and are used for making eligibility decisions. It is important to note that through the IDEA, parents are allowed to request a formal evaluation to determine special education eligibility at any point in the RTI process. The RTI process cannot be used to delay or deny a formal special education evaluation. It should also be noted that there are various formats for how schools choose to implement RTI. School districts use different approaches to implementation (e.g., hybrid approaches, standard protocol, problem-solving, functional assessment) and have variations to the tiers used to provide RTI services. RTI can be used as a school-wide framework to effectively distribute resources to improve student outcomes. Figure 6-2 shows how instruction and potential placement in special education can be facilitated in an RTI framework (RTI Action Network, 2021).

CHECK FOR UNDERSTANDING

RTI is a continuum. All students receive fantastic evidence-based instruction that captures most students (80% to 90%). However, there are some students who need additional support. These students move to Tier 2 where they receive Tier 1 instruction and Tier 2 instruction (5% to 10%). Students who are still not responding move to Tier 3 for the most intensive interventions (1% to 5%).

Assessment Practices Within the Response to Intervention Framework

The fundamental purpose of assessment within the RTI framework is to identify students who are at risk of school failure and to collect data to determine whether or not instruction is effective to ensure appropriate instructional decisions are made (Hallahan et al., 2019). The most common forms of assessment are screening and progress monitoring. Assessment screening instruments are used by teachers or even school psychologists to identify students who may be at risk for school failure. Typically, the screening instruments are administered to a whole group of students and can be given to a large group of students within a short time period. The results of the screening are used to identify students who require additional progress monitoring and need to move to Tier 2 for further instruction. In the next section, we will discuss progress monitoring in detail.

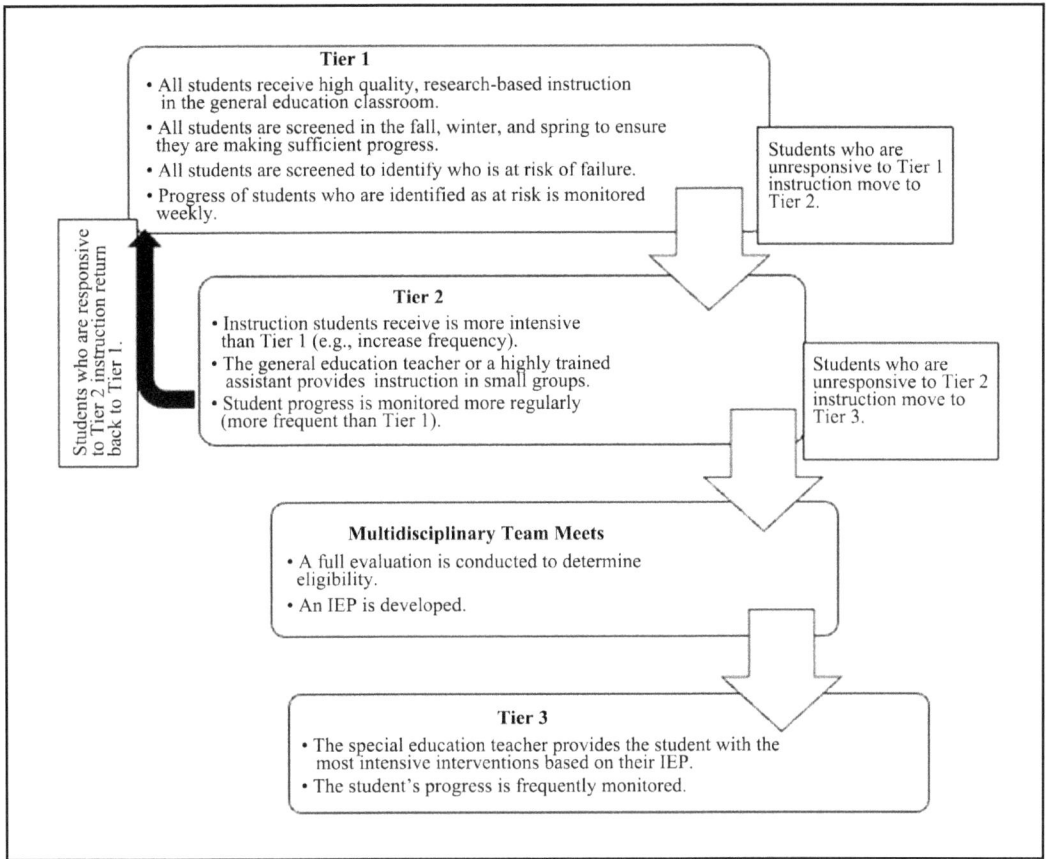

Figure 6-2. Three-tiered RTI framework. (Adapted from Hallahan, D. P., Kauffman, J. M., & Pullen, P. C. [2019]. *Exceptional learners: An introduction to special education* [14th ed.]. Pearson.)

Check for Understanding

RTI is *not* an assessment tool. It is a multi-tiered framework or model that teachers use to systematically ensure students are getting quality evidence-based instruction at increasing levels of intensity to meet their academic needs. Progress monitoring is done within the framework to ensure students' needs are being met.

Progress Monitoring

A key component of RTI is progress monitoring. Progress monitoring is a type of formative assessment used to regularly evaluate student learning (IRIS Center, 2021b). Progress monitoring provides valuable feedback regarding student performance to both the teachers and the students themselves. Teachers are able to evaluate the effectiveness of their instruction by monitoring students' progress over time, to quantify the rate of students' improvement or responsiveness to instruction, and to evaluate the effectiveness of instruction (National Center on Response to Intervention, 2013). Progress monitoring can be used for an entire class or for individual students (McLane, n.d.-a). Progress monitoring can also be used to help educators design effective individualized plans for students with disabilities (National Center on Response to Intervention, 2013).

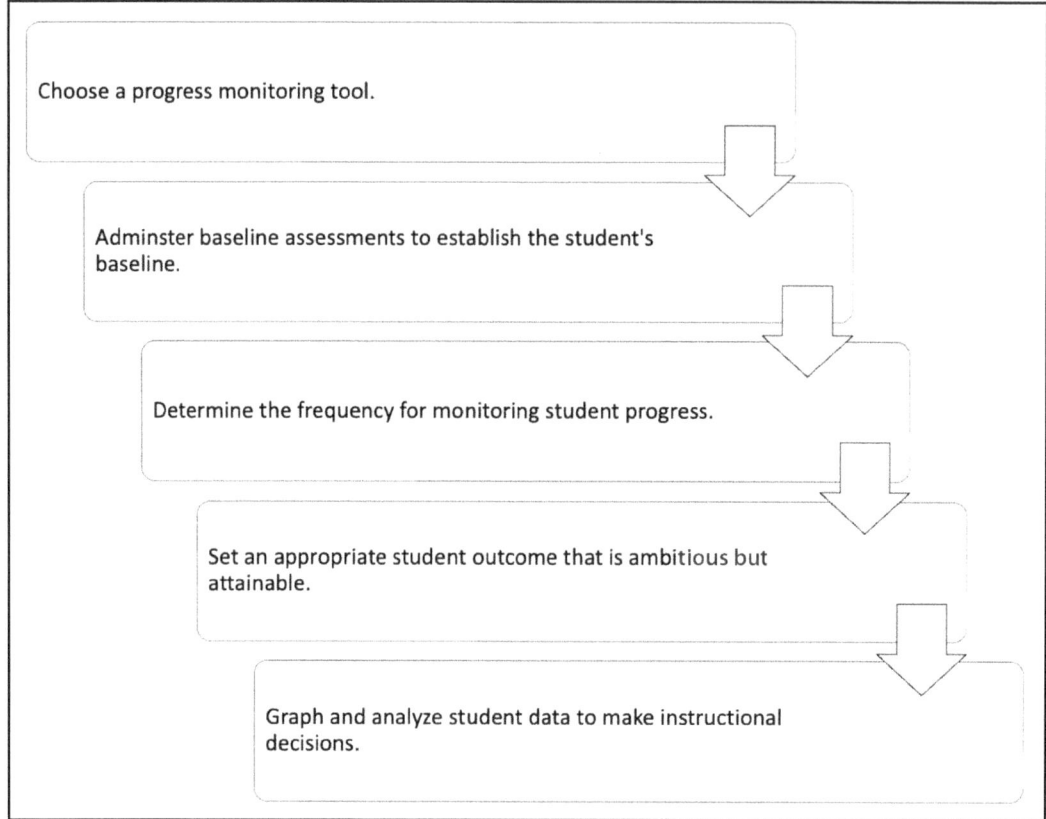

Figure 6-3. Steps for progress monitoring.

Teachers use progress monitoring to determine appropriate goals for a student's Individualized Education Program (IEP). Teachers use the state standards for the student's grade level to develop measurable goals that are tracked through progress monitoring (McLane, n.d.-a). For example, a student may have a reading goal to read a specific number of words per minute by the end of the school year. The teacher creates a goal, using the standards, and begins instruction. Each week the teacher measures the student's progress toward meeting the goal. The difficulty level of the tests is the same, which provides accurate information of student progress. The teacher takes the results of each test and compares how much the student is expected to have learned with the student's actual rate of learning. If a student's performance on a measurement does not meet expectations, then the teacher can make changes to their teaching (e.g., grouping arrangement, method of teaching being used, amount of instructional time) or some different aspect of teaching (McLane, n.d.-a). The goal for the teacher is to look for the amount and type of instruction that will allow students to make progress toward their academic goals. Progress monitoring measures are only meant to take between 1 and 5 minutes, which prevents the students from feeling like they are constantly taking tests. Frequent progress monitoring (typically once a week) allows teachers the opportunity to revise instruction when data show the students need it rather than waiting until an end-of-unit test or state assessment shows the student's needs are not being met. Figure 6-3 shows the steps needed to appropriately monitor student progress.

Implementation of Progress Monitoring

Implementing progress monitoring successfully is a result of purposeful planning and thoughtful practices (National Center on Response to Intervention, 2013). According to the National Center on Response to Intervention, it is important to make a progress monitoring plan to ensure all the important aspects of progress monitoring are included:

- Decide on a progress monitoring tool that is reliable, valid, and age appropriate per grade level
- Create a preset schedule for when progress monitoring data will be collected throughout the year
- Create a set agenda and schedule for meeting to discuss and evaluate progress monitoring data
- Determine what the rules will be for making decisions to help guide the decision-making process and follow-up tasks
- Establish practices that will be used to ensure fidelity of the progress monitoring process

After careful planning, the first step of progress monitoring involves identifying an appropriate measure to use for data collection. A valid progress monitoring tool accurately measures the primary concept it is intended to measure (National Center on Response to Intervention, 2013). The tool being used must also be appropriate for the grade level and be associated to instruction being provided. For example, in kindergarten and first grade, typically progress is measured using assessments involving letter names, letter sounds, and words in isolation. Oral reading fluency is measured when students are able to read connected text. Maze fluency is a comprehension measure to be used starting in late elementary school. When thinking about math, number identification, missing number (orally identify the missing number in a sequence of numbers), and quantity discrimination (when given two numbers, identify which number is larger) are assessed in kindergarten and first-grade students. Around second grade and beyond, math concepts and applications as well as computation are appropriate for monitoring students' progress.

The most common types of data collection are CBM (curriculum-based measurement) and MM (mastery measurement; Filderman & Toste, 2018). Both tools are important in providing the most information on students' growth. MM determines a student's understanding and mastery of a specific target skill and is used to evaluate a student's level of performance. On the other hand, CBM is a general outcome measure and is used to measure a student's progress across the entire curriculum. CBM and MM will be discussed in detail further down in this chapter. *Because Parker was struggling with reading, Mrs. Miller decided CBM assessing fluency and comprehension using oral reading fluency and maze.*

After an appropriate progress monitoring measure has been identified, baseline data need to be collected to assess the targeted skills. Baseline data are used to determine the student's current level of performance (IRIS Center, 2021a). The student's progress is monitored based on the student's instructional level rather than the grade level. For example, if a student is in the fourth grade, but their reading level is at first grade, rather than administering a fourth-grade reading passage to measure (or probe) reading fluency, the teacher may consider administering a word identification fluency probe instead. Teachers administer three probes within about a week to get a reliable estimate of the student's level of performance. For students already receiving Tier 2 instruction, teachers can use the last three data points as a baseline for the student.

The next step in the process is to determine how frequently progress will be monitored. Schools that are successful at progress monitoring develop a schedule and make certain everyone knows the schedule with the expectation that data will be collected and reviewed based on the schedule (National Center on Response to Intervention, 2013). At a minimum, teachers should be monitoring student progress monthly. However, progress should be monitored more frequently for students in Tiers 2 and 3 who have more severe academic difficulties. According to Filderman and Toste (2018), there are several important questions to consider when making decisions on the frequency of progress monitoring. When looking at baseline data points, consider the following questions:

- What is the student's current level?
- Was there variability (inconsistencies) when the student's baseline data was collected?
- How long will data be tracked overall?

Although recommendations vary for how often data should be collected, Filderman and Toste have found instructional decisions can be made with a minimum of 5 to 6 weeks of data that include multiple data points, particularly if the student shows steady trends when baseline data are collected. Additional data points may be necessary (e.g., at least 20 total data points) for younger students or students with significant challenges and/or variability on performance assessments (e.g., unexpected highs and lows). For example, if a student is reading at a first-grade reading level but is in fourth grade, it may be beneficial to collect more data points. However, if the student was reading at a fourth-grade reading level, the number of data points can be reduced. When data are being collected for a long period of time, one data point per week may be appropriate while a shorter period of time for data collection will require more than one data point collected per week.

Mrs. Miller began Parker at third-grade level instruction but quickly realized that was too difficult and moved him down. It was determined that Parker's baseline data was actually at a first-grade level. Mrs. Miller then administered a first-grade passage to establish his true baseline. She decided she would collect data two times per week for 6 weeks to determine if additional reading instruction was benefiting Parker.

Once baseline data have been collected and frequency of progress monitoring has been determined, the next step in the process is to set student outcome goals. When creating goals for students, it is important to ensure the goal is based on where the student is currently performing and what the expected outcomes are (Filderman & Toste, 2018). It is important for the expected outcomes to be achievable levels of growth. Goals should be ambitious but also realistic. There are several essential questions to ask for determining the best goal for a student:

- What does baseline data show the student to be performing at?
- How long will the student's progress be tracked for meeting the goal?
- Is the goal realistic based on the student's grade level and time-tracking progress?
- Is the goal ambitious based on the student's grade level and time-tracking progress?
- Keeping a balance between ambitious and realistic, what is a goal that is achievable yet rigorous for the student?

Realistic goals are based on a student's expected levels of growth when combined with evidence-based practices that are implemented well (Filderman & Toste, 2018). Ambitious goals are achievable but will involve intensive work to accomplish. Realistic and ambitious goals are appropriate and practical depending on the student, the time available to work with the student, accessibility to materials, and the teacher's comfort level with instructional methods required. When teachers keep these points in mind, the most appropriate decisions for students are made on an individual basis. The National Center on Intensive Intervention website (www.intensiveintervention.org) is a resource for comparing instruction and grade-level goals.

The next step in effectively monitoring progress is to plot student progress. Plotting student progress is an essential step for deciding when and how to adapt instruction to meet student needs (Filderman & Toste, 2018). There are different ways student data can be graphed. Graphs for measuring student progress can be created by teachers. Additionally, graphing software often accompanies commercially available progress monitoring measures (IRIS Center, 2021a). The horizontal axis represents the number of weeks instruction occurs, and the vertical axis represents the range of potential scores a student can achieve on the probe. Once the student's baseline data are plotted on the graph, draw a goal line between the median of the scores and the goal. Table 6-1 provides steps required for graphing students' progress monitoring data (Filderman & Toste, 2018). Graphing and analyzing data is an essential step in progress monitoring to ensure each student's needs are being met and appropriate instructional decisions are being made. Questions to consider include:

Table 6-1. Steps for Graphing Student Progress Monitoring Data

Step 1: Find and plot the average baseline data point.
Step 2: Calculate a realistic and ambitious outcome goal— average baseline + (estimated average growth × weeks of monitoring progress).
Step 3: Plot the outcome goal.
Step 4: Draw a line from the baseline average to the outcome goal.
Step 5: Collect the student's data.
Step 6: Draw a trend line through data based on best fit from data seen (through the middle while adjusting for outliners).
Step 7: Use the points-below or slope method. • Points-below: Ask yourself, are the last three points below, above, or below and above the trend line? • Slope: Do the trend line and outcome slopes match?
Step 8: Based on data graphed, decide to adjust or continue instruction.
Adapted from Filderman, M. J., & Toste, J. R. (2018). Decisions, decisions, decisions: Using data to make instructional decisions from struggling readers. *TEACHING Exceptional Children, 50*(3), 130-140.

- What progress monitoring tool is being used?
- Based on the progress monitoring tool being used, what are recommendations for how data should be collected?
- What is the student's instructional level?
- How variable is the student's performance when considering baseline data collected?

Administering and scoring probes should occur regularly (e.g., weekly or biweekly; IRIS Center, 2021a). Generally, the probes can be administered quickly (e.g., math concepts in 10 minutes, maze fluency in up to 3 minutes). Each time a probe is administered, the score is recorded on the graph, and a line is drawn to connect it to the previous data point.

Often students are not involved in monitoring or graphing their progress (Furey & Loftus-Rattan, 2022). However, research has shown that students who are actively involved in performance feedback and goal setting having improved motivational and academic outcomes. Students who are active participants are more responsible for their learning and are more aware of their performance. Furey and Loftus-Rattan recommend a six-step protocol for a progress monitoring performance feedback and goal setting (PFGS) routine.

1. Provide explicit performance feedback. After measuring the student's progress, the teacher can say, "To calculate your score, I am going to count how many (e.g., problems solved correctly, words read)," and then tell the student what their score is.
2. Provide specific, true, and positive feedback on the student's performance. For example, "I liked how you _____." or "I noticed that you _____."
3. Collaborate when graphing data by showing the student their graph, which can be on paper or computer-generated. The teacher can invite the student to add the new score to their progress monitoring graph.
4. Collaborate to analyze the data by making observations on what the graph looks like. Specifically notice if the score goes up, down, or stays the same compared to the last score.

5. Ask reflective questions and listen and take notes over what the student says. The student can be asked what they believe they have done to help to continue improving. The student can also be asked questions about the goal they created from the previous session. Was the student able to accomplish their goal?

6. Collaboratively set a goal for the next session and listen and take notes. The student can be asked how the teacher can help the student improve. Another goal can be set for what the student will do to improve until the next time. Once the student has created the goal, it is important to restate the goal. A scale of 1 to 10 can be used to see how confident the student is in reaching their goal.

Research has supported the PFGS routine being effective for improving academic skills in reading, writing, and math (Furey & Loftus-Rattan, 2022). The skill and will of students can easily be supported by teachers who are implementing academic interventions. PFGS practices help students overcome task avoidance and poor motivation which can contribute to skill deficits for students with learning disabilities. Graphing progress provides visual, frequent, and objective evidence of a student's improvement.

It is helpful when schools have a progress monitoring team (e.g., principal, RTI coordinator, teachers). Teams should meet regularly (e.g., monthly), and the meetings should be set on the school calendar with the knowledge that additional meetings may need to be held if the number of students needing more specific attention increases or if it is determined the prescheduled meetings are not sufficient (National Center on Response to Intervention, 2013). Including an agenda and appointing a leader to facilitate the meetings can also be helpful to ensure all information is covered and done so in a timely manner.

Guidelines should be developed regarding the number of data points needed to make a comprehensive decision (National Center on Response to Intervention, 2013). There are several important points to keep in mind. First, with more data points included, there is a decreased chance of measurement error, meaning that more data points included provide confidence the student's scores are representative of the actual skill of the student. Before any decisions are made, it is essential enough data points have been included to ensure the student's skill level has been accurately measured. Additionally, it is important to allow enough time for an intervention to work. Typically, it takes a minimum of 6 to 10 data points to know if an intervention is successful for the student. When thinking about the number of data points to collect, the time in which data is collected is important to consider. If data are only collected one time every 2 weeks, months can go by before determining if an intervention is working. On the other hand, collected data daily for 2 weeks is also not helpful because assessment tools are not sensitive enough to detect day-to-day growth. However, there are tools that are more sensitive, and those tools can be used more frequently. For example, it should be expected that a second grader increases fluency by about 1.5 words per week. A passage-reading fluency assessment is sensitive enough to be used weekly. On the other hand, on a maze assessment, the typical increase for a first grader is 0.40 words per week, which does not lend itself to frequent use, but using it every 2 or 3 weeks would provide more meaningful data on the number of words the student knows.

Schools should also plan to assess fidelity, ideally at the same time as RTI is implemented (National Center on Response to Intervention, 2013). Schools need to build in procedures for monitoring the fidelity of assessment, instruction, and adherence to DBDM practices into the yearly RTI plan for implementation, and the plan should be reviewed at least quarterly. Monitoring student progress and results from the data when making instructional decisions is a critical component of RTI implementation. Valuable time is spent monitoring student progress, and it is crucial the data are not wasted.

Table 6-2. Web-Based Curriculum-Based Measurement Tools

CBM TOOL	WEBSITE	GRADE LEVEL	CONTENT	EXTRA INFORMATION
aimwebPlus	https://app.aimswebplus.com/	PK–12	Reading Math	Add-on screeners for behavior and dyslexia-comprehension
DIBELS	https://dibels.uoregon.edu/dibels8	K–8	Fluency Dyslexia screening	
easyCBM	https://easycbm.com/	K–8	Reading Math	Spanish version
FASTBRIDGE	https://www.illuminateed.com/products/fastbridge/	PK–12	Reading Math Social-emotional behavior	

Check for Understanding

Planning is a critical part of progress monitoring to be most effective. Progress monitoring tools, the frequency of monitoring, and appropriate goals must be based on individual student's needs. Instructional decisions need to be data-based.

Curriculum-Based Measurement in the Classroom

CBM is a type of progress monitoring system used by teachers to track how students are performing in academic areas including math, reading, writing, and spelling and to evaluate effectiveness of instruction (Deno, 1985). CBM involves frequent (e.g., weekly) short, simple measures that sample students' academic performance. Teachers use CBM to determine how well students are progressing in their content areas. Additionally, CBM is used to monitor the success of instruction students receive. When CBM shows students who are not meeting expectations, teachers are quickly able to make changes to ensure sufficient progress is made toward meeting academic goals.

Typically, students are assessed weekly with probes lasting 1 to 5 minutes (McLane, n.d.-b). Table 6-2 provides a list of web-based CBM tools. The student's score is determined by counting the number of correct and incorrect answers made by the student in the allotted time. The score is recorded on a graph and compared to the expected performance on the specific content being assessed. The graph is a visual tool to see how a student's performance compares to expectations. Once scores have been recorded, the teacher is able to determine whether instruction should be continued in the same way or changed. A change would be necessary if the student's rate of learning is lower than is needed to meet goals set for the year. See Figures 6-4 and 6-5 for an example of a student's CBM graph. Changes to instruction may include increasing instructional time, changing the teaching technique or how material is presented, or changing the group arrangement (e.g., rather than small group instruction, provide individual instruction).

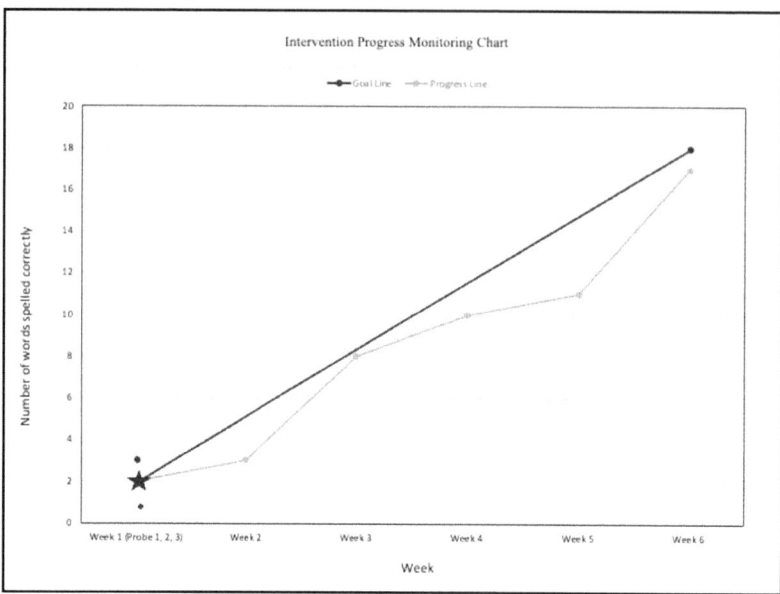

Figure 6-4. Student making progress toward goal line.

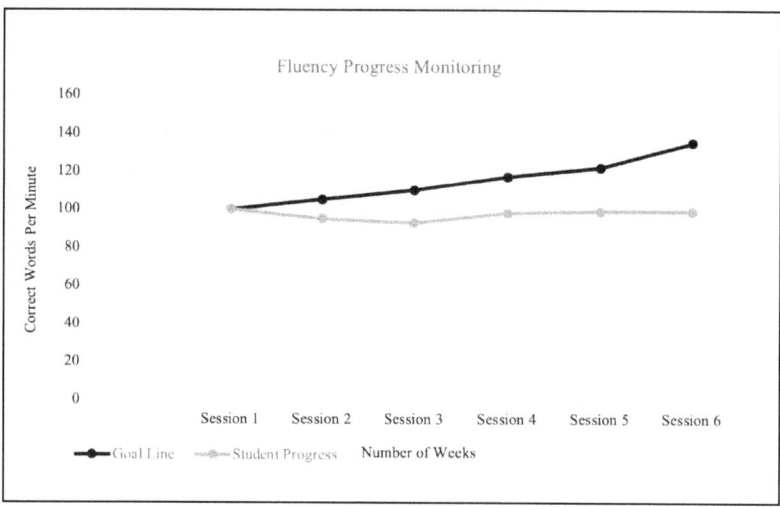

Figure 6-5. Student not making progress toward goal line.

TABLE 6-3. COMPARISON OF CURRICULUM-BASED MEASUREMENT AND MASTERY MEASUREMENT

CHARACTERISTIC	CBM	MASTERY MEASUREMENT
Skills being assessed are aligned with curriculum.	X	X
Assessments are quick and easy to implement.	X	X
Students' skills are frequently assessed.	X	X
Assessment results are available immediately.	X	X
The assessments are cost-effective.	X	X
Information from the assessments is used to evaluate the effectiveness of the instruction allowing teachers to design better instructional programs.	X	X
Assessments are aligned with a sequenced curriculum.	X	
Assessments are given multiple times in a unit of study for each set of skills.	X	
Assessments monitor achievement of a specific skill.	X	
Assessments monitor student growth across the year.		X
Different assessments are available that are equal in difficulty.		X
Standardized assessment measures, guidelines for administration, and scoring procedures are included.		X
Assessments predict student performance on standardized achievement tests.		X
Assessments identify students not making adequate progress and students needing additional or different instruction.		X

Mastery Measurement

While CBM is used to assess students' progress across an entire curriculum, MM evaluates a student's understanding of and proficiency in a single target skill (IRIS Center, 2022). A teacher can ensure a student has measured one specific skill before moving to another skill when using MM. Instructional changes can be made in a timely manner when a student is not mastering the specific target skill. As the school year progresses, the target skills are broken into subskills that are sequenced, and one subskill is included per measure. Each measure is administered on a frequent basis (typically weekly). The data from the measure are used by the teacher to determine if students are on the right track to master the skill by the end of the instructional unit or if they will need additional support. When the student achieves mastery of the specific skill, the next skill is introduced and subsequently assessed.

Although CBM and MM are both types of progress monitoring and have many similarities, they are also different. Table 6-3 provides a comparison between CBM and MM.

Check for Understanding

Two of the most common types of progress monitoring are CBM and MM. CBM tracks a student's progress across the entire curriculum, and MM tracks a student's mastery of a target skill.

Summary

It is important to understand the RTI framework and how DBDM through the use of progress monitoring fits into the RTI framework. When we are working with our students, we must come from a place of making informed decisions based on data. When we make data-based decisions, use appropriate CBM, and move our students through the RTI framework, we are better able to meet the needs of our students. Effective progress monitoring prevents the idea of "wait to fail" because students are being worked with at all levels. Remember, effective progress monitoring using CBM or MM is not time intensive but is effective in tracking student progress. Teachers need to have the knowledge and skills to implement numerous evidence-based interventions to address significant needs of students (Filderman & Toste, 2018). Ongoing progress monitoring is essential to determine students' RTI programs utilized and determine if and when adjustments to instruction are needed.

Case Study Wrap-Up

In the RTI process, Parker moved from Tier 1 instruction to Tier 2 instruction where he could receive more specific instruction to help him reach his reading goals. After collecting baseline data, Mrs. Miller created a realistic and ambitious goal and created a graph to plot Parker's data. Two times each week for 6 weeks, Mrs. Miller plotted Parker's data. At the end of the 6 weeks, Mrs. Miller found that although Parker was making some progress, the outcome slope was not matching the trend line. It was determined that Parker would need to move to Tier 3 for even more intensive interventions and a comprehensive evaluation to establish how to best support him.

Chapter Review

1. What are teachers' roles and responsibilities in the assessment process?
2. Describe how progress monitoring fits within response to intervention.
3. Discuss the progress monitoring steps and discuss why following the steps is so important.
4. Look through the online web-based curriculum-based measurement tools. What are the benefits and challenges of the curriculum-based measurement tools presented? Discuss which curriculum-based measurement tool(s) you can see yourself using most and why.
5. What can you interpret from looking at the following graph (on page 105)? Describe recommendations would you give to the teacher implementing the intervention.

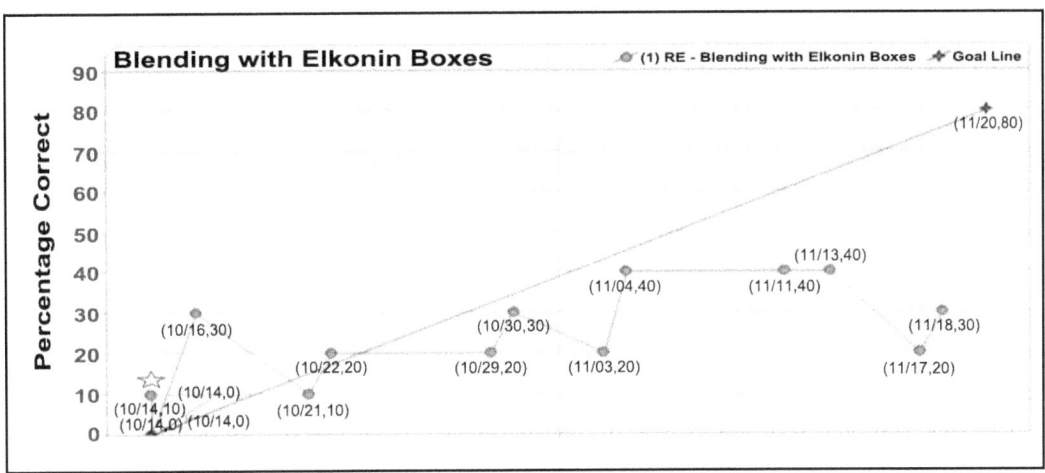

References

Cornelius, K. E., & Johnson-Harris, K. M. (2017). Progress monitoring: Your classroom itinerary. In W. W. Murawski & K. L. Scott (Eds.), *What really works with exceptional learners*. Corwin Press, Council for Exceptional Children.

Deno, S. L. (1985). Curriculum-based measurement: The emerging alternative. *Exceptional Children, 52*(3), 219-232. https://doi.org/10.1177/001440298505200303

Filderman, M. J., & Toste, J. R. (2018). Decisions, decisions, decisions: Using data to make instructional decisions for struggling readers. *TEACHING Exceptional Children, 50*(3), 130-140. https://doi.org/10.1177/0040059917740701

Furey, J., & Loftus-Rattan, S. M. (2022). Actively involving students with learning disabilities in progress monitoring practices. *Intervention in School and Clinic, 57*(5), 329-337. https://doi.org/10.1177/10534512211032618

Hallahan, D. P., Kauffman, J. M., & Pullen, P. C. (2019). *Exceptional learners: An introduction to special education* (14th ed.). Pearson.

Individuals with Disabilities Education Improvement Act, Public Law 108-446, 108th Congress (2004).

IRIS Center. (2021a). *How can school personnel use data to make instructional decisions? Page 3: Progress monitoring.* https://iris.peabody.vanderbilt.edu/module/dbi2/cresource/q2/p03/#content

IRIS Center. (2021b). *What is data-based individualization? Page 1: Overview of data-based individualization.* https://iris.peabody.vanderbilt.edu/module/dbi2/cresource/q1/p01/#content

IRIS Center. (2022). *Progress monitoring: Mastery measurement vs. general outcome measurement.* https://iris.peabody.vanderbilt.edu/module/pmr/cresource/q1/p02

Lingo, A. S., Barton-Arwood, S. M., & Jolivette, K. (2011). Teachers working together: Improving learning outcomes in the inclusive classroom—Practical strategies and examples. *TEACHING Exceptional Children, 43*(3), 6-13. https://doi.org/10.1177/004005991104300301

McLane, K. (n.d.-a). *Student progress monitoring: What this means for your child.* Reading Rockets. https://www.readingrockets.org/article/student-progress-monitoring-what-means-your-child

McLane, K. (n.d.-b). *What is curriculum-based measurement and what does it mean to my child?* Reading Rockets. https://www.readingrockets.org/article/what-curriculum-based-measurement-and-what-does-it-mean-my-child

National Center on Response to Intervention. (2013). *Progress monitoring brief #1: Common progress monitoring omissions: Planning and practice.* U.S. Department of Education, Office of Special Education Programs, National Center on Response to Intervention.

No Child Left Behind Act, Public Law 107-110, 107th Congress (2001).

RTI Action Network. (2021). *Learn about RTI: What is RTI?* http://www.rtinetwork.org/learn/what/whatisrti

Stecker, P. M., Lembke, E. S., & Foegen, A. (2008). Using progress-monitoring data to improve instructional decision making. *Preventing School Failure, 52*(2), 48-58. https://doi.org/10.3200/PSFL.52.2.48-58

Assessing Behavior

CHAPTER OBJECTIVES
- Define behaviors.
- Describe the differences between direct and indirect methods of measuring behavior and delineate examples of both.
- Outline the steps to appropriately assess students who exhibit challenging behaviors.

KEY TERMS

- **antecedent:** An antecedent is the thing that happens right before a problem behavior occurs. The antecedent can be events, conditions, activities, or times.
- **behavior intervention plan (BIP):** An individual plan directly based on the results of a student's functional behavior assessment, designed to support the needs of the student through the treatment of problem behaviors. It describes how the behaviors will be changed by creating a plan to change the social context in which the behaviors occur. It also describes in specific detail how teachers, parents, and others working with the student will change their behavior.
- **direct data:** Direct data collection involves a person directly observing or seeing the behaviors occur and collecting data on the problem behavior. Examples include ABC observations, event recording, latency recording, and interval recording. Direct data collection is a part of the functional behavior assessment process.
- **duration:** Duration is a type of frequency recording when the observer records the length of time a student engages in the problem behavior.
- **event recording:** Event recording is a type of frequency count where the observer makes a tally every time a behavior occurs within a specific period of time.
- **frequency count:** The frequency count involves counting each time a student's problem behavior occurs.
- **functional behavior assessment (FBA):** A formal assessment process designed to determine why problem behaviors are occurring.
- **indirect data:** Indirect data collection does not involve any direct observations of behavior. It involves looking at records or asking the opinion of others who directly witness the behaviors or know the student well. Indirect data collection is done through the use of rating scales or interviews. Indirect data collection is a part of the functional behavior assessment process.
- **interval recording:** Interval recording is a type of frequency recording where the observer breaks up a specific period of time into intervals and notes, with a + or –, if the problem behavior occurs within the interval.
- **interviews:** Interviews are conversations with the student, family members, teachers, and anyone else who works with the student who is exhibiting challenging behaviors. The interview is an indirect form of data and is designed to hear the perspective of the student with challenging behaviors and those who work closely with the student to help determine the potential function of the behaviors.
- **latency recording:** Latency recording is a type of frequency recording where the observer records how long it takes for the problem behavior to occur.
- **positive behavioral interventions and supports (PBIS):** An example of a multi-tiered framework that is data-driven and designed to support all students through a continuum of evidence-based practices to meet the specific needs of students.
- **rating scale/surveys/questionnaires:** Rating scales, surveys, and questionnaires are a form of indirect data and can be done with students, family members, teachers, and anyone else who works with the student who is exhibiting challenging behaviors. The person filling out the form rates the behaviors of the student with challenging behaviors as a way to help potentially determine the function of the problem behaviors.
- **records:** Records are considered written documentation of the student's academic, behavior, and medical history. Examples can include report cards, testing scores, medical assessments, Individualized Education Program documentation, or office referrals. Reviewing records is a form of indirect data to get an understanding of the student and the potential function of a student's behavior.
- **scatterplot:** A scatterplot is a form of direct data and is designed to get a week-long perspective of a student's behavior to see if there are patterns in the days/times the student exhibits challenging behaviors. A tally mark is added to the days/times the defined behavior of concern is observed.

KEY ABBREVIATIONS

- BIP: behavior intervention plan
- FBA: functional behavior assessment
- IEP: Individualized Education Program
- PBIS: positive behavioral interventions and supports

Case Study

Jordan is a third-grade student at Cedar Ridge Elementary School. Jordan joined Cedar Ridge Elementary School when he was in first grade. Although his parents are no longer married, they are supportive of Jordan and are actively engaged with his schooling. Jordan has a hard time sitting still, and he easily gets upset when he does not like something his teachers or classmates say or do. Jordan would often crumple up assignments and refuse to do them. Each year at Cedar Ridge has gotten more challenging for Jordan. Academically, he is an average-performing student, but his behaviors often cause him to be in the principal's office. A few of Jordan's teachers came to talk to Mrs. Wright, his second-grade teacher, before the school year started to talk about his behaviors and how wild he was in their classrooms. They also felt like his parents were too pushy and did not believe Jordan needed to be put on medication for being hyperactive. Mrs. Wright listened to them but knew it was important for her to form her own opinion of Jordan and his family. She also knew it would be important for her to form a positive relationship with them at the start of the school year.

An important environment for students, families, educators, and community members to grow, learn, and teach is the school system. Students and their teachers are in school for about 180 days for 6 hours or more during those days. The school environment has the potential to be a stable, positive, and predictable environment for students where they have the opportunity to have positive adult and peer role models and learn and grow academically and socially (Sugai et al., 2000). Each year, schools are being asked to do more with fewer resources while educators are teaching an increasingly heterogeneous group of students. For example, students are coming into school with significant learning and/or behavior problems, mental health problems, limited family support, and families who may be facing financial barriers. The purpose of this chapter is to discuss a framework to seamlessly meet the needs of all students, particularly students with challenging behaviors, through a multi-tiered system of support and functional behavior assessment (FBA). Schools are faced with the challenge of meeting the needs of all their students yet lack the capacity to sustain practices and policies to effectively meet the needs of all the students. To help meet the needs of students, it is first important to learn how to properly define behaviors. The chapter highlights indirect and direct methods of data collection. We discuss the difference between a brief FBA and a comprehensive behavior assessment. The chapter ends by going through the steps of an FBA and how the assessment supporting the implementation of a behavior intervention plan (BIP).

Multi-Tiered System of Support

A school system is responsible for ensuring their students achieve academic success. Educators know they are required to teach the academic subjects they have been hired to teach. There is an understanding that students need to be taught how to read, write, do math, and so on. Although most students typically engage in school-appropriate behaviors, there are some students who struggle in this area and need additional support to learn appropriate behaviors. Research has shown that zero tolerance and practices of punishment and control are unsuccessful at preparing students who struggle with their behavior to be successful in school or in society (e.g., Center on PBIS, 2022a; Sugai et al., 2000; Yell et al., 2013). However, when multi-tiered frameworks, such as positive behavioral interventions and supports (PBIS) or multi-tiered system of support (MTSS) are utilized, not only do students show an increase in academic achievement but also these frameworks increase positive social, emotional, and behavioral needs of students (Center on PBIS, 2022a).

A multi-tiered framework has three levels of support and is a preventative and proactive framework to support the needs of all students. Tier 1 involves all students and sets the foundation for being proactive and prevents unwanted behaviors (Center on PBIS, 2022b). Being consistent with preventative and proactive measures will capture most students; however, there will be some students who need additional support. Students who need extra support with their behavior are much like students who need support academically. We know we need to provide extra support for students academically, but sometimes we can forget that there are students who need support with their behaviors. These students move to Tier 2 (Center on PBIS, 2022c). Tier 2 practices are designed to support students who are not successful with only Tier 1 interventions and involve small group instruction where students can learn social skills and self-management skills and get academic support. Students at Tier 2 are still receiving Tier 1 supports as well as Tier 2 supports. At most schools, only 1% to 5% of students need to move to Tier 3 because supports at Tier 1 and Tier 2 have not connected. Students at Tier 3 need more individualized and intense support to improve their academic and behavioral outcomes (Center on PBIS, 2022d). When a student moves to Tier 3, they are still receiving support at Tier 1 and Tier 2. At Tier 3, an FBA is completed to determine how to best support the individual needs of a student.

Check for Understanding

An MTSS, such as PBIS, is a framework used to support all students and includes universal strategies for all students and more targeted strategies for students who need additional support.

Behavior Defined

Behaviors are both observable and measurable. When behaviors are defined, it is important to be objective rather than subjective. To effectively assess problem behaviors, the first step in the process is to operationally define the behavior. The operational definition of a behavior should be clear and describe what the behavior is including the frequency, intensity, or duration (Harlacher & Rodriguez, 2018). It is important for behaviors to be operationalized so there is consistency between the individuals who are rating the behaviors (Yell et al., 2013). Additionally, operationally defining behaviors ensures teachers and the student understand exactly what behavior needs to be increased or decreased. When operationally defining behaviors, be thinking, what does the behavior look like? For example, Maggie is too active. What does "too active" look like? If there were two people observing Maggie, each person would have a different idea of what "too active" looks like. The example here is subjective, meaning based on a person's one perspective, and poorly defined. Active could mean walking around the room, bouncing around on the floor or in a seat, fidgeting with things on or around a desk, or any other number of things. On the other hand, if we were to say Maggie leaves her seat when her teacher is teaching the class, we can easily count the number of times Maggie gets out of her seat. This example is objective because it is clear and specific. Two people could observe Maggie in class to see how many times she leaves her seat during instructional time. Table 7-1 provides examples of problem behaviors defined in objective terms and subjective terms. These definitions are not all-inclusive; students show behaviors in different ways, which is why it is important to be objective when providing operational definitions of problem behaviors.

TABLE 7-1. EXAMPLES OF DEFINING PROBLEM BEHAVIORS

SUBJECTIVE DEFINITION—NONOBSERVABLE	OBJECTIVE, OPERATIONALLY DEFINED—OBSERVABLE AND MEASURABLE
Defiant	Student refuses to comply with directions given by the teacher by verbally saying, "You can't make me!" or yelling, "No!" followed by leaving the room.
Anger	In a loud, raised voice the student will say, "I am going to punch you!" and clenches their fists together.
Sad	The student cries when asked to work on their math assignment independently. The student becomes quiet and withdraws from the group with their head down.
Off-task	The student is up out of his seat walking around the classroom when the class is doing independent work. The student draws on his paper and does not complete the assignment.
Noncompliant	The student refuses to complete an independent task by putting their head on the desk, not moving, and not answering the teacher when they tell them to begin working or ask why they are not working.
Aggression	The student tears paper into pieces and throws them at the teacher. The student slams their fist on the table and throws their pencil. The student yells profanity.
Academic engagement	The student is actively looking at the teacher when they are talking and participates in group discussions by raising their hand to answer questions and writing notes in their journal.

Behaviors are defined by frequency, duration, latency, and amplitude in the field of social-emotional assessment (Yell et al., 2013). When behaviors are defined in these terms, other individuals are able to understand assessment outcomes because the behaviors are observable. Table 7-2 provides a definition for the ways we can observe behaviors (Yell et al., 2013). It is important to refine the problem behaviors to be able to determine if the behavior is a problem because of (1) the nature of the behavior (e.g., threatening), (2) how frequently the behavior occurs (e.g., getting out of seat 100 times per day), (3) lasting too long (e.g., takes 10 minutes to go to the carpet), or (4) being too intense (e.g., yelling so loud the class across the hall could hear; Scott, 2017). When thinking about this list, threatening is the only negative behavior. Although the other behaviors are appropriate, the ways they are done make them inappropriate. Behaviors become inappropriate when they occur at a low or high frequency, for a short or long time, or at a low or high intensity. For example, it is considered inappropriate for a student to physically strike another student. However, what if the strike is a mild shoulder tap and only happened two times in the last year? In contrast, what if the strike is defined as a closed-fist blow to the chest and occurs multiple times a week? It is clear when defining behaviors that more than just a description of what the behavior is must be included. Figure 7-1 provides example questions to ask when defining behaviors (Scott, 2017).

Table 7-2. Examples of Observable Terms for Measuring Behavior

FREQUENCY	DURATION	LATENCY	AMPLITUDE
Measures the number of times an event (behavior) occurs.	Measures the length of time the event (behavior) occurs.	Measures time between an instruction given and a response.	Measures the force of a specific behavior. Typically, this is measured qualitatively.
Colton left his seat during instruction 15 times in 20 minutes.	Sean looked out the classroom door for 14 of 20 minutes.	After being told, Addison took 8 minutes to get her paper out.	Claudia punched the wall, leaving a hole in the wall.
Andrew talked out 7 times in 15 minutes.	Nathan sat on the floor for 20 out of 20 minutes.	After directions were given, Eli took 5 minutes to begin working.	Grace threw a rock at the window; the window cracked.

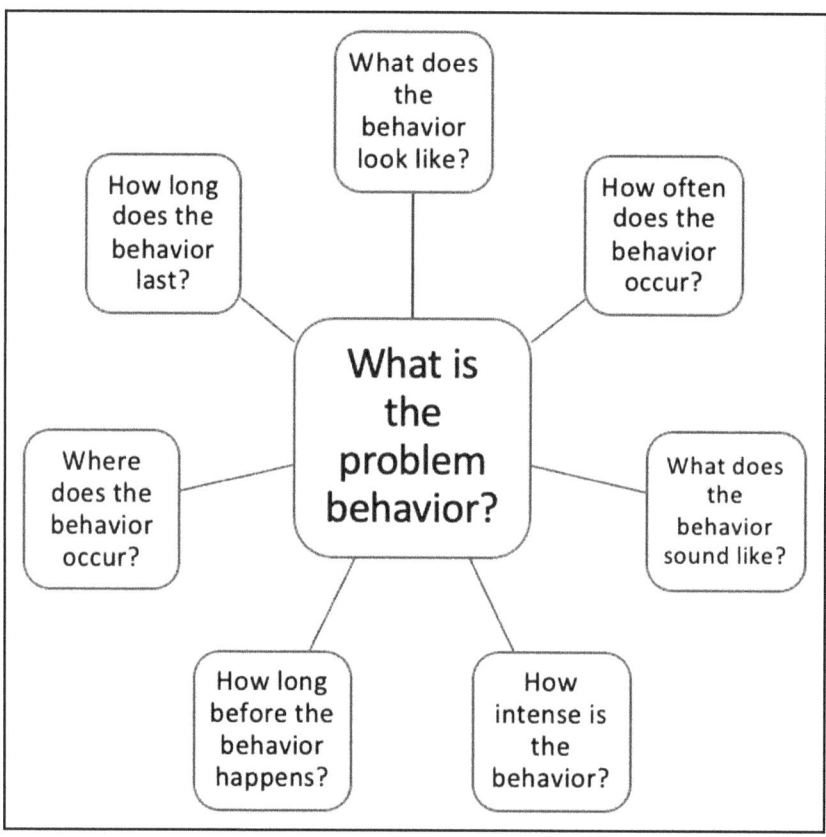

Figure 7-1. Example questions to help define behavior. (Adapted from Scott, T. M. [2017]. *Teaching behavior: Managing classrooms through effective instruction*. Corwin.)

Check for Understanding

When defining behaviors, it is important that the definition is both observable and measurable. Defined behaviors must be objective rather than subjective.

An important part of operationally defining problem behaviors is to determine whether there are (1) skill deficits where the student has not learned the appropriate behavior and therefore needs to be taught, (2) fluency problems where the student knows how to perform the appropriate behavior but struggles doing it well, or (3) performance problems where the student knows how to do the behavior and has practiced the behavior but is not doing the desired behavior in the environmental situation desired (Harlacher & Rodriguez, 2018). Additionally, it is critical to determine if a problem behavior is competing with a desired behavior or if the problem behavior is more effective for the student to get their needs met. It is important to understand how problem behaviors are working for a student and also help build appropriate interventions.

PREDICTING BEHAVIOR

After defining the problem behavior, it is important to think about when the behavior occurs. Being able to predict when the behavior occurs can provide focus for when and where to best initiate the intervention (Scott, 2017). The intervention will always be much bigger and more complex if the problem behaviors occur everywhere all the time compared to an intervention focused on completing independent work during writing. Additionally, knowing that a behavior occurs under a specific set of circumstances is helpful in determining why the behavior is occurring or its purpose for the student, which will provide information needed to make the intervention simple but effective.

Predictors of problem behaviors can be referred to as antecedents, the things (i.e., events, conditions, activities, times) that happen directly before the problem behavior occurs (Scott, 2017). When there is a consistent antecedent or group of antecedent conditions directly before a behavior occurs, we can say those specific antecedent condition(s) are the predictors of behavior. It is important to note that predictors do not necessarily imply cause; rather, they signal the student to engage in a specific behavior. For example, when a student lays their head down during independent work, the independent work does not cause the student to lay their head down; it simply signals the student that putting their head down will work. The student has a choice to not put their head down, so there is not a causal connection. It is, however, the outcome of the behavior that makes it happen. Figure 7-2 provides example questions to consider when predicting behaviors (Scott, 2017).

The example questions from Figure 7-2 elicit follow-up question to consider. The goal is to focus on a particular set of predictor conditions with the least number of questions (Scott, 2017). It is most efficient to begin with the bigger questions and then narrow down. For example, if a student refuses to complete adult requests, it would be important to ask if it is a specific adult or all adults. It is most logical when the actual questions asked and the sequence in which they are asked are based on the behavior and as much introductory and related information as possible. Figure 7-3 is an example flowchart for asking a sequence of questions about a behavior.

DON'T FORGET!

When you are trying to predict a problem behavior, ask yourself, when and where does the behavior occur? What causes the behavior to occur? Figuring out these answers will help you figure out the "why" of the behaviors.

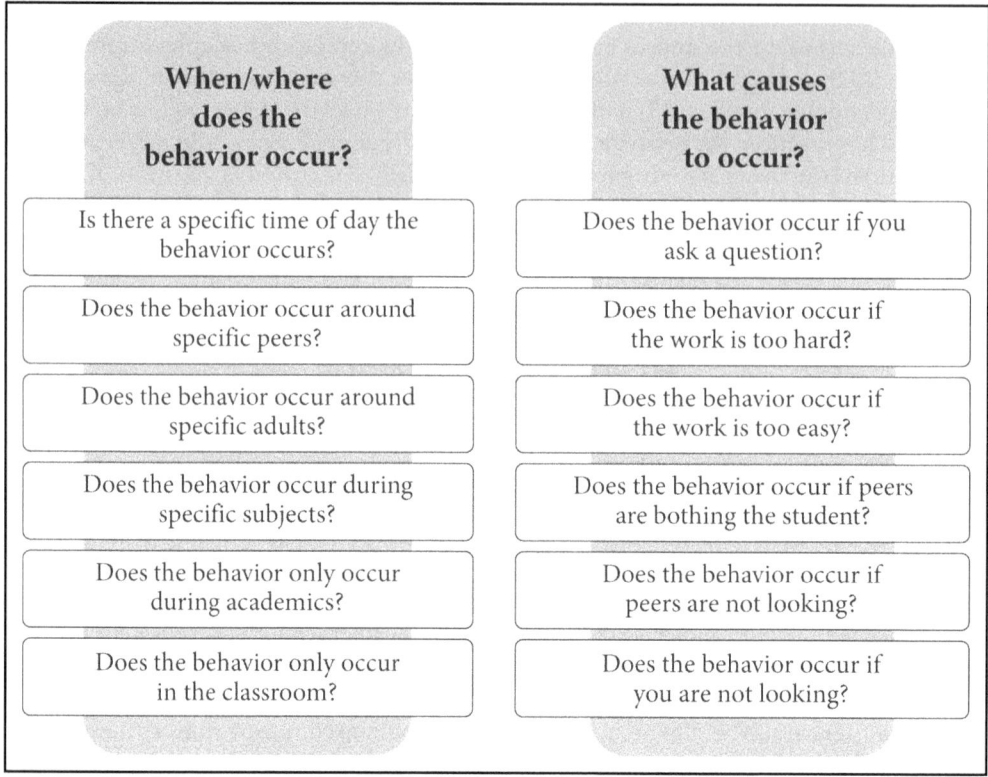

Figure 7-2. Example questions for predicting behaviors. (Adapted from Scott, T. M. [2017]. *Teaching behavior: Managing classrooms through effective instruction.* Corwin.)

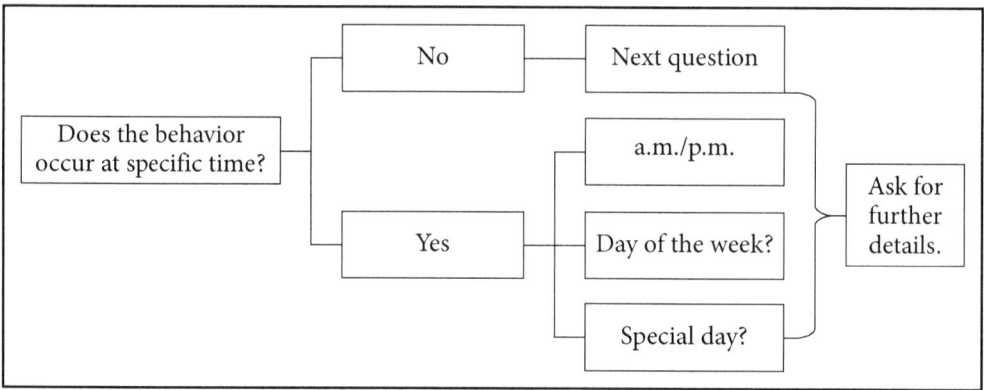

Figure 7-3. Example flowchart of questioning sequence. (Adapted from Scott, T. M. [2017]. *Teaching behavior: Managing classrooms through effective instruction.* Corwin.)

Purpose of Behavior

The final question to consider when thinking about behaviors is to consider what the purpose of the behavior might be, or what is the reason for the continued behavior under some specific circumstance (Scott, 2017). When we think about the purpose of behaviors, it is important to ask a few questions:

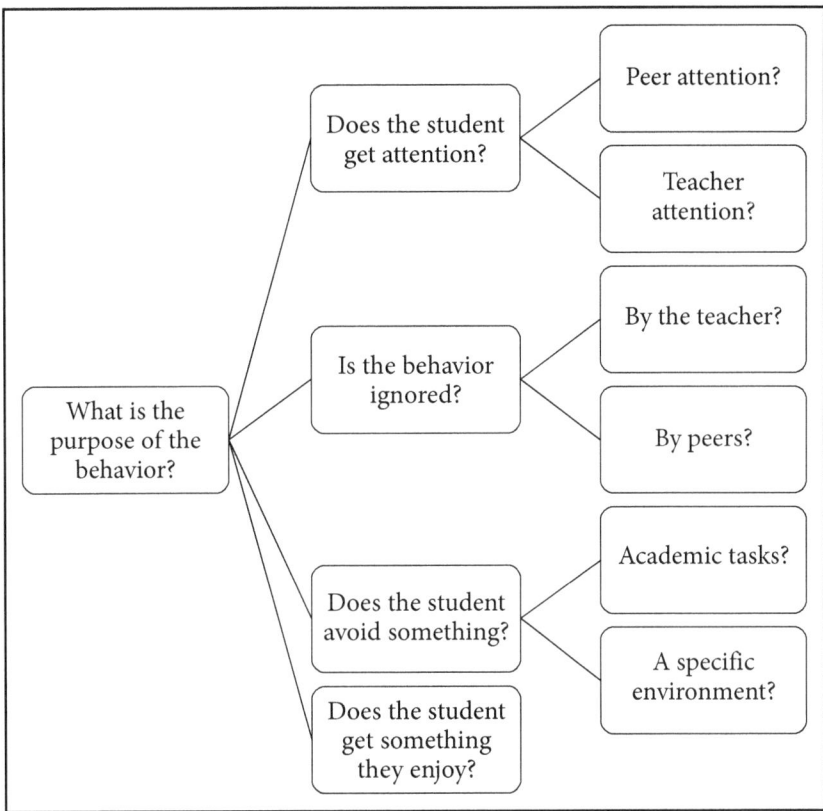

Figure 7-4. Example questions to determine the purpose of behaviors.

1. Why would the student want to exhibit the behavior?
2. What is in it for the student?
3. What needs of the student are being met by the environment when the behavior occurs?
4. How does the behavior benefit the student to be rewarded by the environment?

When an FBA is being completed, one question asked is, what is the function of the behavior (Scott, 2017)? In other words, what is the purpose of the behavior? Determining the function of the behavior is important because it tells us why the student continues engaging in the problem behavior. Students engage in behaviors for a reason; they either get something they like, or they avoid something they do not like. For some students, when they engage in problem behaviors, they are getting a benefit while also avoiding the thing they do not want to do. Figure 7-4 provides example questions to think about when determining the purpose of behaviors. When we understand why the behaviors occur, it helps educators determine what interventions will and will not be effective. For example, let's say you have twin boys in fifth grade, and they both scream. We learn that Asher screams to gain the attention of his peers and teachers. However, his brother, Grant, screams when given attention. Any time a peer or the teacher approaches him about doing his work, Grant begins screaming, and people will back away from him. Grant has learned that if he screams proactively when he sees the teacher or his peers approach, they will stop approaching and stay away. Asher screams when he wants the attention of his peers or teacher, but Grant screams to avoid attention from his peers and teacher. In both cases, we need to teach the students a better way to get what they want, but we would not want to conduct the same intervention for both students because the function is different even though the behavior is the same. Asher needs to be taught appropriate ways to seek attention from his teacher and peers, while Grant needs to be taught appropriate ways to escape the attention of his teacher and peers.

It is important to remember a behavior can serve more than one purpose. Although the purpose of the behavior is essential in developing an intervention, defining the behavior, predicting the behavior, and learning the purpose of the behavior all play in important role in developing an appropriate plan for the student.

> **DON'T FORGET!**
>
> When you are trying to determine the purpose of function of a behavior, it can serve more than one purpose. As yourself the foregoing questions to determine the purpose of behaviors.

EXAMPLES OF MEASURING BEHAVIORS

Behaviors can be measured both indirectly and directly. There are various ways to measure behaviors indirectly and directly. In the section that follows, we will outline what indirect and direct observations are, and we provide examples for the different methods that can be used to measure behaviors.

Indirect

Indirect data collection involves gathering information about a student and the student's challenging behaviors from the student and from individuals who have direct contact with the student. Indirect data are relying on the perspective of others to help determine the potential function of the student's challenging behaviors and identify reinforcers for behaviors of concern (IRIS Center, 2022).

Interviews

An interview can be formal or informal conversation with the student, family members, and teachers. Interviews can be used as a first tool for assessing the function of a student's behavior (IRIS Center, 2022). Interview questions are geared to understand (1) background information concerning the challenging behaviors and/or target behaviors, (2) potential antecedents and consequences connected with the challenging behaviors, (3) times of day and settings where the problem behavior is most likely and least likely to occur, and (4) strategies that have already been tried. Typically, interviews take between 10 and 30 minutes to complete. Interviews can be done individually or with a group (e.g., paraprofessional and teacher, mom and dad). Generally, the interview questions are straightforward, but there are times when probing for additional information is needed. See Figures 7-5, 7-6, and 7-7 for an example of a teacher interview, parent interview, and student interview, respectively.

Records

Reviewing records is one way to help the team identify a student's academic, behavioral, and medical history (Center on PBIS, 2022f). If an intervention plan has been done in the past or there are any prior data collected, information can help identify strategies from the past that were and were not effective. Examples of records to review can include (1) medical documents; (2) previous Individualized Education Programs (IEPs), BIPs, or data collected; (3) report cards; (4) office referrals; (5) psychoeducation reports, including reports from outside evaluations; and (6) any other evaluation report (e.g., speech/language). It is important to note that a record review cannot provide current information on environmental events triggering and/or maintaining the behaviors of concern. However, the information can be used to help the team understand the student's past experiences.

Student: _____   Date of Birth: _____

Interviewer: _____   Date of Interview: _____

Respondent: _____   Title of Respondent: _____

1. Describe the behavior(s) of concern.
2. How often do the behavior(s) occur?
3. How long do the behavior(s) last?
4. When and where are the behavior(s) most likely to occur?
5. When and where are the behavior(s) least likely to occur?
6. Describe what conditions set off the student's behavior(s).
7. Can you tell when the behavior is going to start? If so, how?
8. Describe what happens after the behavior(s) occur.
9. What do you think may serve as the function of the student's behavior(s)?

Figure 7-5. Example of a teacher interview.

Student: _____   Date of Birth: _____

Interviewer: _____   Date of Interview: _____

Name of Parent/Family Member: _____

Relationship to Student: _____

1. Describe your child's behaviors at home.
2. If you are seeing concerning behaviors at home, explain the situation surrounding the behaviors. For example, who are the behaviors most likely to occur with? When are the behaviors most likely to occur? Where are the behaviors most likely to occur?
3. If you are seeing concerning behaviors at home, how are the behaviors handled at home?
4. Are there any factors you can think of that may be causing your child stress?
5. When do you believe your child began to experience problems at school?
6. What do you think may be causing the challenging behaviors at school?
7. Can you think of anything else that we need to consider when addressing the challenging behaviors?

Figure 7-6. Example of a parent interview.

> Student: _____   Date of Birth: _____
>
> Interviewer: _____   Date of Interview: _____
>
> 1. Tell me about things you like about school.
> 2. Tell me about things you don't like about school.
> 3. Tell me things you like about home or other places you go outside of school.
> 4. Tell me things you don't like about home or other places you go outside of school.
> 5. What is your favorite subject/class at school? Why?
> 6. What is your least favorite subject/class at school? Why?
> 7. Talk to me about when you feel you have the most problems at school. Think about where you are, what time of day it is, and who is with you.
> 8. Talk to me about when you feel you have the least problems at school. Think about where you are, what time of day it is, and who is with you.
> 9. Tell me about your peers at school.

Figure 7-7. Example of a student interview.

Rating Scales/Surveys/Questionnaires

Rating scales are a set of questions or statements for parents, the student, and teachers to respond to. The information from the responses provides information on antecedent events that may be happening before the problem behaviors occur as well as responses that occur following the challenging behaviors (Center on PBIS, 2022f). Individuals who work most closely with the student and have observed the problem behaviors can provide rich information about events happening with the environment. The student can also complete one of these forms. Getting information from numerous people can provide a comparison to help identify where there is agreement and disagreement on environmental triggers. Interview questions may be arranged into a rating scale, survey, or questionnaire format. A Google document or a Qualtrics survey is an online format for individuals to complete a rating scale, survey, or questionnaire.

CHECK FOR UNDERSTANDING

Indirect data involve relying on the perspective of others to understand the function of student behaviors and includes interviews and/or rating scales.

ABC Observation Sheet

Student: _____   Date: _____

Observer: _____   Time of Observation: _____

Class and Teacher: _____

Antecedent	Behavior	Consequence
Example: The bell rings.	S walks into class.	T asks S, "Where have you been? Go sit in your seat."

S – student; T – teacher

Figure 7-8. Example of an ABC observation sheet.

Direct

One way to measure behavior is through direct observations, meaning a person is directly observing a student in the classroom setting and is collecting data on challenging behaviors that are occurring. The observer can be the teacher, behavior analyst, another teacher, school psychologist, or school counselor (Scott, 2017). Direct observations can provide insight into how often a behavior occurs, how long the behavior lasts, when the behavior is most and least likely to occur, and where the behavior is most and least likely to occur (IRIS Center, 2022).

ABC Observation

An ABC observation is used to identify the (A) antecedents that set the stage for the (B) challenging behavior to occur and the (C) consequences appearing to maintain the problem behavior (IRIS Center, 2022; Figure 7-8). The person observing the student records what is happening during the observation and also includes the time of day and setting in which the observation is taking place. During the observation, the recorder is writing down exactly what happens, providing as clear of a picture as possible of what is occurring in the room. For example, if the student being observed says something, and the class laughs, the consequence would be the class laughing. If the behavior continues, we may learn that the cause of the challenging behavior is peer attention. Multiple observations should occur in order to have enough information to see an ABC pattern.

Event Recording Sheet

Student: _____ Date: _____

Observer: _____

Class and Teacher: _____

Behavior Defined: _____

Add a tally mark for each time the behavior defined above occurs.

Time	Tally	Total
Example: 9:00 – 9:30 a.m.	/////	5

Figure 7-9. Example of an event recording sheet.

Frequency Count

It is important to know how often problem behaviors occur. One way to do this is to observe the frequency of a student's problem behaviors by counting the number of times the problem behavior occurs, which can be measured through event or interval recordings (IRIS Center, 2022). Event recordings involve tallying every time the behavior (event) occurs within a given period of time. See Figure 7-9 for an example of an event recording sheet. Tally marks on a piece of paper or using a handheld tally counter are two ways to complete an event recording. An interval recording involves recording whether or not the problem behavior occurred within a specific period of time. Figure 7-10 provides an example of an interval recording sheet. The periods can be broken down into 30-second intervals or even minute-long intervals. The difference in an interval recording is that the observer is not counting how many times a behavior occurs within a specific period of time; rather, the observer is just noting if the behavior did or did not occur within a specific period of time.

Duration

When measuring the duration of a behavior, the observer is measuring the length of time the student engages in the problem behavior (IRIS Center, 2022; Figure 7-11). To do this, the observer uses a handheld stopwatch or phone stopwatch when the student begins to engage in the problem behavior and then stops the time when the behavior ends.

Latency

Latency recording is similar to duration recording in that the observation is about length of time. Figure 7-12 provides an example of a latency recording sheet. However, with latency recording, the observer records how long it takes for the problem behavior to occur (IRIS Center, 2022). A stopwatch is used for latency recording, but the observer starts the stopwatch when the behavior should begin and then stops when the behavior actually begins. For example, if a student is asked to begin independent work, the observer would start the stopwatch when the student is asked to begin the independent work and ends the stopwatch when the student begins the independent work.

Interval Recording Sheet

Student: _____   Date: _____

Observer: _____   Start/Stop Times: _____

Class and Teacher: _____   Length of Interval: _____

Behavior Defined: _____

+ behavior occurs

− behavior does not occur

Interval	Behavior
	Example:
30'	+
60'	−
90'	+
120'	
150'	
180'	
210'	
240'	
270'	
300'	

Figure 7-10. Example of an interval recording sheet.

Scatterplot

A scatterplot is a type of frequency data collection and is used to determine when behaviors are most and least likely to occur over a period of time (Yell et al., 2013). Typically, a scatterplot is done over the course of a week, and tally marks are added for each time the problem behavior occurs. Figure 7-13 provides an example of a scatterplot recording sheet. At the end of the week, a scatterplot should be able to see if there are patterns when problem behaviors occur. For example, there may be a specific day of the week when problem behaviors occur or are worse than during other days. There may also be times of the day when problem behaviors are most or least likely to occur.

Duration Recording Sheet

Student: _____   **Date:** _____

Observer: _____

Class and Teacher: _____

Behavior Defined: _____

Time begins when at the beginning of the defined behavior and stops when the defined behavior stops.

Start Time	End Time	Total Duration
Example: 12:32 p.m.	12:43 p.m.	11 minutes

Figure 7-11. Example of a duration recording sheet.

Latency Recording Sheet

Student: _____   **Date:** _____

Observer: _____

Class and Teacher: _____

Behavior Defined: _____

Time begins when the prompt is given, and the time ends when the student complies with request.

Start Time of Request or Prompt	Time Student Complies	Total Latency
Example: Start independent work 2:30 p.m.	Time student began work – 2:35 p.m.	5 minutes
Reminder to continue independent work 2:42 p.m.	Time student begins independent work – 2:44 p.m.	2 minutes

Figure 7-12. Example of a latency recording sheet.

Scatterplot Recording Sheet

Student: _____ Date: _____

Observer: _____

Behavior Defined: _____

Activity	Time (Start-Stop)	Monday	Tuesday	Wednesday	Thursday	Friday	Total
Science							
Social Studies							
Math							
Recess							
Lunch							
Reading/Language Arts							
Specials PE – M, T, Th Music – W Art – F							

Figure 7-13. Example of a scatterplot recording sheet.

Check for Understanding

Direct data collection involves directly observing the problem behaviors when they occur and documenting the behaviors through frequency recordings or an ABC observation.

Functional Behavior Assessment

FBA is a formal assessment process designed to determine why problem behaviors are occurring (Center on PBIS, 2022e). Conducting an FBA allows teams to identify not only why behaviors are occurring but also interventions most likely to support the individual student in being successful. According to Yell et al. (2013), an FBA should identify the following information:

1. A description of the challenging behaviors and daily routines
2. Consequences that are maintaining the problem behaviors
3. Antecedent events triggering the problem behaviors
4. Setting events that increase the likelihood of the challenging behaviors

A formal FBA process includes strategies to prevent unwanted behaviors from occurring, teach appropriate behaviors, provide positive reinforcement for desired behaviors, reduce rewarding unwanted behaviors, and ensure the safety of students (Center on PBIS, 2022e). When developing interventions to support students with challenging behaviors, it is crucial to minimize the payoff for competing problem behavior while concurrently shaping and encouraging the student's skill set to engage in increasingly desired behaviors (Harlacher & Rodriguez, 2018).

FBA became a significant concept in the 1997 amendments to the Individuals with Disabilities Education Act (IDEA). According to the IDEA (1997), when appropriate, a child's IEP must consider strategies including PBIS for a child whose behavior impedes their learning or the learning of others to help address the behaviors. When schools fail to use PBIS for students who are receiving special education services and exhibit behaviors resulting in the suspension of the child, the local educational agency (LEA) must assemble an IEP meeting to develop an assessment plan to appropriately address the behaviors of concern. However, if the child already has a BIP, the IEP team needs to review the student's plan and modify it as necessary to address the behaviors. Although PBIS and FBA are not new, having them included in IDEA 1997 and again in the Individuals with Disabilities Education Improvement Act (2004) represents an important effort to improve the quality of behavior interventions and behavioral support planning for students with challenging behaviors, particularly students with disabilities (Yell et al., 2013).

The positive impact of function-based interventions grounded on data from FBA has been well documented for more than 20 years (Center on PBIS, 2022e). However, some districts and schools struggle implementing effective individualized interventions. One barrier to effectively implementing Tier 3 interventions is the misconception district personnel have that an FBA should be conducted as a last resort or is only for students who have an IEP. There is a perception that district-level behavior specialists or outside experts are needed to create a time-intensive and comprehensive BIP only when challenging behaviors have begun to significantly impact educational success. For students who demonstrate less severe problem behavior or who do not need special education services, valuable resources and time are underutilized by implementing interventions that are less effective and do not address the function of the student's challenging behaviors. When an FBA is only conducted in response to the most intensive problem behaviors, school personnel lose the opportunity to use a function-based intervention earlier in the PBIS continuum to address less severe challenging behaviors and prevent them from developing into a more serious problem. Developing and providing a continuum of Tier 3 supports is one way school personnel can ensure all students who require an individualized behavior support plan needs are met while also maximizing the efficient use of valuable resources and time.

Within a multi-tiered framework, students with persistent problem behaviors not addressed within Tier 1 or 2 should receive support for their behavior that is designed to address the function of the behaviors (Center on PBIS, 2022e). At Tier 3, information is collected, through the FBA process, about the student, their behavior, and the learning context to best understand what the function or purpose of the challenging behavior is for the student. The type of FBA implemented can vary depending on the complexity of the student's needs. For students who have severe and intensive behaviors (e.g., self-injury, aggression), a comprehensive FBA process is needed. However, benefits have been seen from a streamlined and less resource-intensive FBA process, or brief FBA, for students who engage in persistent but non-dangerous challenging behaviors (e.g., work avoidance, out of seat behavior, talk-outs). Team members of a brief FBA include the student, family members, school personnel who are most familiar with the student (e.g., classroom teacher), and a trained school-based professional. If the student is receiving special education services, individuals who are a part of the student's IEP team should be included to ensure consistency in services provided. On the other hand, team members of a comprehensive FBA include the student, family members, school personnel most familiar with the student, appropriate district and school support staff, and behavioral experts trained in developing and implementing intensive interventions for students with intensive challenging behaviors (e.g., behavior specialist, school psychologist; Center on PBIS, 2022f).

When thinking about a brief versus comprehensive FBA, it is important to note that there should not be two distinct FBA processes but rather a continuum. The goal of a brief FBA is to prioritize one or two behaviors of concern and identify what is happening (e.g., independent work, group work, lunch, recess) when the behaviors are most likely to occur (Center on PBIS, 2022e). After receiving parent permission to conduct the brief FBA, the process includes a focused interview (about 30 to 45 minutes) with teachers/staff who work most closely with the student and direct observations of the student during the time prioritized and/or a review of the student's existing data (e.g., office referrals) to capture a clear picture of the challenging behavior within the typical school routines and identify common patterns in the behavior. Once the team feels confident enough data have been collected to understand the function of the challenging behaviors, the team meets to design a brief BIP. The brief BIP will be discussed in detail further in the chapter. On the other hand, a comprehensive FBA is needed for students who have intensive challenging behaviors (e.g., aggression, self-injury). The process includes an initial extensive review of the student's records, multiple interviews (e.g., parents, students, teachers), and direct observations. Data collection should be ongoing and should be performed across multiple settings, days, and times. The main goal of a comprehensive FBA is to create a comprehensive BIP, which is often done as part of a student's IEP. The comprehensive BIP is discussed later in the chapter. Table 7-3 provides a side-by-side comparison of the brief and comprehensive FBA and BIP process.

DON'T FORGET!

The brief FBA and comprehensive FBA are considered a continuum rather than two distinct and separate processes.

STEPS TO COMPLETING A COMPREHENSIVE FUNCTIONAL BEHAVIOR ASSESSMENT

There are multiple steps to complete a comprehensive FBA. Before the FBA process begins, a team is formed that best meets the needs of the students (e.g., student, parent, educators, behavior specialist, counselor; IRIS Center, 2022). Once the team is established, roles and responsibilities (e.g., coach to keep team focused, primary implementers to engage in discussion and provide information about the student) should be decided on for team members to ensure the process is efficient and activities are carried out as intended (Center on PBIS, 2022f). It is important to remember that schools may have a different group of professionals who are involved in the process (IRIS Center, 2022). Each student's needs will be different and require different professionals, but regardless of who participates, the process is the same (see Table 7-4 for the steps; Center on PBIS, 2022f; IRIS Center, 2022; Sugai et al., 2000). *When thinking about our case study with Jordan, it was determined that a comprehensive FBA was needed. Mrs. Wright has a positive relationship with Jordan and his family. She had implemented Tier 2 strategies with Jordan, but his behavior was impeding his instruction and the learning of those in the classroom. His team included Mrs. Wright, the special education team leader, the counselor, the principal, Jordan, and his parents.*

TABLE 7-3. OVERVIEW OF BRIEF VERSUS COMPREHENSIVE FUNCTIONAL BEHAVIOR ASSESSMENT AND BEHAVIOR INTERVENTION PLAN PROCESS

FEATURE	BRIEF FBA	COMPREHENSIVE FBA
Team members	<ul><li>School-based professional trained in conducting brief FBA</li><li>School personnel, such as the general education teacher, most familiar with the student</li><li>The student</li><li>Family members</li></ul>	<ul><li>Expert personnel, such as a behavior specialist or school psychologist, trained to develop and implement interventions for students with severe challenging behaviors</li><li>School personnel most familiar with the student</li><li>Relevant school and district support staff</li><li>Community agencies that are applicable to the student, such as mental health</li><li>The student</li><li>Family members</li></ul>
Training involved to lead FBA	<ul><li>District training on process of completing a brief FBA</li><li>Personnel with extensive training for implementing Tier 3 support who will provide continuous on-site coaching support</li></ul>	<ul><li>Graduate degree in fields such as special education, behavioral analysis, or school psychology</li><li>Training in conducting FBAs</li><li>Training and experience in crisis response management</li><li>Experience conducting function-based interventions for student with significant challenging behaviors</li><li>Training and experience in facilitating wraparound services and person-centered planning</li></ul>
Behaviors	<ul><li>A small number of behaviors that occur frequently but are *not* dangerous such as work refusal, talking out, out-of-seat behavior</li><li>Universal and/or targeted interventions have not been effective for the student</li><li>School personnel are easily able to identify patterns of the behavior using a simple interview format</li><li>Behaviors occur in one to two school routines such as lunch, recess, or the classroom</li></ul>	<ul><li>Chronic and high-intensity behaviors or behaviors that are dangerous such as destruction of property, throwing objects, hitting, self-injurious behaviors</li><li>Behaviors serve more than one function such as behaviors served by escape and student attention</li><li>Behaviors occur in three or more school routines or throughout the entire school day</li></ul>

(continued)

Table 7-3 (continued). Overview of Brief Versus Comprehensive Functional Behavior Assessment and Behavior Intervention Plan Process

FEATURE	BRIEF FBA	COMPREHENSIVE FBA
Sources of data collection	• Interview with school personnel who work most closely with the student (30 to 45 minutes) • Observe the student in setting where behaviors occur, considered the priority setting • Review of existing data	• Interviews with school personnel who work most closely with the student, parents, and the teacher • Archival records review • Direct observations of numerous occurrences of the student's challenging behaviors across a variety of school settings • Any additional data collection and assessment to help better understand skill deficits and influences on the student's behavior outside of the school context

Intervention strategies	• Functionally equivalent replacement behaviors that will allow the student to have their needs met
	• Practical strategies for:
	   ◦ Preventing challenging behaviors
	   ◦ Teaching and reinforcing replacement behaviors
	   ◦ Minimizing the reinforcement of challenging behaviors
		• Functionally equivalent replacement behaviors
		• There may be more than one replacement behaviors to be able to effectively address more than one function of problem behaviors
		• Plan includes multiple components
		• Antecedent strategies to prevent challenging behaviors
		• Explicitly teaching and reinforcing replacement behaviors
		• Shaping toward appropriate desired behaviors
		• Changing response to problem behaviors
		• If appropriate, crisis response planning
		• If appropriate, person-centered planning and wraparound interventions to include community supports and family members

Adapted from Center on PBIS. (2022f). *Tier 3 comprehensive functional behavior assessment (FBA) guide.* https://www.pbis.org/resource/tier-3-comprehensive-functional-behavior-assessment-fba-guide

TABLE 7-4. STEPS OF FUNCTIONAL BEHAVIOR ASSESSMENT PROCESS

DETERMINE THE FUNCTION OF THE BEHAVIOR

1. Identify and objectively define target behaviors and replacement behaviors.
2. Collect indirect data (e.g., rating scales, interviews).
3. Form initial hypothesis statement.
4. Collect direct data (e.g., frequency recording, ABC observation).
5. Formalize hypothesis statement.

DEVELOPMENT AND IMPLEMENTATION OF A FUNCTION-BASED INTERVENTION

6. Design a function-based intervention plan.

EVALUATE EFFECTIVENESS OF THE INTERVENTION

7. Collect data on the effectiveness of the plan.
8. Adjust or redesign plan based on information from the evaluation.

TABLE 7-5. EXAMPLE TARGET AND REPLACEMENT BEHAVIOR

TARGET BEHAVIOR	REPLACEMENT BEHAVIOR
During independent work time, Jace gets out of his seat and roams around the room.	During independent work time, Jace will stay in his seat to complete his work. He will raise his hand if he has a question or needs help.
When frustrated, Morgan will shout, "I can't do this! This is stupid!" She will throw her pencil and other objects on her desk.	When Morgan is feeling frustrated, she will ask to take a break by going to the quiet corner or asking for help from an adult or a peer.

After the team has been established, the first step in the FBA process is to identify, prioritize, and define the problem behaviors (target behaviors) the student exhibits that the team would like to decrease as well as the behaviors the team would like to increase (replacement behaviors). The selected behaviors need to be defined in measurable and observable terms. We shared how to appropriately define behaviors at the beginning of the chapter. It is important to simultaneously work to decrease and eliminate problem behaviors while reinforcing more acceptable replacement behaviors (IRIS Center, 2022). See Table 7-5 for an example. *The target behaviors for Jordan included not being able to stay in his seat, crumpling his papers and throwing them across the room, refusing to complete tasks asked of him by putting his head down on his desk, raising his voice when he becomes upset about work he is asked to complete, and leaving the room. The team decided replacement behaviors for Jordan included raising his hand to ask a question or ask for help when he does not understand an assignment. When Jordan begins to feel upset or needs a break, Jordan will go to the cool-down corner in the classroom to take a break. He can also ask to go get a drink of water down the hall if he needs to leave the room.*

Once the team operationally defines the target behaviors, data are collected. The purpose of indirect data collection is to gather information about setting events, antecedents, and consequences connected to the problem behaviors (Yell et al., 2013). Indirect data collection relies on the informant's memory and may or may not be accurate, which is why it is important to verify information

TABLE 7-6. EXAMPLE OF SUMMARY HYPOTHESIS STATEMENT

SETTING EVENTS	ANTECEDENTS	BEHAVIOR	CONSEQUENCES

BEHAVIOR	WHEN	STUDENT WILL	FUNCTION
Target behavior			
Replacement behavior			

through direct data collection. Although indirect collection does not prove the function of the behavior, data lead to a hypothesis statement about the potential function of the problem behavior. The summary statement provides a hypothesis and connects the function-based intervention plan and BIP because it suggests which antecedents, consequences, and setting events need to be changed to decrease problem behaviors and indicates new behaviors that can be taught to replace the challenging behaviors. Information from indirect data helps the team learn in which environments the students should be directly observed (e.g., environments where the likelihood of problem behavior is high, environments where the likelihood of problem behavior is low; Center on PBIS, 2022f). It is important to recognize the environments where the problem behavior is most and least likely to occur, to understand what/why triggers in other environments set the problem behaviors off, and also help determine potential interventions. Once direct data in multiple settings are collected, the hypothesis statement is finalized. The hypothesis statement includes the main antecedents (e.g., setting events), the target behavior, and the function, which are based on triggers of the problem behaviors and responses to the problem behavior. The function of the target behavior is divided into two categories:

- Avoid/delay/escape
  - An activity or an object
  - The attention or presence of peers or adults
  - Sensory conditions
- Gain/access
  - An activity or an object
  - The attention or presence of peers or adults
  - Sensory conditions

A chart, like the chart in Table 7-6, can be used to help summarize the hypothesis statement for a student's problem behaviors.

The purpose of an FBA is to determine why problem behavior occurs (Yell et al., 2013). Once the function of a student's behaviors is determined through indirect and direct data collection, a function-based intervention plan (BIP) is developed and implemented (IRIS Center, 2022). The summary hypothesis statement ensures all interventions are logically related to the statement and serves as the backbone of the BIP. Table 7-7 provides an example of a completed summary hypothesis statement.

Indirect data were collected by interviewing Jordan, his parents, and Mrs. Wright. Mrs. Wright also completed a questionnaire. It was determined that when Jordan feels overwhelmed with an assignment, he avoids the academic task by exhibiting target behaviors. Direct observations confirmed academic task avoidance was the main function of Jordan's behavior. However, it was determined that he was also seeking attention from Mrs. Wright and the counselor. He would get one-on-one time with them when they were trying to talk to him and calm him down.

TABLE 7-7. EXAMPLE SUMMARY HYPOTHESIS STATEMENT FOR JORDAN

BEHAVIOR	WHEN	STUDENT WILL	FUNCTION
Target behavior	When Jordan must sit for a long period of time or is presented with an academic task he does not understand or enjoy.	Jordan will leave his desk and walk around the room, crumple his assignment and throw it across the room, refuse to complete the assignment by putting his head down, or leave the room. He will raise his voice when he is confronted about his behavior. Jordan will visit with the counselor or Mrs. Wright for one-on-one time.	Jordan is avoiding academic tasks. Jordan is seeking attention from his teacher and the counselor.
Replacement behavior	When Jordan does not understand an academic task.	Jordan will raise his hand to ask for help if he does not understand an assignment. When he is feeling overwhelmed or frustrated, Jordan will go to the cool-down corner or ask for a drink of water. Jordan can request to stand to complete his work and can sit on a wobble chair to move around. Jordan will visit with Mrs. Wright at the beginning of the day and the end of the day to check in and chat. Jordan will visit with the counselor before lunch to say hi and check in. If he is needing extra help, he can ask to visit with the counselor. He also has an option to earn an incentive of lunch with the counselor or lunch with the teacher.	Jordan will complete the academic tasks. Jordan will have one-on-one attention with Mrs. Wright and the counselor before he exhibits academic work refusal.

BEHAVIOR INTERVENTION PLAN

A BIP, or behavior support plan, is directly based on a student's FBA and should include strategies to prevent problem behavior from occurring by addressing antecedents that may be triggering undesired behaviors, teaching replacement behaviors, and reinforcing replacement behaviors, in turn supporting the student's use of appropriate behaviors (Center on PBIS, 2022e). The idea is to promote desired behaviors while minimizing the reinforcement of undesired behaviors. Sometimes students need to be taught how to express their needs without engaging in problem behaviors. The central concepts of prevention, function, teaching, and reinforcement should stay the same across all support planning within Tier 3; however, depending on the intensity of the student's needs and the nature of the challenging behaviors, the way function-based supports are designed and implemented will vary to meet the specific, individual needs of the student.

A brief BIP specifies replacement behaviors that allow the student to communicate their needs without engaging in the problem behaviors and a few individualized strategies designed to (1) prevent challenging behaviors by changing antecedents found to be triggers and encouraging desired behaviors, (2) teach and reinforce replacement behaviors that help the student communicate needs and feel success, and (3) redirect the student to use desired behaviors and minimize the reinforcement of the challenging behaviors (Center on PBIS, 2022e). On the other hand, the goal of a comprehensive BIP is to (1) include strategies for antecedents, behaviors, and consequences; (2) identify safety responses when the student engages in behaviors that are a serious or imminent risk to themselves or others; and (3) incorporate mental health supports that can extend to both the home and community settings.

Once a function-based BIP is created, the team should meet regularly to coordinate implementation of the plan, create protocols and evaluation plans for data collection, monitor fidelity of the plan once it is implemented (Did we do what we said we would do?) and student outcome data (Is our plan working?), modify the plan to increase the effectiveness, and when appropriate, help with transitioning to less intensive interventions (Center on PBIS, 2022e). A brief BIP should include the following:

- Short- and long-term goals for student progress that are both reasonable and measurable
- Timelines and procedures to collect and evaluate fidelity and student outcome data
- Process for summarizing data in a way that is understandable (e.g., tables, graphs)
- Decision rules to support team-based decision making regarding the fidelity and effectiveness of the plan
- A schedule for the team to meet for data evaluation
- A process to regularly share data with family members

To enhance and streamline feasibility of the brief FBA and BIP process, whenever possible, it is recommended to make modifications to existing data collection tools school personnel are familiar with when collecting student data (Center on PBIS, 2022e). For example, as part of Tier 2, data collection may include a behavior rating scale that can be modified and used to collect data on more specific and individualized goals. It is beneficial to have a checklist when implementing the plan to regularly check the rate of implementation of BIP strategies. Additionally, it is recommended for the team lead/coach to meet regularly (e.g., weekly, biweekly) with the implementers to conduct observations of the plan being implemented and collect data on the behaviors of concern (e.g., frequency and duration) during the school day, especially within the first few weeks the plan is implemented.

When developing a comprehensive BIP, teams need to select a minimum of four FBA-based interventions (Center on PBIS, 2022f):

1. Determine one support/intervention that can directly modify the antecedent (trigger) so it no longer triggers the target behavior, in turn preventing the behavior from occurring.
2. Decide on a support/intervention that can directly teach replacement behaviors. It is important for the replacement behaviors to maintain the same function as the target behaviors. The replacement behavior can teach the student a way to directly communicate the function. For example, a student with off-task behavior to avoid a task can be taught to ask for a break instead. The replacement behavior can also be an alternative skill, which is a behavior that is appropriate. For example, our student who is off-task can be taught to be academically engaged during a nonpreferred task rather than getting off-task, which can include having the student complete the engaged academic behavior for a particular period of time (e.g., 5 minutes) or for a specific amount of work (e.g., one reading passage). Being academically engaged could earn the student a short break (escape) from the task.
3. Determine a support/intervention that reinforces the replacement behavior. The scenario described previously is an example of a reinforcement for staying on-task. The reinforcement can be more powerful. For example, if the student stays on-task for a longer period of time without needing a break, a longer break from the nonpreferred activity could be earned (e.g., 15 minutes).

4. Determine a support/intervention that prevents reinforcement for the target behavior. A behavior plan is effective when the target behavior no longer serves the student. The team should also develop an intervention/support for redirecting the student to use the replacement behavior rather than the target behavior to get the function. For example, at the first sign of off-task behavior, the teacher can immediately redirect a student to request a break.

It is important to determine how, when, where, and by whom the BIP will be implemented (Sugai et al., 2000). Contingency plans should be created for responding to emergencies, collecting data, and appropriately training staff. Additionally, resources and any assistance from other agencies (e.g., mental health) need to be included. A checklist is a helpful tool to use to ensure a BIP is implemented with fidelity (Yell et al., 2013). A fidelity checklist can serve as a visual prompt to help remind the teacher what steps are needed to perform each strategy (Center on PBIS, 2022f). An observer (e.g., behavior specialist) can use an implementation fidelity observation form (IRIS Center, 2022). A percentage is calculated based on the number of steps completed with fidelity. It is important to note that issues with implementation fidelity should be addressed prior to making changes to the intervention itself.

The final step in the FBA process is to evaluate the BIP to ensure the plan is effective (IRIS Center, 2022). Steps for monitoring progress of the interventions/supports should be included in the BIP. It is helpful if the team has systematic guidelines for how often progress is monitored (e.g., weekly) and when meetings will occur (e.g., every 3 weeks after the plan is implemented; Center on PBIS, 2022f). A structured agenda for reviewing data and when decisions will be made based on data trends should also be included in the BIP. To make the most informed decisions, progress monitoring meetings include data on student outcomes and implementation fidelity. Baseline data are compared to intervention data to determine if the anticipated changes in behavior are actually occurring (IRIS Center, 2022). Data collection for the implementation of interventions/supports help the team determine how well the plan is working and whether or not changes need to be made. Data-based decision making should be a cyclical process (Center on PBIS, 2022f). After the team makes a decision based on data, the team develops an action plan for changes made to implementation and decides when to meet again to review new implementation data. If it is decided that individualized supports are no longer necessary, it is important to ensure the student is still provided with a continuum of behavioral supports in Tier 2. If the BIP results in behavior improvements, a plan for gradually fading supports should occur. It is important to note that abruptly discontinuing behavior interventions/supports should never occur.

SUMMARY

The school system is a great place where students, families, teachers, service providers, and community members can work collaboratively to create a positive impact on all students. When a multi-tiered framework of support is utilized, underresourced school systems have a more seamless approach and can better meet the academic and behavioral needs of students (Center on PBIS, 2022a). A multi-tiered approach ensures students' needs are met at all levels. Additionally, when thinking about meeting the needs of students with challenging behaviors, it is important to think about the type of FBA needing to be conducted (i.e., brief or comprehensive). The FBA process does not need to be cumbersome when we think about the process delineated in this chapter. The ultimate goal is to create an individualized plan to support the specific needs of a student. When the FBA and BIP processes are done with fidelity, students with challenging behavior needs are met and led to their success in school and beyond.

CASE STUDY WRAP-UP

Jordan and the rest of his team worked to create a BIP to support his replacement behaviors to decrease the target behaviors. The team created a plan for teaching replacement behaviors and for when and how data would be collected and created short- and long-term goals for Jordan. The team also decided to meet every 2 weeks to begin, and once short-term goals were met, would meet monthly to ensure Jordan was on his way to meeting his long-term goals. It was determined a meeting could be scheduled as needed. The team also created a fidelity checklist to help make sure the team was implementing replacement behaviors correctly and collecting data regularly.

Jordan and the team worked hard to help Jordan decrease his target behaviors and increase his replacement behaviors. Implementing the FBA helped guide an individualized BIP tailored to meet Jordan's needs. He was able to achieve his long-term goals, and the team decided to continue the plan because it was working. Jordan regularly checked in with Mrs. Wright and the counselor and would ask for breaks and help from a friend in the class when he was unsure of an academic task. At the end of the school year, the team met to determine the best teacher placement for fourth grade and met with the teacher prior to the start of the school year to help support Jordan in having a successful year.

CHAPTER REVIEW

1. Provide three examples of a good definition describing behavior.
2. Describe how behaviors are assessed.
3. What is the purpose of a functional behavior assessment?
4. When does a functional behavior assessment occur?
5. Describe the steps for completing a functional behavior assessment.

REFERENCES

Center on PBIS. (2022a). *Supporting and responding to student's social, emotional, and behavioral needs: Evidence-based practices for educators* (Version 2). Center on PBIS. https://www.pbis.org/resource/supporting-and-responding-to-behavior-evidence-based-classroom-strategies-for-teachers

Center on PBIS. (2022b). *Tier 1*. https://www.pbis.org/pbis/tier-1

Center on PBIS. (2022c). *Tier 2*. https://www.pbis.org/pbis/tier-2

Center on PBIS. (2022d). *Tier 3*. https://www.pbis.org/pbis/tier-3

Center on PBIS. (2022e). *Tier 3 brief functional behavior assessment (FBA) guide.* https://www.pbis.org/resource/tier-3-brief-functional-behavior-assessment-fba-guide

Center on PBIS. (2022f). *Tier 3 comprehensive functional behavior assessment (FBA) guide.* Center on PBIS. https://www.pbis.org/resource/tier-3-comprehensive-functional-behavior-assessment-fba-guide

Harlacher, J. E., & Rodriguez, B. J. (2018). *An educator's guide to schoolwide positive behavioral interventions and supporting: Integrating all three tiers.* Marzano Research.

Individuals with Disabilities Education Act, Public Law 105-17, 105th Congress, (1997). https://www.govinfo.gov/content/pkg/PLAW-105publ17/html/PLAW-105publ17.htm

Individuals with Disabilities Education Improvement Act, Public Law 108-446, 108th Congress, (2004). https://www.govinfo.gov/content/pkg/USCODE-2011-title20/pdf/USCODE-2011-title20-chap33.pdf

IRIS Center. (2022). *Functional behavioral assessment: Identifying the reasons for problem behavior and developing a behavior plan.* https://iris.peabody.vanderbilt.edu/module/fba/#content

Scott, T. M. (2017). *Teaching behavior: Managing classrooms through effective instruction.* Corwin.

Sugai, G., Horner, R. H., Dunlap, G., Hieneman, M., Lewis, T. J., Nelson, C. M., Scott, T., Liaupsin, C., Sailor, W., Turnbull, A. P., Rutherford Turnbull, H., Wickham, D., Wilcox, B., & Ruef, M. (2000). Applying positive behavior support and functional behavioral assessment in school. *Journal of Positive Behavior Interventions, 2*(3), 131-143.

Yell, M. L., Meadows, N. B., Drasgow, E., & Shriner, J. G. (2013). *Evidence-based practices for educating students with emotional and behavioral disorders* (2nd ed.). Pearson.

Assessments of Reading

CHAPTER OBJECTIVES

- Discuss the similarities between dyslexia and a specific learning disability in reading.
- Describe the key features of informal reading assessments.
- Describe the key features of formal reading assessments.
- Explain the similarities and differences of informal and formal reading assessments.

KEY TERMS

- **alphabetic principle:** The foundation for the development of word identification and is the first stage in reading and spelling development.
- **basic reading skills:** The ability to use systematic correspondences between the sounds and spellings (e.g., decoding) to attain a bank of words that can be read by sight.
- **blending:** The ability to hear the individual sounds in a word, put the sounds together, and then say the word.
- **curriculum-based measurements of reading (R-CBM):** A common way of assessing reading fluency. R-CBM features words read correct per minute and graphs students' performance.
- **dyslexia:** A neurobiological disorder that causes significant impairments in the ability to read and spell.
- **formal reading assessments:** Structured tests with specific guidelines. These assessments require that examiners be highly trained in standardized administration procedures and can interpret the assessment findings.
- **high-leverage practices (HLPs):** "Practices that can be used to leverage student learning across different content areas, grade levels, and student abilities and disabilities" (McLeskey et al., 2017, p. 9).
- **informal reading assessments:** Not as structured as standardized (i.e., formal) assessments of reading, have broader guidelines, and tend to be more authentic.
- **informal reading inventories (IRIs):** Consist of graded series of passages that increase with difficulty. IRIs are used to determine a child's oral reading strengths and weaknesses, word identification strategies, and oral reading fluency.
- **orthographic awareness:** The knowledge of the writing system and visual awareness of reading, spelling, letters, and letter patterns.
- **orthography:** Includes the symbols of a writing system: numbers, punctuation, letters, and letter patterns and speech sounds depicted by letters or letter combinations.
- **phonics:** A reading method that is used to teach individuals how to decode words by identifying the sounds of letters.
- **phonological awareness:** The ability to recognize, think about, and manipulate sounds in spoken words.
- **reading fluency:** The ability to read a passage accurately, quickly, and with appropriate spoken expression.
- **running records:** A method for measuring oral reading accuracy and for identifying reading behaviors such as self-correcting, rereading, and monitoring for meaning.
- **segmenting:** The ability to pull sounds of a word apart.
- **sight word recognition:** The ability to quickly read words without using structural analysis or decoding strategies.
- **structural analysis:** The ability to break words into smaller parts or units (e.g., syllables) to make complex words easier to pronounce.

KEY ABBREVIATIONS

- BRI: *Basic Reading Inventory*
- CALT: Certified Academic Language Therapist
- CBM: curriculum-based measurement
- CTOPP-2: *Comprehensive Test of Phonological Processing, Second Edition*
- DIBELS: *Dynamic Indicators of Basic Early Literacy Skills*
- FAR: *Feifer Assessment of Reading*

- GORT-5: *Gray Oral Reading Test, Fifth Edition*
- HLP: high-leverage practice
- IDA: International Dyslexia Association
- IDEA: Individuals with Disabilities Education Act
- IRIs: informal reading inventories
- OWLS-II: *Oral and Written Language Scales, Second Edition*
- R-CBM: curriculum-based measurements of reading
- SLD: specific learning disability
- TOC: *Test of Orthographic Competence*
- TOSWRF-2: *Test of Silent Word Reading Fluency, Second Edition*
- TOWRE-2: *Test of Word Reading Efficiency, Second Edition*
- TWS-5: *Test of Written Spelling, Fifth Edition*
- WCPM: words correct per minute
- WIF: word identification fluency
- WRC: words read correctly
- WRMT-III: *Woodcock Reading Mastery Tests, Third Edition*

CASE STUDY

Carrie is an 8-year-old girl who is a second grader at the Best Elementary School Ever. Mr. and Mrs. Hernandez, Carrie's parents, are involved in Carrie's educational programming and are concerned about her academic progress. Parents report a family history (paternal) of learning difficulties and dyslexia, respectively. According to Mrs. Hernandez, Carrie met all her developmental milestones at age-appropriate rates, developed language appropriately, and has had no significant health issues. In addition, Carrie passed the vision and hearing screening, unaided.

Carrie attended the Best Elementary School Ever beginning in PK and has had access to high-quality instruction. According to Ms. Mast, Carrie's kindergarten teacher and private tutor, Carrie was retained in kindergarten because she was a "young kindergartner" and needed time to develop. The second time in kindergarten, Carrie was able to identify the initial sounds of all the letters in the alphabet. However, Carrie had difficulty grasping concepts (in comparison to her peers) and was not able to identify the complex sounds of the alphabet. Ms. Mast also reported that a typical kindergartner should know 25 sight words, and Carrie only recognized 10 to 12 sight words on the Fry's 100 Sight Word List. At this point, Ms. Mast began to have concerns there might be more than "developmental issues" and started to suspect a reading disability. As such, Mr. and Mrs. Hernandez hired Ms. Mast as Carrie's private tutor. Tutoring was conducted after school for 30 to 45 minutes one time a week. The focus of these tutoring sessions was on the alphabetic principle.

Carrie was then promoted to first grade where she still struggled to obtain grade-level standards even though private tutoring continued one afternoon weekly and accommodations were being made (e.g., reduced spelling tests, tests in reading lab). Moreover, Carrie also began "pre-flight" dyslexia training in the reading lab by Mrs. Tucker, a certified academic language therapist (CALT). Mrs. Tucker noted Carrie has difficulty retaining and recalling information and struggles with phonemic awareness but is making slow progress.

As a second grader Carrie receives Take Flight dyslexia training in the reading lab. In addition, private tutoring with Ms. Mast increased to two afternoons per week for 1½ hours each for a total of 3 hours weekly. The primary focus of these tutoring sessions is on the alphabetic principle, sight word instruction, vocabulary development, and book chats. Moreover, Carrie receives accommodations such as reduced spelling tests, testing in the reading lab, and oral accommodations for reading tasks in the classroom.

Ms. Jones, Carrie's second grade-teacher, notes Carrie has a great personality, takes responsibility, and shows personal initiative. However, Carrie continues to struggle with grade-level demands. Ms. Jones's chief concern is Carrie's reading skills. Carrie is reading at a Rigby Level 5 (beginning of first grade). Typically developing second graders are reading at Rigby Levels 17–18. On a recent Renaissance STAR Reading assessment, Carrie was estimated to be reading at the pre-primer level as she was not allowed to continue past the practice assessment because she scored too low. Although Carrie is obtaining passing marks in the classroom and on her report cards, Ms. Jones notes Carrie receives a modified curriculum (e.g., reduced spelling tests, oral accommodations) and would not be passing had the curriculum not been modified.

DEFINING DYSLEXIA AND READING DISABILITIES

Although many educational organizations, states, and school districts have attempted to define dyslexia, there remains no universally accepted definition (Mather & Wendling, 2012). In addition, there is often confusion between what constitutes dyslexia versus a reading disability. However, for the purposes of this chapter, the authors contend "dyslexia" and "reading disabilities" are interchangeable terms. Siegel and Mazabel (2013) state, "The terms 'reading disability' and 'dyslexia' are actually synonymous" (p. 187). Even though dyslexia and reading disabilities are used interchangeably and are synonymous, it is useful to understand the nuances of each definition.

Individuals with Disabilities Education Act (2004) defines a specific learning disability (SLD) as:

(i) General. Specific learning disability means a disorder in one or more of the basic psychological processes involved in understanding or in using language, spoken or written, that may manifest itself in the imperfect ability to listen, think, speak, read, write, spell, or to do mathematical calculations, including conditions such as perceptual disabilities, brain injury, minimal brain dysfunction, dyslexia, and developmental aphasia.

One key aspect of the SLD definition is it includes the term "dyslexia," but it also acknowledges many individuals with SLD have difficulties with one or more aspects of reading in general (i.e., "imperfect ability to listen, think, speak, read . . ."). Moreover, Mather and Wendling (2012) suggest SLD is a broad category that is made up of many disorders. The definition of SLD is more inclusive and encompasses many aspects of reading such as basic reading skills, reading comprehension, and/or reading fluency. Whereas IDEA is broader and more inclusive of many different types of reading disorders, the definition of dyslexia is more limited.

The International Dyslexia Association (IDA; 2002) defines dyslexia as follows:

Dyslexia is characterized by difficulties with accurate and/or fluent word recognition and by poor spelling and decoding abilities. These difficulties typically result from a deficit in the phonological component of language that is often unexpected in relation to other cognitive abilities and the provision of effective classroom instruction. Secondary consequences may include problems in reading comprehension and reduced reading experience that can impede growth of vocabulary and background knowledge.

The IDA definition of dyslexia asserts dyslexia is a language-based disorder originating from a basic problem with phonological processing. The primary indicators are slow and/or inaccurate word reading and poor spelling and decoding (Mather & Wendling, 2012). In addition, Siegel and Mazabel (2013) state, "The problems of the beginning reader or the disabled reader are clearly at the level of the word (p. 187)." Although making meaning of the written word is the ultimate goal of reading, the IDA definition of dyslexia identifies reading comprehension as a secondary consequence of reading difficulties at the word level.

In summary, dyslexia and reading disabilities are interchangeable terms highlighting a breakdown at the word level of reading. Thus, reading comprehension is a secondary consequence of the difficulties at the word level.

CHECK FOR UNDERSTANDING

Dyslexia and reading disabilities are interchangeable terms highlighting a breakdown at the word level of reading. These difficulties originate from deficits in phonological processing. Thus, reading comprehension is a secondary consequence of difficulties at the word level.

INFORMAL READING ASSESSMENTS

High-leverage practice 4 (HLP 4) advises teachers to collect data from multiple sources including informal sources such as observations, work samples, curriculum-based measurements (CBMs), information from families and key stakeholders, and analysis of the curriculum (McLeskey et al., 2017). Because teachers should collect informal assessment data to help drive instruction, these assessments can be conducted routinely in the classroom by the teacher and can take place in any student–teacher interaction, whole class, small group, or one-on-one level (Ruiz-Primo & Furtak, 2007).

Informal reading assessments have broad guidelines and are not as structured as standardized (i.e., formal) assessments of reading. Moreover, informal assessments tend to be more authentic and provide valuable information in determining students' reading abilities and instructional strengths and needs (Spinelli, 2008).

CHECK FOR UNDERSTANDING

HLP 4—"Teachers should collect, aggregate, and interpret data from multiple sources (e.g., informal and formal observations, work samples, curriculum-based measures, functional behavior assessments [FBA], school files, analysis of curriculum, information from families, other data sources" (McLeskey et al., 2017, p. 42).

Table 8-1 includes descriptions of informal reading assessment that focus on the foundations of reading. It does not include higher-level reading skills such as reading comprehension, inferencing, and vocabulary.

INFORMAL ASSESSMENTS OF PHONOLOGICAL AWARENESS

Pullen et al. (2002) define phonological awareness as "the conscious sensitivity to the sound structure of language" (p. 101). Children who possess strong phonological awareness skills are able to identify, match, blend, segment, and manipulate speech sounds (Pullen et al., 2002). Therefore, to be successful at reading, children must understand the relationship between the sounds in speech and how these sounds relate to the printed words on the page (Uhry, 2005). This relationship between the sounds and symbols (i.e., letters) is referred to as the alphabetic principle. The alphabetic principle is the foundation for the development of word identification and is the first stage in reading and spelling development (Mather & Wendling, 2012).

| **TABLE 8-1. INFORMAL READING ASSESSMENTS** ||
INFORMAL ASSESSMENT	DESCRIPTION
Informal assessments of phonological awareness	Measure a child's ability to perceive and manipulate sounds (Mather & Wendling, 2012). Examples of tasks include blending, segmenting, and isolating sounds.
Informal assessments of basic reading skills and spelling	Measure word recognition skills and the ability to spell regular and irregular words. Examples of word reading include reading lists of real and nonsense words as well as reading text. Informal spelling tasks include analysis of spelling errors from tests and writing samples.
Informal assessments of orthographic awareness	Measure the ability to recall letter patterns and letter strings. In essence, orthographic awareness is the ability to picture how a word appears in the mind (Mather & Wendling, 2012). Examples of these types of tasks include writing name, writing the alphabet, recognizing letters and words.
Informal assessments of oral reading	Measure the ability to read orally—accuracy, rate, and prosody. Examples of informal assessments include informal reading inventories, running records, and curriculum-based measurements of reading.

Two of the most important phonological awareness abilities for reading and spelling development are blending and segmenting (Mather & Wendling, 2012). Blending is the ability to hear the individual sounds in a word, put the sounds together, and then say the word (e.g., /c/ /a/ /t/). Segmenting is the ability to pull the sounds apart (e.g., what three sounds are in the word "dish?"; Reading Rockets, n.d.).

Blending

The ability to blend individual phonemes is an essential phonics application skill when encountering an unfamiliar word. When teaching blending, teachers should first start with compound words such as "sunshine" and move progressively toward smaller units of words such as syllables and individual sounds once the child has mastered the skill of blending compound words (Mather & Wendling, 2012; Reading Rockets, n.d.).

Segmenting

Teachers can informally assess phonological awareness skills by engaging students in various blending and segmenting games and strategies in their classrooms. One proven strategy for developing segmenting skills is through the use of Elkonin boxes (Figure 8-1). The following steps provide instruction on how to use Elkonin boxes (Mather & Wendling, 2012; Reading Rockets, n.d.).

1. Say the word slowly, emphasizing each sound.
2. Invite the child to repeat the word.
3. Draw boxes or squares on a piece of paper or dry erase board with one box for each phoneme or syllable.

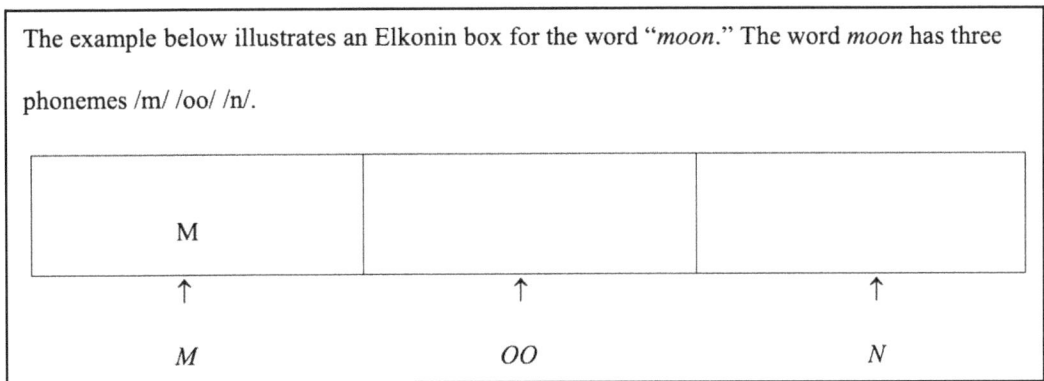

Figure 8-1. Elkonin box example.

4. Invite the child to count the number of phonemes (i.e., sounds) or syllables in the word—recognizing that sometimes a word may have more letters than phonemes or syllables, for example, /d/ /i/ /sh/ has three phonemes but four letters.
5. Provide the child with a token (e.g., bean, tile) and have them slide the token for each phoneme to the corresponding box while they say each sound aloud.

Check for Understanding

Blending and segmenting are two of the most important phonological awareness abilities for reading and spelling development (Mather & Wendling, 2012).

Introduction to Basic Reading Skills

A skilled reader derives meaning from text accurately and efficiently. Basic reading skills, or decoding, are the ability to use systematic correspondences between the sounds and spellings to attain a bank of words that can be read by sight (Mather & Wendling, 2012; McCardle et al., 2001). These skills enable readers to pronounce familiar and unfamiliar words. Basic reading skills include decoding using phonics, structural analysis of words, and sight word recognition (Mather & Wendling, 2012).

Phonics is a reading method used to teach individuals how to decode words by identifying the sounds of the letters (Mather & Wendling, 2012). Structural analysis is the ability to break words into smaller parts or units (i.e., syllables) to make complex words easier to pronounce. Sight word recognition is the ability to quickly read words without using structural analysis or decoding strategies (Mather & Wendling, 2012). Common sight words include words such as *and*, *the*, *that*, *be*, *with*, and *when*. The Dolch Word List contains 220 commonly used words and is organized by grade level. The Fry Sight Word List expanded the Dolch Word List and includes 1,000 words from Grades 3 to 9.

Assessing Basic Reading Skills

One of the proven methods for assessing basic reading skills at the word level is by using the word identification fluency (WIF) assessment technique (Zumeta et al., 2012). WIF consists of students reading words from a list. The words on the list are presented in a graduated sequence so children can experience success reading words at the top of the list (Zumeta et al., 2012). Similarly, rapid word recognition charts have been used to assess sight word recognition. Word recognition charts include high-frequency words that occur regularly in printed form. In addition, word recognition charts using irregular words, such as *said, were, they*, can also be used to evaluate children's sight word recognition. This assessment method is easy for teachers to use in the classroom. Using a chart of high-frequency words or irregular words, the teacher provides a brief review of the words on the chart, then the student is timed for 1 minute while reading the words aloud. At the end of the minute, students count and graph the number of words read correctly (Mather & Wendling, 2012).

Graphing the number of words read correctly permits the student and the teacher to monitor the progress of sight word recognition. By graphing the words read correctly, the teacher is using principles of CBM (Deno, 2003). CBMs can also be used to monitor students' performance in an entire classroom, track progress toward year-end goals, or for screening students at an individual point in time to determine if they are at risk for academic failure (Deno, 2003; Zumeta et al., 2012).

The *Dynamic Indicators of Basic Early Literacy Skills* (DIBELS; University of Oregon, 2018) and the *Basic Reading Inventory* (BRI; Johns, 2005) are informal assessments that include word recognition as part of their assessments. Moreover, DIBELS and BRI are designed to be used in the classroom by teachers. Even though DIBELS and BRI are informal in nature, teachers must be trained on the administration procedures prior to their use.

Check for Understanding

Basic reading skills include decoding using phonics; structural analysis of words, which is the ability to break words into smaller parts; and sight word recognition (Mather & Wendling, 2012).

Assessing Spelling

According to Beirne-Smith and Riley (2009), good spellers are accurate and fluent readers who possess a high degree of word knowledge. Moreover, they recognize when words look correct and have strong phonemic awareness and knowledge of spelling patterns (Norton, 1997). Conversely, children who have difficulty in spelling seem to lack understanding of the basic orthographic features of the English language and do not appear to recognize words correctly.

Informal assessment of spelling skills should include collection of data from a wide variety of sources. Specifically, samples from dictated spelling tests, writing samples, responses to written questions, and other independent writing assignments (Beirne-Smith & Riley, 2009). By gathering data from a wide variety of sources, teachers are able to evaluate students' ability to generalize spelling skills across content areas and various forms of written communication (Beirne-Smith & Riley, 2009).

When evaluating student spelling, teachers can analyze errors at the word level, syllable level, letter sequences, or in sound clusters (Beirne-Smith & Riley, 2009). In addition, Beirne-Smith and Riley advise that analysis at the whole word level yields only information about the number of correct and incorrect responses, and while this approach is beneficial for students who possess adequate spelling skills, it is insufficient for students with significant difficulties with spelling. For these students, teachers need to look closely at errors contained in individual words. The ability to spell in English depends on two fundamental prerequisite skills: phoneme awareness and letter–sound knowledge (Caravolas et al., 2001). Caravolas and colleagues emphasize that encouraging beginning spellers to write phonologically reasonable spellings of words, coupled with direct instruction in spelling, may help lay the foundation for the development reading and spelling.

> **CHECK FOR UNDERSTANDING**
>
> The ability to spell depends on two prerequisite skills: (1) phoneme awareness and (2) letter–sound knowledge.

INFORMAL ASSESSMENTS OF ORTHOGRAPHIC AWARENESS

Orthography encompasses the symbols of a writing system: numbers, punctuation, letters, and letter patterns (Mather & Wendling, 2012) and where speech sounds are depicted by letters or letter combinations (Stubbs, 1980). Thus, orthographic awareness is knowledge of the writing system and visual awareness of reading, spelling, letters, and letter patterns (Mather & Wendling, 2012).

Informal assessments of orthographic awareness measure the ability to recall letter patterns and letter strings (Mather & Wendling, 2012). Characteristics of poor orthographic awareness include difficulty learning how to write letters, confusion of similar letters (e.g., b for d), tendency to reverse letters or numbers, trouble remembering how words look, trouble reading irregular words, slow reading speed, using different spellings for the same word, omitting word endings, and overreliance on the phonological system rather than on the visual aspects of words. Moreover, since orthography includes numbers, readers with poor orthographic awareness can also experience difficulty in mathematics (Mather & Wendling, 2012). By understanding the signs of poor orthographic awareness, teachers are better able to identify children who may be struggling with orthography.

> **CHECK FOR UNDERSTANDING**
>
> Difficulty with writing letters, confusion of similar letters (b for d), reversing letters, and having difficulty remembering how words look are indicators of weaknesses with orthographic awareness.

INFORMAL ASSESSMENTS OF ORAL READING

An example of an informal assessment of oral reading is reading inventories. Informal reading inventories (IRIs) assess multiple aspects of a child's reading skills in authentic classroom situations (Paris & Carpenter, 2003). The purpose of an IRI is to identify the instructional level a child should be taught and to identify the level the child should be expected to read independently (Provost et al., 2010).

IRIs consist of a graded series of passages that increase with difficulty and are used to determine a child's oral reading strengths and weaknesses, word identification strategies (Barr et al., 2007), and oral reading fluency (Paris & Carpenter, 2003). The most important reason for using IRIs is to diagnose reading difficulties early so the teacher can design targeted instruction. IRIs provide useful information to students, parents, and key stakeholders about achievement and skills needing improvement. In addition, IRIs provide evidence to teachers about the appropriateness of instruction and information regarding their decision-making skills.

Although there are several commercial IRIs on the market, teachers can create IRIs for use in their classrooms. One of the benefits of using teacher-created IRIs is to provide information to general and special educators in differentiating instruction. A key factor in designing or selecting a commercially produced IRI for the classroom is to select appropriate reading passages based on the

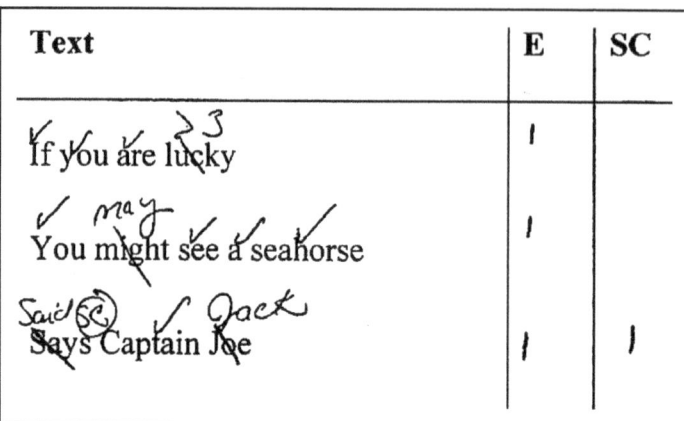

Figure 8-2. Running record example: *Pete the Cat: Scuba Cat*.

instructional reading level of the child (Provost et al., 2010). There are many articles that speak to designing teacher-created IRIs, and the reader should consult additional resources before designing their own IRI. Alternatively, a teacher may want to use commercial-created IRIs.

Running Records

Running records are a method for measuring oral reading accuracy and for identifying reading behaviors such as self-correcting, rereading, and monitoring for meaning (Barone et al., 2020). Running records are typically used within guided reading and reading conferences. Although there are many ways to record oral reading (symbols, marks), teachers should use a common method within a school or district so they can be shared with other professionals and able to be compared over time (Barone et al., 2020).

The following is an excerpt of Carrie's running record taken when she read a book from her favorite series, Pete the Cat: Scuba Cat *(Dean, 2016, para. 3). This excerpt was taken from a larger running record sample and represents only a small segment of the record (Figure 8-2). Thus, the error rate, self-correction rate, and accuracy rate discussed subsequently are based only on this excerpt.*

Carrie was presented with a passage consisting of 12 total words. She read eight words correctly as indicated by the check marks, self-corrected one error (SC), and committed three total errors. Words read incorrectly are written above the word in the passage. For example, Carrie attempted to read the word "might" but instead read "may," and "Jack" for "Joe." The word "lucky" was provided when Carrie hesitated for 3 seconds. This is noted by the >3 written above "lucky." Although the word "says" appears to be an error with the word "said" written above, Carrie self-corrected as indicated by the notation of SC. When an error is immediately self-corrected, the previous substitution is not counted as an error.

In addition to the qualitative analysis of the child's reading behavior and reading comprehension, the information collected during a running record can help teachers identify the child's error rate, self-correction rate, and accuracy rate in determining the child's reading level. The following formulas (error, self-correction, and accuracy) are according to guidance from Reading A-Z (n.d.).

The error rate is expressed as a ratio. It is calculated by using the following formula: total words / total errors = error rate (12/3 = 4) and is expressed as 1:4. This means that for each error Carrie made, she read four words correctly.

The self-correction rate is also expressed as a ratio. It is calculated by using the following formula: number of errors + number of self-corrections/numbers of self-corrections = self-correction rate (3 + 1/1 = 4) and is expressed as 1:4, which means Carrie corrects approximately one out of every four errors she commits and is having difficulty self-monitoring her reading. A self-correction rate of 1:3 or less indicates the child self-monitors their reading.

The following formula was used to calculate the accuracy rate: total words read – total errors/total words read × 100 (12 – 3 = 9/12 × 100 = 75%). An accuracy rate of 75% indicates this passage was at Carrie's frustrational level. Table 8-2 depicts accuracy rate categories and provides guidelines for determining a child's reading level.

TABLE 8-2. ACCURACY RATE CHART

CATEGORY	DESCRIPTION	RANGE
Independent	The level is easy for the child to read independently.	95% to 100%
Instructional	The level is for the classroom (i.e., guided reading groups).	90% to 94%
Frustrational	The level is too difficult and will frustrate the child.	89% and below

Adapted from Reading A-Z. (n.d.). *Scoring and analyzing a running record*. https://www.readinga-z.com/helpful-tools/about-running-records/scoring-a-running-record/

```
One hundred years ago in Paris, when theaters and music halls      11
drew traveling players from all over the world, the best place to  23
stay was at the widow Gateau's, a boardinghouse on English         33
Street  Acrobats, jugglers, actors, and mimes from as far away     43
as Moscow and New York reclined on the widow's feather             53
mattresses and devoured her kidney stews  Madame Gateau            61
worked hard to make her guests comfortable, and so did her         72
daughter, Mirette  The girl was an expert at washing linens,       82
chopping leeks, paring potatoes, and mopping floors.  She was      91
a good listener too.  Nothing pleased her more than to overhear   102
the vagabond players tell of their adventures in this town and    113
that along the road.                                              117
```

Figure 8-3. Reading curriculum-based measurement example: *Mirette on the High Wire*.

Curriculum-Based Measurements

Reading fluency is an integral component in the assessment of oral reading. One of the most common ways of assessing reading fluency is by using curriculum-based measurements of reading (R-CBM). The child's instructional reading level should be used as a benchmark when selecting passages for reading fluency assessments (Provost et al., 2010).

A typical guideline for oral reading fluency is the number of words read correctly (WRC) per minute. Sometimes this is referenced as words correct per minute (WCPM). Within each grade and semester, there are expected range of WRC per minute. For example, a second grader should correctly read 51 to 106 words during the fall semester, 72 to 125 words during the winter semester, and 89 to 125 words during the spring semester (Mather & Wendling, 2012).

Figure 8-3 provides an example of an R-CBM excerpt taken from a popular children's book, *Mirette on the High Wire* (McCully, 1992, para. 1-3).

Administering a Curriculum-Based Measurement of Reading

The administration of an R-CBM is fairly straightforward. The child is provided a copy of the passage, also known as a probe, and the teacher retains a copy of the passage with the number of words for each line noted on the right margin. While the child is reading, the teacher marks each error with a slash (/). At the end of 1 minute, the last word read is marked with a bracket (]). Errors that are marked include mispronunciations, word substitutions, omitted words, hesitations (words that are not read aloud in 3 seconds), and reversals (when two or more words are transposed). If the child skips an entire line in the passage, then a straight line is drawn through the skipped line (Fuchs & Fuchs, 2011).

To calculate the total number of words read (TWR), sum together the numbers of words attempted for each line. If the child reads a partial sentence, add only the words the child attempted (Fuchs & Fuchs, 2011). For example, in this passage, the TWR is 63. Because the child skipped the seventh line of text in this passage, the words in this line are not counted in the total. To calculate the WRC, subtract the errors from the TWR. In this example, the child committed six errors as indicated by the slash marks. These six errors are subtracted from the total words read: 63 – 6 = 57. Fifty-seven is the number of words the child read correctly in 1 minute.

Charting Curriculum-Based Measurement Data

CBM data are represented on graphs. The most common types of graphs used are line graphs and bar graphs. The steps for charting CBM (Stephens, n.d.) include:
1. Determine the academic behavior that will be measured.
2. Determine which type of graph (line or bar) to represent the academic behavior.
3. Label the vertical axis with the academic behaviors and the numbers representing the academic behaviors.
4. Label the horizontal axis that describes when the probes were administered (e.g., dates, number of testing sessions, number of weeks).
5. Identify the number of instructional weeks that the CBM data will be graphed.
6. Administer CBM to obtain baseline data.

Figure 8-4 depicts a line graph demonstrating the oral reading fluency CBM chart. The vertical axis represents the number of words read correctly per minute, and the horizontal axis represents the testing session that each probe was administered. On the right-hand side of the graph is the number 23, which represents the goal of 23 words read correct per minute. The line with the bullseye is the aim line. Directions for setting appropriate goals and establishing aim lines are described in detail in Chapter 6.

Figure 8-4 illustrates that a total of eight R-CBM probes were administered. On the first probe, Carrie read 13 WCPM and on the sixth and eighth probes she read 19 WCPM. The data on the graph indicate Carrie has not reached her goal of reading 23 WCPM, but she is making progress toward her goal.

CHECK FOR UNDERSTANDING

When administering informal assessments of oral reading fluency, the child's instructional reading level should be used when selecting passages (Provost et al., 2010).

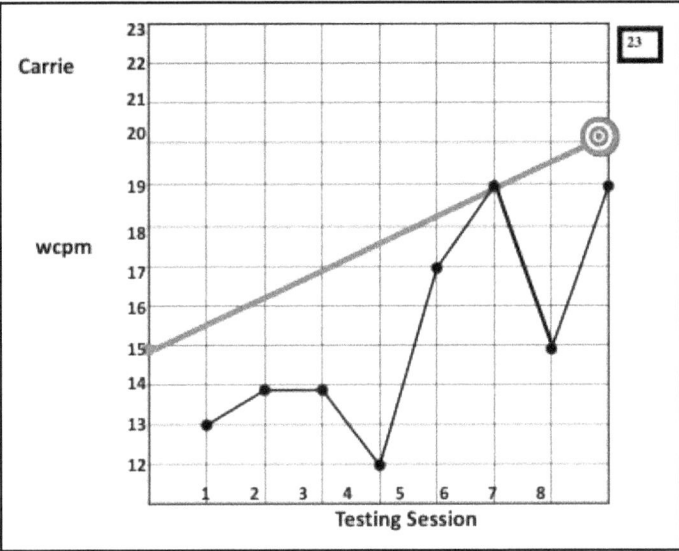

Figure 8-4. Progress morning chart: Oral reading fluency example. (Reproduced with permission from Stephens, T. L. [n.d.]. *Curriculum based measurement: Charting and interpreting CBM data* [PowerPoint slides].)

FORMAL READING ASSESSMENTS

Formal reading assessments require that examiners are highly trained in standardized administration procedures and able to interpret the assessment findings (Mather & Wendling, 2012). This means examiners are typically required to take graduate-level classes that focus on standardized assessment practices and procedures and interpreting and reporting test results. Table 8-3 provides frequently used measures of standardized assessments of reading. However, the list is not exhaustive, and many other diagnostic reading assessments exist.

SUMMARY

Although there is no universally accepted definition of dyslexia and there is often confusion between what constitutes dyslexia and a reading disability, the authors of this chapter contend "dyslexia" and "reading disabilities" are interchangeable terms highlighting a breakdown at the word level of reading. That said, the purpose of this chapter was to describe informal assessments of reading that can be used in the classroom to aid in lesson planning for children who are struggling to read.

CASE STUDY WRAP-UP

Carrie was administered a variety of reading and writing measures. These instruments ranged from general measures to diagnostic measures of reading and writing. Importantly, the data reveal Carrie is a young lady who is experiencing profound difficulties with all aspects of reading and is expending a significant amount of cognitive energy to read even simple words. In particular, Carrie's overreliance on sounding out individual phonemes and blending phonemes together as her main strategy for identifying unknown words will adversely impact her ability to attack more complex or irregular words as the content demands increase. Moreover, it will adversely impact her ability to read fluently and requires a great deal of effort on her part.

TABLE 8-3. STANDARDIZED ASSESSMENTS OF READING	
NAME	PURPOSE
Comprehensive Test of Phonological Processing, Second Edition	The CTOPP-2 is a norm-referenced test that measures phonological processing abilities related to reading (Wagner et al., 2013).
Feifer Assessment of Reading	The FAR examines the underlying cognitive and linguistic processes that support proficient reading skills (Feifer & Nader, 2015).
Gray Oral Reading Test, Fifth Edition	The GORT-5 is an individually administered measure of oral reading ability (Wiederholt & Bryant, 2012).
Oral and Written Language Scales, Second Edition	The OWLS-II evaluates listening comprehension, oral expression, reading comprehension, and written expression (Carrow-Woolfolk, 2012).
Test of Orthographic Competence	The TOC assesses aspects of the English writing system that are integral to proficient reading and writing (Mather et al., 2008).
Test of Silent Word Reading Fluency, Second Edition	The TOSWRF-2 provides a reliable and valid measure of students' ability to recognize printed words accurately and efficiently (Mather et al., 2014).
Test of Word Reading Efficiency, Second Edition	The TOWRE-2 is a measure of an individual's ability to pronounce printed words (sight word efficiency) and phonemically regular nonwords (phonemic decoding efficiency) accurately and fluently (Torgesen et al., 2012).
Test of Written Spelling, Fifth Edition	The TWS-5 is an accurate and efficient instrument that uses a dictated-word format to assess spelling skills in school-age children and adolescents (Larsen et al., 2013).
Woodcock Reading Mastery Tests, Third Edition	The WRMT-III is a comprehensive battery of individually administered tests that measure reading readiness and reading achievement (Woodcock, 2011).

In addition, Carrie's weakness in orthographic processing is negatively impacting her ability to read fluently. Children with weak orthographic processing skills are unable to picture words in their brains (Linde & Clayton, n.d.). These students rely completely on phonics to read and write words. Because they decode all words instead of learning words by sight, their reading is choppy and not fluent. Moreover, letter shapes are easily confused because their brains do not retain the memory of letters or letter patterns. They may mistake "b" and "d" often, or substitute known words for unknown words because they start with the same letter. For example, house and home—relying on the first letter "h" to guess the word (Linde & Clayton, n.d.).

Eligibility Statement

Based on multiple measures of assessment (formal and informal), Carrie is exhibiting difficulty in learning to read, spell, and write even though she has had high-quality instruction, adequate sociocultural opportunities, and intellectual functioning. Despite average cognitive abilities and access to high-quality instruction (e.g., private tutoring, Take Flight), Carrie is experiencing significant disruptions in reading specifically in phonological awareness and reading-related tasks such as spelling and writing. Therefore, Carrie meets the criteria as a child with dyslexia, an SLD in the area of reading.

Chapter Review

1. In collaboration with a peer, describe three to four instructional reading strategies that you can use in your classroom for a child who is struggling with phonemic awareness (blending, segmenting, etc.).
2. In collaboration with a peer, describe three to four instructional reading strategies that you can use in your classroom for a child who is struggling with orthographic awareness.
3. In collaboration with a peer, describe three to four instructional reading strategies that you can use in your classroom for a child who is struggling with reading fluency.
4. In collaboration with a peer, practice administering and scoring a running record.
5. In collaboration with a peer, create a presentation that describes dyslexia and reading disabilities.

References

Barone, J., Khairallah, P., & Gabriel, R. (2020). Running records revisited: A tool for efficiency and focus. *The Reading Teacher, 73*(4), 525-530. https://doi.org/10.1002/trtr.1861

Barr, R., Blachowicz, C. L. Z., Bates, A., Katz, C., & Kaufman, B. (2007). *Reading diagnosis for teachers: An instructional approach* (5th ed.). Pearson.

Beirne-Smith, M., & Riley, T. F. (2009). Spelling assessment of students with disabilities. *Assessment for Effective Intervention, 34*(3), 170-177. https://10.1177/1534508408318844

Caravolas, M., Hulme, C., & Snowling, M. J. (2001). The foundations of spelling ability: Evidence from a 3-year longitudinal study. *Journal of Memory and Learning, 45*(4), 751-774. https://doi.org/10.1006/jmla.2000.2785

Carrow-Woolfolk, E. (2012). *Oral and Written Language Scales* (2nd ed.). Pro-Ed.

Dean, J. (2016). *Pete the cat: Scuba cat*. Harper, HarperCollins Publishers.

Deno, S. L. (2003). Developments in curriculum-based measurement. *Journal of Special Education*, 37, 184-192. https://doi:10.1177/00224669030370030801

Feifer, S. G., & Nader, R. G. (2015). *Feifer Assessment of Reading*. PAR.

Fuchs, L. S., & Fuchs, D. (2011). *Using curriculum-based measurement for progress monitoring in reading*. National Center on Student Progress Monitoring.

Johns, J. (2005). *Basic reading inventory: Pre-primer through grade twelve and early literacy assessments* (9th ed.). Kendall Hunt.

Individuals with Disabilities Education Act. Sec. 300.8 (c) (10). (2004). https://sites.ed.gov/idea/regs/b/a/300.8/c/10

International Dyslexia Association. (2002). *Definition of dyslexia*. https://dyslexiaida.org/definition-of-dyslexia

Larsen, S. C., Hammill, D. D., & Moats, L. (2013). *Test of Written Spelling* (5th ed.). Pro-Ed.

Linde, S., & Clayton, J. (n.d.). *What is orthographic processing?—Definition & explanation*. https://study.com/academy/lesson/what-is-orthographic-processing-definition-explanation.html

Mather, N., Hammill, D. D., Allen, E. A., & Roberts, R. (2014). *Test of Silent Word Reading Fluency* (2nd ed.). Pro-Ed.

Mather, N., Roberts, R., Hammill, D. D., & Allen, E. A. (2008). *Test of Orthographic Competence*. Pro-Ed.

Mather, N., & Wendling, B. J. (2012). *Essentials of dyslexia assessment and intervention*. John Wiley & Sons.

McCardle, P., Scarborough, H. S., & Catts, H. W. (2001). Predicting, explaining, and preventing children's reading difficulties. *Learning Disabilities Research & Practice, 16*(4), 230-239. https://doi.org/10.1111/0938-8982.00023

McCully, E. A. (1992). *Mirette on the high wire*. G. P. Putnam's Sons.

McLeskey, J., Barringer, M-D., Billingsley, B., Brownell, M., Jackson, D., Kennedy, M., Lewis, T., Maheady, L., Rodriguez, J., Scheeler, M. D., Winn, J., & Ziegler, D. (2017). *High-leverage practices in special education*. Council for Exceptional Children & CEEDAR Center.

Norton, D. E. (1997). *The effective teaching of language arts* (5th ed.). Prentice Hall.

Paris, S. G., & Carpenter, R. D. (2003). FAQs about IRIs. *The Reading Teacher, 56*(6), 578-580.

Provost, M. C., Lambert, M. A., & Babkie, A. M. (2010). Informal reading inventories: Creating teacher-designed literature-based assessments. *Intervention in School and Clinic, 45*(4), 211-220. https://doi.org/10.1177/1053451209353444

Pullen, H. B., Pullen, P. C., Eisele, M. R., & Jordan, L. (2002). Phonological awareness assessment and instruction. *Preventing School Failure: Alternative Education for Children and Youth, 46*(3), 101-110. https://doi.org/10.1080/10459880209603354

Reading A-Z. (n.d.). *Scoring and analyzing a running record.* https://www.readinga-z.com/helpful-tools/about-running-records/scoring-a-running-record

Reading Rockets. (n.d.). *Blending and segmenting games.* https://www.readingrockets.org/strategies/blending_games

Ruiz-Primo, M. A., & Furtak, E. M. (2007). Exploring teachers' informal formative assessment practices and students' understanding in the context of scientific inquiry. *Journal of Research in Science Teaching, 44*(1), 57-84.

Siegel, L. S., & Mazabel, S. (2013). Basic cognitive processes and reading disabilities. In H. Lee Swanson, K. R. Harris, & S. Graham (Eds.), *Handbook of learning disabilities* (2nd ed., pp. 186-213). Guilford Press.

Spinelli, C. G. (2008). Introduction: The benefits, uses, and practical application of informal assessment procedures. *Reading & Writing Quarterly, 24*(1), 1-6. https://doi.org/10.1080/10573560701753005

Stephens, T. L. (n.d.). *Curriculum-based measurement: Charting and interpreting CBM data* [PowerPoint slides].

Stubbs, M. (1980). *Language and literacy: The sociology of reading and writing.* Routledge & Kegan Paul.

Torgesen, J. K., Wagner, R. K., & Rashotte, C. A. (2012). *Test of Word Reading Efficiency* (2nd ed.). Pro-Ed.

Uhry, J. K. (2005). Phonemic awareness and reading: Research, activities, and instructional materials. In J. R. Birsh (Ed.), *Multisensory teaching of basic language* skills (pp. 83-111). Paul H. Brookes.

University of Oregon. (2018). *Dynamic Indicators of Basic Early Literacy Skills* (DIBELS; 8th ed.). https://dibels.uoregon.edu

Wagner, R. K., Torgesen, J. K., Rashotte, C. A., & Pearson, N. A. (2013). *Comprehensive Test of Phonological Processing* (2nd ed.). Pro-Ed.

Wiederholt, J. L., & Bryant, B. R. (2012). *Gray Oral Reading Test* (5th ed.). Pro-Ed.

Woodcock, R. W. (2011). *Woodcock Reading Mastery Tests: WRMT-III. Manual.* Pearson.

Zumeta, R. O., Compton, D. L., & Fuchs, L. S. (2012). Using word identification fluency to monitor first-grade reading development. *Exceptional Children, 78*(2), 201-220.

Assessments of Writing

CHAPTER OBJECTIVES

- Define dysgraphia.
- Define written expression disorder.
- Identify informal measures for handwriting and written expression.
- Describe formal assessment measures for handwriting and written expression.

KEY TERMS

- **dysgraphia:** Written language disorder in serial production of strokes to form a handwritten letter.
- **occupational therapy:** Therapy focused on everyday skills including balance, coordination, and motor skills.
- **structural error analysis:** Set of procedures for identifying, explaining, and describing a learner's errors.
- **visual-motor integration:** The ability to translate an image into a motor action such as copying shapes and perceiving and copying letters and numbers.
- **written expression:** Conceptual aspects of writing, which include grammar, capitalization, idea generation, organization, sentence structure, and coherence.

KEY ABBREVIATIONS

- Beery VMI: *Beery-Buktenica Developmental Test of Visual-Motor Integration, Sixth Edition*
- FAW: *Feifer Assessment of Writing*
- KTEA-3: *Kaufman Test of Educational Achievement, Third Edition*
- OWLS-II: *Oral and Written Language Scales, Second Edition*
- THS-R: *Test of Handwriting Skills, Revised*
- TOC: *Test of Orthographic Competence*
- TOWL-4: *Test of Written Language, Fourth Edition*
- WJ IV ACH: *Woodcock-Johnson IV Tests of Achievement*

CASE STUDY

Janice is a bubbly third grader in Mrs. Beck's language arts classroom. Mrs. Beck has noticed Janice is able to provide oral answers without any issues but seems to struggle to get her ideas on paper. She will often sit and not start writing assignments. When she does get her thoughts on paper, her handwriting is often hard to decipher. Mrs. Beck has met with Janice's mom, and her mother noted that writing has always been a struggle for Janice. Janice's mother also observed she had an awkward pencil grasp until second grade and attributed that to her problem with handwriting. Mrs. Beck is concerned Janice will have trouble with the state-mandated writing assessment and wants to provide her with tools and strategies needed for her to be successful. Mrs. Beck decides to meet with Mrs. Olander, the campus dyslexia specialist, to ascertain what formal and informal assessments might be available to assess Janice's writing skills.

DEFINING WRITTEN EXPRESSION

In order to improve writing instruction, teachers must understand the challenges students face and design instruction to address those challenges. "Students' writing improves when teachers learn to give more specific recommendations for improvement" (Parr & Timperly, 2010, p. 68). Writing involves the integration of various constructs and is one of the most complex, higher-level language skills. "At the most complex level, writing has been described as the simple act of using symbols to produce written letters and words. At the most complex level, writing is a complicated act of planning, organizing, writing, and editing text" (Stephens et al., 2020, p. 6). The process of writing integrates visual, motor, and conceptual abilities and requires sustained attention and concentration. It also requires the student to use executive functioning skills, including planning, organizing, and reasoning.

The terms *dysgraphia* and *disorder* in written expression are often used interchangeably. Both describe challenges related to writing. The concept of writing encompasses a broad spectrum of tasks from transcription of letters to the process of drafting, revising, editing, and conceptualizing. Dysgraphia is defined as a written language disorder in serial production of strokes to form a handwritten letter (Texas Education Agency, 2021). Berringer et al. (2015) define dysgraphia as a neurodevelopmental disorder resulting in graphomotor function (hand movements) and/or storing and retrieving orthographic codes (letter formation). The *Diagnostic and Statistical Manual of Mental Disorders, Fifth Edition* (DSM-5; American Psychiatric Association, 2013), includes dysgraphia under the specific learning disability category but does not define it as a separate disorder. According to the DSM-5, symptoms of a learning disorder must be present for 6 months and include symptoms such as (1) inaccurate or slow and effortful word reading; (2) difficulty understanding the meaning of what is read; (3) difficulty with spelling; (4) difficulty with written expression; (5) difficulties mastering number sense, number facts, or calculation; and (6) difficulties with mathematical reasoning. In schools, the Individuals with Disabilities Education Act (IDEA; 2004) is used to diagnose a learning disability. IDEA (2004) defines a specific learning disability as:

> The child does not achieve adequately for the child's age or to meet State-approved grade-level standards in one or more of the following areas, when provided with learning experiences and instruction appropriate for the child's age or State-approved grade-level standards: oral expression, listening comprehension, written expression, basic reading skills, reading fluency skills, reading comprehension, mathematics calculation, or mathematics problem solving.

For the purposes of this text, the authors will use "dysgraphia" to describe the technical aspects of handwriting, such as letter formation and handwriting, and will refer to written expression disorder regarding the conceptual aspects of writing, which include grammar, capitalization, idea generation, organization, sentence structure, and coherence.

CHECK FOR UNDERSTANDING

Dysgraphia is defined as a written language disorder in serial production of strokes to form a handwritten letter.

HANDWRITING

Children's experimentation around handwriting usually begins around 2 years of age with a child experimenting with performing hand movements such as up-down, left-right, and progressing to drawing vertical and horizontal lines and shapes (Feng et al., 2019). Classroom instruction in handwriting usually begins in kindergarten or first grade. Chung and Patel (2015) posit children spend approximately half the day engaged in the act of writing. Handwriting objectives often focus on letter formation, letter size, proportion and alignment, spacing, line quality, and slant. Numerous factors may contribute to difficulties: motor problems, visual processing issues, visual memory, and lack of motivation. Occasional reversals, omissions, and poor spacing are normal and usually not a cause for concern; however, if issues continue for a long period of time, assessment may be warranted. In the school system, handwriting difficulties are often referred to occupational therapy (Benson et al., 2016). Morgan et al. (2021) note, "Handwriting is developmentally valuable because it involves

TABLE 9-1. CHARACTERISTICS OF DYSLEXIA

Excessive erasures and cross outs
Heavy pressure and hand fatigue
Poor spacing between letters and words
Awkward pencil grip
Letter and number reversals beyond the early writing stage
Poorly shaped or formed letters
Slow copying and writing with legible or illegible handwriting
Incorrect student posture and positioning when writing

Adapted from the 2021 *Texas Dyslexia Handbook*.

a complex process including visual perception and decoding skills, activating working memory, and establishing connections to language centers that access and process information" (p. 12). In recent years, challenges in the area of handwriting have targeted increased attention on the identification of dysgraphia. Chung and Patel (2015) define "dysgraphia" as a difficulty in writing that may manifest itself through "letter illegibility, slow rate of writing, difficulty spelling, and problems of syntax and composition" (p. 7). Characteristics of dysgraphia are presented in Table 9-1.

Informal Assessment of Handwriting

Unlike other academic skills, few standardized tests measure handwriting. Often informal measures are used. Teachers can obtain diagnostic information by visually examining a student's handwriting. While observing handwriting activities, the teacher should note possible problem areas by answering the following questions (Mercer et al., 2015):

- Does the student grip the pencil correctly and in a comfortable and flexible manner?
- Is the student's paper in the proper position on the writing surface?
- Does the student sit correctly when writing?
- Does the student consistently write with the same hand?
- Does the student appear extremely fatigued, frustrated, or emotional when writing?

Additionally, teachers may analyze writing for letter formation, letter size, letter proportion, alignment, spacing, line quality, slant, and rate (Mercer et al., 2015). Probes can be used to assess specific handwriting skills. Writing probes are easy to administer either individually or in a group. The student is provided lined paper and asked to do tasks such as repeatedly writing the same letter, the student's first or last name, lower- or uppercase letters, or words. The student is given 1 minute, and daily performance on the probe sheet is charted to show progress. See Figure 9-1 for an example of a handwriting probe worksheet.

Rubrics may also be used to informally assess handwriting. Using an analytic rubric, a teacher can make explicit what is being assessed, list the characteristics of the different degrees of quality, and provide a rating scale to differentiate among the degrees (Powell, 2019). Not only are rubrics used for assessment, they can also be an instructional tool. Figure 9-2 is an example of an informal handwriting rubric potentially used to evaluate handwriting.

Assessments of Writing 155

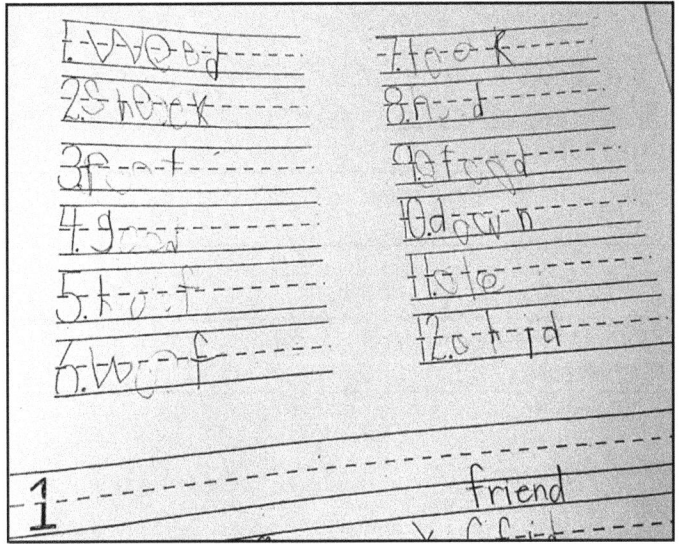

Figure 9-1. Handwriting probe worksheet.

Overall Writing	Unsatisfactory 0 points	Needs Improvement 1 point	Satisfactory 2 points
Letter Legibility	Few letters are legible	70% of letters are legible	90% of letters are legible
Spacing	50% or less of spaces between words are the correct size	51-75% of spaces between words are the correct size	76-100% of spaces between words are the correct size
Neatness	Paper appears cluttered with more than 5 extra marks or smudges	Paper contains 3-5 marks or smudges	Overall paper is neat; no extra smudges are evident
Letter Formation	Less than 50% of letters are formed correctly	75% of letters are formed correctly	76-100% of letters are formed correctly
Line Awareness	The size of more than 7 letters is slightly larger or smaller than the space allowed by the line	The size of 4-6 letters is slightly larger or smaller than the space allowed by the line	The size of 1-3 letters is slightly larger or smaller than the space allowed by the line

Figure 9-2. Informal handwriting rubric.

TABLE 9-2. DESCRIPTIONS OF SELECTED *FEIFER ASSESSMENT OF WRITING* SUBTESTS

SUBTEST	DESCRIPTION
Alphabet Tracing Fluency	Examinee constructs legible letters by completing a partial stencil of letters.
Executive Working Memory	Examinee is required to write one sentence using two words that best fit a verbal prompt.
Isolated Spelling	Examinee writes a series of letters and/or spells words of increasing difficulty.

Formal Assessment of Handwriting

While informal assessments are often used to diagnose handwriting issues, there are standardized assessments on the market that may be used to assess handwriting. One example of a formal assessment is the *Feifer Assessment of Writing* (FAW; Feifer, 2020). The FAW is a diagnostic achievement test designed to examine the underlying cognitive, motoric, and linguistic processes that support proficient written language skills. The FAW includes a Graphomotor Index score, which assesses performance in alphabet tracing fluency, motor sequencing, copying speed, and motor planning. It is normed for students PK through college. Examples of subtests comprising the FAW are described in Table 9-2.

TEST AT A GLANCE

Feifer Assessment of Writing (FAW)
- Type of assessment: Norm-referenced
- Type of administration: Individual
- Administration time: 20 to 65 minutes
- Age/grade level: PK to college
- Scores: Graphomotor Index, Dyslexic Index, Executive Index

An additional formal measure of handwriting is the *Test of Handwriting Skills, Revised* (THS-R; Milone, 2007). The THS-R is an untimed assessment used to assess neurosensory integration skills both in print and cursive handwriting. It is appropriate for ages 6 years, 0 months through 18 years, 11 months and can be administered in approximately 25 minutes via individual or group administration. Participants are asked to perform tasks including writing from memory the letters of the alphabet in alphabetical sequence, writing from dictation letters of the alphabet, and copying uppercase letters out of alphabetical sequence. Additionally, the THS-R measures speed of writing, letter reversals, and case substitutions. THS-R scores are based on the characteristics of individual letters. Each letter or number the participant produces is related on a 4-point scale with 0 being the worst or missing and 3 the best. The examiner scores each item based on a set of criteria and compares it to an exemplar. Each score is summed to obtain a raw score, which is converted to a scale score. The scaled scores are summed and converted to a standard score.

TEST AT A GLANCE

Test of Handwriting Skills, Revised (THS-R)
- Type of assessment: Norm-referenced
- Type of administration: Individual or group
- Administration time: 25 minutes
- Age/grade level: 6-0 to 18-11
- Scores: Scaled scores, standard scores

Research has consistently identified significant correlations between visual-motor integration and handwriting (Pfeiffer et al., 2015). One measure often used to assess a person's ability to integrate visual and motor skills is the *Beery-Buktenica Developmental Test of Visual-Motor Integration, Sixth Edition* (Beery VMI; Beery et al., 2010). The Beery VMI assessment involves copying geometric forms used to determine the level of integration between the visual and motor systems and is appropriate for individuals from 2 to 100 years. It can be administered in approximately 10 to 15 minutes. Scores provided include standard scores, percentiles, and age equivalents, and it is often used by occupational therapists to diagnose visual-motor integration delays that may cause a child to struggle with copying numbers and letters correctly. Children with visual-motor integration issues may display handwriting that is disjointed and lacks flow. The Beery VMI is not only an assessment tool but is also used as an outcome measure to determine if visual-motor integration skills improve after handwriting interventions (Howe et al., 2013).

TEST AT A GLANCE

The Beery-Buktenica Developmental Test of Visual-Motor Integration, Sixth Edition (Beery VMI)
- Type of assessment: Norm-referenced
- Type of administration: Individual
- Administration time: 15 to 20 minutes
- Age/grade level: 2 to 100 years full form, 2 to 7 years for short form
- Scores: Standard score, percentile ranks, age equivalents

The final formal assessment of handwriting included in this chapter is the *Test of Orthographic Competence* (TOC; Mather et al., 2008). Orthography refers to the way "letter and punctuation marks form words, a process called spelling" (Mather et al., 2008, p. 1). This assessment is comprised of nine subtests (see Table 9-3 for subtest descriptions) and assesses aspects of the English writing system including letters, spelling, punctuation, abbreviations, and special symbols. The test yields scaled scores, percentile ranks, and index scores. The TOC is generally used for three purposes (Mather et al., 2008). One purpose of the TOC is to identify students who score significantly below their peers and might require intervention to improve orthographic skills. Another purpose of the TOC is to ascertain a student's strengths and weaknesses in orthographic skills. The final purpose for administering the TOC is to assist with research studies focused on the relationship between reading and spelling and orthographic skills.

Table 9-3. Test of Orthographic Competence Subtest Descriptions

SUBTEST	DESCRIPTION
Signs and Symbols	Examinee looks at a series of signs and symbols and tells what each one signifies.
Grapheme Matching	Examinee identifies two identical shapes within a 2-minute time limit.
Homophone Choice	Examinee matches picture with correct choice of spelling.
Punctuation	Examinee supplies missing punctuation to a list of printed sentences.
Abbreviations	Examinee is asked to write the meaning of each abbreviation presented in response booklet.
Letter Choice	Examinee is required to write letters missing from words within a 2-minute time limit.
Word Scramble	Examinee rearranges letters to spell real words within a 2-minute time limit.
Sight Spelling	Examinee is asked to fill in missing letters to complete the spelling of a word.
Word Choice	Examiner reads a word, and the examinee circles the correct answer from an array of words.

The TOC should only be administered to students between the ages of 6 years, 0 months and 17 years, 11 months by an examiner knowledgeable with testing, statistics, and general procedures that govern test administration and interpretation (Mather et al., 2008). Results from the TOC can be used to devise individual intervention for students who require direct instruction in spelling and punctuation and can also be used to assess students having reading difficulties due to poor knowledge about the English writing system.

Test at a Glance

Test of Orthographic Competence (TOC)
- Type of assessment: Norm-referenced
- Type of administration: Individual
- Administration time: 20 to 60 minutes
- Age/grade level: 6-0 to 17-11
- Scores: Scaled scores, percentile ranks, index scores

Written Expression

Effectively communicating thoughts and ideas is a fundamental writing skill necessary for student success (Furey et al., 2016). The National Council of Teachers of English (NCTE; 2016) describes writing as a means "through which ideas, thoughts, and feelings can be expressed and communicated, enabling individuals to communicate, reflect, explain, and influence." Writing requires one to coordinate everything from fine motor skills to executive functions to produce written work (Molitor et al., 2016). The skill of written expression is often not fully acquired until the individual has extensive exposure and experience in reading, spelling, and verbal expression. Written

Figure 9-3. Student example of a writing prompt. Student is asked to describe an activity in which they excel.

expression is "the most complex language arts skill and is based on listening, talking, handwriting, reading, and spelling" (Mercer et al., 2015, p. 359).

Individuals who demonstrate a weakness in expressing their thoughts in writing may have a written expression disorder, which is often characterized by writing that is disorganized and lacks appropriate grammar and punctuation; however, they may be able to orally tell a story with great clarity and detail. Students with written expression problems may benefit from instructional time allocated for writing and the review and editing of written products. Informal and formal assessment data can provide teachers with the information needed to develop appropriate instructional activities.

Informal Assessment of Written Expression

In most informal assessments of written expression, the student is asked to produce a writing sample in response to a prompt that may be a picture or question about the student's experience (Figure 9-3). Informal assessment of writing is "seen as valuable for use in planning and delivering daily classroom instruction because student writing samples are continually collected and examined and progress is monitored on an ongoing basis" (Scott & Vitale, 2000, p. 67). In informal assessment of writing, five components are often analyzed. Those components include fluency, syntax, vocabulary, structure, and content. Table 9-4 provides a description of each of the five components. Too often teachers focus their primary concern on the surface features of a student's writing, particularly focusing on the mechanical aspects of writing. A balanced approach to informally assessing writing includes the five components listed in Table 9-4.

A simple measure for fluency is the total number of words written during a writing assessment. When fluency is the focus, the examiner does not measure spelling, punctuation, capitalization, or word choice. The number of words written could be compared to writers at the same age or grade level.

As a student progresses in writing, they move from writing one word to connecting words into phrases and sentences, also referred to as *syntax*. Beginning writers often produce sentences that follow a subject, verb, object sequence, such as "I go store." As students mature in writing ability, the sentence pattern becomes more complex. For example, a student might progress from writing, "I go

Table 9-4. Informal Writing Assessment Measures

COMPONENT OF WRITING	DESCRIPTION
Fluency	Measure of the number of words written
Syntax	Measure of the construction of words into meaningful phrases
Vocabulary	Measure of the choice of words used in writing
Structure	Measure of the mechanics of writing
Content	Measure of the organization of thoughts and ideas

store" to "I went to the store to pick up several items for our trip to Jamaica." Assessing syntax requires the examiner to look for syntactic maturity (Issacson, n.d.). This is the transition from simple words and sentences to more complex sentences whereby the student incorporates items such as subordinate clauses and adverbial or gerund clauses.

Vocabulary is another variable assessed in informal writing. When assessing vocabulary, the examiner is evaluating a student's maturity of words (Issacson, n.d.). The examiner might evaluate the writing for words used repetitiously (e.g., big or large) to ascertain if the student is growing in the use of more mature words (replacing "big" with "gigantic" or "enormous").

Structure, also referred to as *convention*, involves spelling, punctuation, capitalization, grammar, word usage, and handwriting. When assessing a writing sample, the examiner evaluates the writing to make sure it meets grade-level standards. A rubric may be used so the student can also evaluate their paper prior to submission.

The fifth area often assessed in informal writing is content. The examiner evaluates the writing for cohesion, accuracy, and originality (Issacson, n.d.). The examiner may review the writing sample and ask questions, such as "Is there a logical sequence?" "Does the student have a clear beginning and end?" "Who is the audience?" and "Are transitions used?" Again, a rubric can be helpful in assessing the writing sample. Self-assessment with a rubric can assist students in taking ownership of their writing and help them internalize the strategies they are learning during classroom instruction. See Figure 9-4 for a sample analysis chart.

Check for Understanding

In an informal assessment of writing, what five components are often analyzed?

Another informal measure used for written expressions is a structural error analysis. The term *error analysis* was coined by Corder (1967). In short, error analysis is the study of language forms deviating from the standard of the target language that occurs during learners' language learning. James (1998) described five categories of error analysis, which include grammatical errors (e.g., adjectives, adverbs, articles, pronouns), substance errors (e.g., capitalization, punctuation, spelling), lexical errors (e.g., word formation and selection), syntactic errors (e.g., sentences structure and ordering), and semantic errors (e.g., ambiguous communication and miscommunication). With using error analysis, the teacher obtains a writing sample and performs a frequency count of errors. For example, the teacher can review the sample and count the number of punctuation errors. The

Error Analysis Type	Frequency Count	Examples
Grammatical Errors (adjectives, adverbs, articles, etc.)	13	"She got doll" Article missing: She got a doll
Substance Errors (capitalization, punctuation, spelling)	7	"The doctor was not in his offce" Misspelled office
Lexical Errors (word formation/selection)	3	"The tennis march ended in a tie" Error: Used march instead of match
Syntactic Errors (sentence structure/order)	23	"She store the went to." Error: Word order She went to the store.
Semantic Errors (communication/miscommunication/substitutions)	11	"Please leave your values at the front desk when you leave." Error in communication: Please leave your valuables at the front desk when you leave.

Figure 9-4. Sample analysis chart.

Name: Date:

One day I was walking in the park by my house when I spotted a dog running toward me growling!

Figure 9-5. Curriculum-based measurement writing probe example.

frequency of specific errors can be recorded to target individual weaknesses. Data from the error analysis allow teachers to glean information through observations and interviews. Thus, the teacher can observe various stages of the writing process and query students regarding purpose and audience for the writing, and ascertain a student's thought process as the draft is being written.

Curriculum-based measurements (CBMs) are another type of informal, formative assessment that may be used to measure growth in written expression (Figure 9-5). A CBM may be used to measure instructionally useful data including the total number of words written, correctly spelled words, and correct writing sequences (Furey et al., 2016). These probes may be administered in a group in a short time period and yield a method for monitoring a student's progress in mechanics and conventions of writing. CBM was discussed in detail in Chapter 6.

TABLE 9-5. TEST OF WRITTEN LANGUAGE, FOURTH EDITION SUBTEST DESCRIPTIONS

SUBTEST	DESCRIPTION
Vocabulary	Examinee writes a sentence that includes the presented stimulus word.
Spelling	Examinee writes words dictated by examiner.
Punctuation	Examinee writes sentences dictated by the examiner using proper punctuation.
Logical Sentence	Examinee edits an illogical sentence.
Sentence Combining	Examinee integrates the meaning of several short sentences into one.
Contextual Conventions	Examinee writes a story in response to a stimulus.
Story Composition	Examiner evaluates story relatives to the quality using the examiner manual as a guide.

A final informal assessment that may be implemented involves portfolio assessment whereby students compile a collection of their works and reflect on growth in writing skills. Portfolio assessment can compare student progress to curricular objectives and instructional methods. Rather than focus on one product, portfolio assessment measures academic achievement over time and relies on monitoring the process (Bryant et al., 2020). Unlike other types of work sample analysis, the goal of the portfolio is not the identification of error patterns. Instead, the task is to determine whether students are able to demonstrate proficiency in the performance of tasks. Weigle (2002) articulates that portfolio assessments "are clearly superior to timed writing tests in terms of authenticity" (p. 203) and provide personal investment and ownership by students as authors. Further, Weigle notes the benefit of opportunities for feedback and reflection and the focus on process rather than product.

Formal Assessment of Written Expression

A student's ability to plan, write, and revise a piece of original writing can be assessed formally using standardized tests. There are several instruments used by examiners to assess written expression. This chapter will highlight a few of the assessments used.

The *Test of Written Language, Fourth Edition* (TOWL-4; Hammill & Larsen, 2009) is a norm-referenced assessment that evaluates both the contrived and spontaneous aspects of writing. This assessment can be administered individually or in a group setting to children ages 9 years, 0 months to 17 years, 11 months with an approximate administration time of 60 to 90 minutes. The TOWL-4 is comprised of seven subtests (Table 9-5).

The TOWL-4 provides three composite scores: Overall Writing, Contrived Writing, and Spontaneous Writing. Overall, the data gleaned from the TOWL-4 are useful for pinpointing weaknesses in a student's basic writing abilities with respect to vocabulary, sentence construction, writing mechanics, and punctuation.

TEST AT A GLANCE

Test of Written Language, Fourth Edition (TOWL-4)
- Type of assessment: Norm-referenced
- Type of administration: Individual/group
- Administration time: 60 to 90 minutes
- Age/grade level: 9-0 to 17-11
- Scores: Composite

The *Kaufman Test of Educational Achievement, Third Edition* (KTEA-3), is a standardized achievement test that evaluates written expression (Kaufman & Kaufman, 2014). The Written Expression subtest requires examinees to complete tasks in the context of a grade-appropriate story format. Students are required to write sentences from dictation, add punctuation and spelling, fill in missing words, complete sentences, combine sentences, and write an essay based on the story. Sample skills that are assessed include writing complete sentences, subject–verb agreement, verb tense, meaningful context, punctuation, capitalization, writing complex sentences, and providing transition words. The examiner is able to assess the number of errors using an error category checkbox to tally errors related to the writing task, sentence structure, word form, capitalization, and punctuation. The examiner should refer to the scoring manual to score each item and for an explanation of the error categories.

TEST AT A GLANCE

Kaufman Test of Educational Achievement, Third Edition (KTEA-3)
- Subtest: Written Expression
- Type of assessment: Norm-referenced
- Type of administration: Individual
- Administration time: 20 to 30 minutes
- Age/grade level: 4-0 to 25-0
- Scores: Raw score, standard score, percentile, age/grade equivalent

Another standardized achievement test that measures written expression is the *Woodcock-Johnson IV Tests of Achievement* (WJ IV ACH; Schrank et al., 2014). The Writing Samples subtest measures a student's ability to write sentences given a verbal and picture cue, write sentences that comply with teacher directions, and devise complex sentence construction. Unlike other items on the WJ IV ACH, "Writing Samples uses a modified holistic procedure that requires examiner judgement when scoring" (Mather & Wendling, 2014, p. 70). Items on the subtest are scored for quality of expression, and students are not penalized for errors pertaining to capitalization, punctuation, and spelling. Written expression is analyzed at the sentential level. Examiners are required to use the examples provided in the Examiner's Manual to score the sentences. Scores ranges include 2 points (exceeds task requirement), 1 point (meets task requirement), to 0 points (illegible or inadequate response). An overall raw score is provided and converted to a standard score, percentile rank, and age/grade equivalent.

Test at a Glance

Woodcock-Johnson IV Tests of Achievement (WJ IV ACH)
- Subtest: Writing Samples
- Type of assessment: Norm-referenced
- Type of administration: Individual
- Administration time: 20 to 30 minutes
- Age/grade level: 2-0 to 90-0
- Scores: Raw score, standard score, percentile rank, age/grade equivalent

A final example of an assessment measuring written expression is the *Oral and Written Language Scales, Second Edition* (OWLS-II; Carrow-Woolfolk, 2011). The OWLS-II provides a Written Expression Scale, which measures expressive acts of written language. Tasks include providing written answers to open-ended questions, requiring the examinee to complete a story or paragraph, filling in blanks, and writing dictated sentences. These writing tests measure text structure (organization, cohesion, details) and the conventions of writing (spelling, punctuation, capitalization, letter formation). The Written Expression subtest from the OWLS-II is appropriate for individuals ages 5 years, 0 months to 21 years, 11 months and can be administered in approximately 15 to 30 minutes. Data from the OWLS-II can be used to identify students with learning disabilities in accordance with IDEA and to design effective intervention for students with writing challenges. Scores provided on this subtest include scaled scores, standard scores, percentile ranks, and age/grade equivalents.

Test at a Glance

Oral and Written Language Scales, Second Edition (OWLS-II)
- Subtest: Written Expression Scale
- Type of assessment: Norm-referenced
- Type of administration: Individual
- Administration time: 15 to 30 minutes
- Age/grade level: 5-0 to 21-11
- Scores: Raw score, standard score, percentile rank, age/grade equivalent

Summary

Writing is a complex skill that integrates visual, motor, and conceptual abilities and is one way that students demonstrate their knowledge of academic learning. Writing involves the mechanical aspects such as grip, slant, and handwriting, but evolves into written expression that requires sustained attention and concentration and the ability to organize thoughts to convey a message. The goal in assessing writing is to identify areas of weakness in the writing process, provide explicit recommendations for instruction, and improve overall writing abilities of students. Assessment for writing can be conducted informally through writing probes, CBMs, rubrics, and portfolio assessment. Formal assessment of writing is conducted by a trained examiner who may use assessments, including the TOWL-4, KTEA-3, WJ IV ACH, or OWLS-II. These norm-referenced assessments are used to compare an individual's performance to a peer group and may be used to design instructional interventions or used for eligibility decisions for special education services.

Case Study Wrap-Up

Following her meeting with the campus dyslexia specialist, Mrs. Beck has several formal and informal assessments to choose from to assess Janice's writing skills. Mrs. Beck has decided to assess Janice's handwriting skills using the Test of Handwriting Skills, Revised, *to gauge her neurosensory integration skills both in print and cursive handwriting. Additionally, she has chosen to measure her written expression skills with the* Oral and Written Language Scales, Second Edition *(Carrow-Woolfolk, 2011), which will provide information regarding text structure and the conventions of writing.*

Chapter Review

1. Develop a writing probe and rubric that could be used to informally assess a student's writing. Be sure to include items such as number of words, errors in spelling, and number of punctuation errors.
2. Describe how assessments can be used to inform writing instruction.
3. Observe a classroom teacher administrating a formal writing assessment. Write a summary of your experience.
4. Discuss the need for informal and formal assessment of writing for students experiencing academic challenges.

References

American Psychiatric Association. (2013). *Diagnostic and statistical manual for mental disorders* (5th ed.). Author.

Beery, K. E., Beery, N. A., & Buktenica, N. A. (2010). *Beery-Buktenica Developmental Test of Visual-Motor Integration* (6th ed.). Pearson.

Benson, J. D., Szucs, K. A., & Mejasic, J. J. (2016). Teachers' perceptions of the role of occupational therapists in schools. *Journal of Occupational Therapy, Schools, and Early Intervention, 9*(3), 290-301. https://doi.org/10.1080/19411243.2016.118158

Berringer, V. W., Richards, T. L., & Abbott, R. D. (2015). Differential diagnosis of dysgraphia, dyslexia, and OWL LD: Behavioral and neuroimaging evidence. *Reading and Writing, 28,* 1119-1153. https://doi.org/10.1007/s11145-015-9565-0

Bryant, D. P., Bryant, B. R., & Smith, D. D. (2020). *Teaching students with special needs in inclusive classrooms* (2nd ed.). Sage.

Carrow-Woolfolk, E. (2011). *Oral and Written Language Scales* (2nd ed.). Pearson.

Chung, P., & Patel, D. R. (2015). Dysgraphia. *International Journal of Child Adolescent Health, 8*(1), 27-36.

Corder, S. P. (1967). The significance of learners' errors. *International Review of Applied Linguistics in Language Teaching, 5*(4), 161-170. https://doi.org/10.1515/iral.1967.5.1-4.161

Feifer, S. G. (2020). *Feifer Assessment of Writing.* PAR.

Feng, L., Lindner, A., Ji, X. R., & Joshi, R. M. (2019). The roles of handwriting and keyboard in writing: A meta-analytic review. *Reading and Writing, 32,* 33-63. https://doi.org/10.1007/s11145-017-9749-x

Furey, W. M., Marotte, A. M., Hintze, J. M., & Shackett, C. M. (2016). Concurrent validity and classification accuracy of curriculum-based measurement for written expression. *School Psychology Quarterly, 31*(3), 369-382. https://doi.org/10.1037/spq0000138

Hammill, D. D., & Larsen, S. C. (2009). *Test of Written Language* (4th ed.). Pro-Ed.

Howe, T. H., Roston, K. L., Sheu, C. F., & Hinojosa, J. (2013). Assessing handwriting intervention effectiveness in elementary school students: A two-group controlled study. *American Journal of Occupational Therapy, 67,* 19-26. http://dx.doi.org/10.5014/ajot.2013.005470

Individuals with Disabilities Education Act, 20 U.S.C. 1400 (2004).

Issacson, S. (n.d.). *Simple ways to assess the writing skills of students with learning disabilities.* https://www.readingrockets.org/articles/simple-ways-assess-writing-skills-students-learning-disabilities

James, C. (1998). *Errors in language learning and use: Exploring error analysis.* Routledge.

Kaufman, A. S., & Kaufman, N. L. (2014). *Kaufman Test of Educational Achievement* (2nd ed.). Pearson.

Mather, N., Roberts, R., Hammill, D., & Allen, E. (2008). *Test of Orthographic Competence.* Pro-Ed.

Mather, N., & Wendling, B. J. (2014). *Examiner's manual. Woodcock-Johnson IV Tests of Achievement.* Riverside.

Mercer, C. D., Mercer, A. R., & Pullen, P. (2015). *Teaching students with learning problems* (8th ed.). Pearson.

Milone, M. (2007). *Test of Handwriting Skills* (rev.). Academic Therapy.

Molitor, S. J., Langberg, J. M., & Evans, S. W. (2016). The written expression abilities of adolescents with attention-deficit/hyperactivity disorder. *Research in Developmental Disabilities, 51,* 49-59. https://doi.org/10.1016/j.ridd.2016.01.005

Morgan, C., Moon, G., Stephens, T. L., & Gardner, R. L. (2021). Understanding the importance of handwriting instruction: Implications on student cognitive and academic development. *The DiaLog, 50*(1), 11-16.

National Council of Teachers of English (NCTE). (2016). *NCTE beliefs about students' right to write.* http://www.ncte.org/positions/statements/students-right-to-write

Parr, J. M., & Timperly, H. S. (2010). Feedback to writing, assessment for teaching and learning and student progress. *Assessing Writing, 15*(2), 68-85.

Pfeiffer, B., Moskowitz, B., Paoletti, A., Brusilovskiy, E., Zylstra, S. E., & Murray, T. (2015). Developmental test of visual-motor integration (VMI): An effective outcome measure for handwriting interventions for kindergarten, first-grade, and second-grade students? *American Journal of Occupational Therapy, 69*(4). https://doi.org/10.5014/ajot.2015.015826

Powell, S. (2019). *Your introduction to teaching: Explorations in teaching.* Pearson.

Schrank, F. A., McGrew, K. S., Mather, N., & Woodcock, R. W. (2014). *Woodcock-Johnson IV.* Riverside.

Scott, B. J., & Vitale, M. R. (2000). Informal assessment of idea development in written expression: A tool for classroom use. *Preventing School Failure: Alternative Education for Education for Children and Youth, 44*(2), 67-71. https://doi.org/10.1080/10459880009599786

Stephens, T. L., Gonzalez, V. G., & Holman, S. B. (2020). Understanding, planning, and conducting a comprehensive dysgraphia evaluation. *The DiaLog, 49*(1), 6-11.

Texas Education Agency. (2021). Dysgraphia. In *The dyslexia handbook: Procedures concerning dyslexia and related disorders, 2021 update* (pp. 59-72). Texas Education Agency.

Weigle, S. C. (2002). *Assessing writing.* Cambridge University Press.

Assessments of Mathematics

CHAPTER OBJECTIVES

- Identify the National Council of Teachers of Mathematics six principles for mathematics.
- Define dyscalculia.
- Define math reasoning and math calculation.
- Summarize informal assessments for math.
- Describe formal assessment measures for math.
- Identify cognitive processes that impact mathematical thinking.
- Describe instructional issues impacting mathematical thinking.

KEY TERMS

- **dyscalculia:** Problems with mathematical problem solving or calculation.
- **executive functioning (EF):** Ability one uses to self-monitor by using working memory, inner speech, attention, and recall of recent information.
- **explicit instruction:** Teaching in a direct, structured format.
- **long-term memory (LTM):** The retention and recall of information.
- **short-term memory (STM):** Ability to hold information in the mind for a short period of time.
- **working memory (WM):** Ability to manage, manipulate, and transform information.

KEY ABBREVIATIONS

- EF: executive functioning
- FAM: *Feifer Assessment of Mathematics*
- KeyMath-3 DA: *KeyMath-3 Diagnostic Assessment*
- LTM: long-term memory
- M-CBM: math curriculum-based measurements
- NCTM: National Council of Teachers of Mathematics
- R-CBM: reading curriculum-based measurements
- STM: short-term memory
- TOMA-3: *Test of Mathematical Abilities, Third Edition*
- WM: working memory

CASE STUDY

Adi is in Mr. Chang's third-grade math class. Adi is one of four children in the Molina household. Although the Molinas' home language is Spanish, both Rafael and Denise, Adi's parents, possess good command of English, and they report that Adi's preferred language is English. Adi attended bilingual preschool and full-day kindergarten. She has good attendance and has no issues with being tardy. Adi has been instructed in an English-speaking classroom from first to third grade.

Although Rafael and Denise own and operate a thriving landscaping business, they are very involved in their children's education. Rafael and Denise reported they had concerns about Adi's progress, and her second-grade teacher recommended Adi be held back, but they did not agree to this. Adi was instructed at home due to the COVID-19 pandemic in second grade. Denise oversaw the lessons but admitted it was a "fight" to keep Adi engaged. Rafael and Denise were happy when Adi returned to in-person learning.

Mr. Chang's class has been reviewing multi-digit addition and subtraction with regrouping. Mr. Chang noticed Adi calculated multi-digit addition problems from left to right rather than right to left. To help her, Mr. Chang has allowed Adi to use grid paper to line up the numbers in the problems, but Adi continues to struggle with the basic concepts of mathematics. Mr. Chang is not sure what steps he needs to follow to assess her skills and develop a plan to address her needs.

Principles of Mathematics

Mathematics impacts the daily life of everyone. From calculating the interest rate on loans to counting money from a transaction, students need to understand basic mathematical principles. Math deficiencies are often identified during the early years in school when children are not able to sort objects by size, match objects, complete basic computation, or solve problems (National Council of Teachers of Mathematics [NCTM], 2000). NCTM has established principles for mathematics, which encompass the following themes:

1. Equity—Excellence in mathematics education requires equity-high expectations and strong support for all students.
2. Curriculum—A curriculum is more than a collection of activities; it must be coherent, focused, and well-articulated across grade levels.
3. Teaching—Effective mathematics teaching requires understanding what students know and need to learn and then challenging and supporting them to learn it well.
4. Learning—Students must learn mathematics with understanding, actively building knowledge from experience and prior knowledge.
5. Assessment—Assessment should support the learning of important mathematics and furnish useful information to both teachers and students.
6. Technology—Technology is useful in teaching and learning mathematics as it enhances students' learning.

Moreover, NCTM (2000) identifies five content standards students should learn spanning PK through Grade 12. The content standards include (1) number and operations, (2) algebra, (3) geometry, (4) measurement, and (5) data analysis and probability. The five content standards are designed to provide a useful base of mathematical knowledge and skills needed during the life span. When students encounter specific challenges in any of these five areas, assessment is often recommended. The assessment conducted may be formal or informal and can be used to design an effective intervention to address the areas of concern.

Dyscalculia

The term *dyscalculia* is rooted in Greek and Latin and means "counting badly." In today's terms, dyscalculia is often associated with difficulty learning or comprehending mathematics or arithmetic. According to the Individuals with Disabilities Education Act (IDEA; 2004), an individual can be identified as having a learning disability in mathematical problem solving or calculation, and these difficulties are often referred to as dyscalculia. The continuing changing diagnostic criteria and varying definitions between the educational and medical community adds a confounder between the two terms (Soares et al., 2017). Adding to this confusion is the fact that it is unclear if these terms are interchangeable or synonymous. For the purpose of this chapter, the terms "dyscalculia" and "math learning disability" will be considered synonymous.

Development of Math Skills

Children's early math skills are an important predictor of later academic success (Duncan et al., 2007). Math development involves building "a series of skills such as number knowledge, spatial reasoning, and pattern knowledge" (Little et al., 2020, p. 1). The development of math skills can be divided into formal and informal (early) math skills. Examples of informal math encompass skills such as non-numeric quantity discrimination (e.g., counting piles of gummy bears), quantity to number–word linkage (e.g., counting the number of gummy bears in a pile), and then to symbolic and nonsymbolic quantity relations (e.g., adding or subtracting gummy bears across piles; Siegler & Lortie-Forgues, 2014). Formal math knowledge involves the mastery of number competencies, including number recognition, number comparisons, and understanding number magnitudes. As the comparisons and magnitudes extend to increasingly more complex systems, mastery of formal math knowledge progresses (Lyons & Ansari, 2015; Mazzocco & Thompson, 2005). While mathematical skills develop rapidly during the elementary school years, the timelines of skill acquisition often are dependent on cognitive and environmental factors (Daucourt et al., 2020; Rittle-Johnson, 2017).

COGNITIVE PROCESSES THAT IMPACT MATHEMATICAL THINKING

Cognitive factors needed for students to progress in mathematics include the ability to form and remember associations, generalize concepts, count, and apply number sense (National Research Council, 2009). For students to obtain these skills, appropriate functioning in working memory (WM) and executive functioning (EF) is required. WM and EF are higher-level cognitive processes affecting a wide range of academic skills such as mathematical thinking and performance. Because WM and EF are interrelated cognitive processes that impact math performance in the classroom and in daily life, the authors present a discussion of each and its relationships to mathematical functioning.

Working Memory

Although WM, short-term memory (STM), and long-term memory (LTM) are often thought to be interchangeable, they are three distinct memory systems that have different but interrelated functions (Dehn, 2008). A good way to remember the three systems of memory is through the following mnemonic device—The Three Houses of Memory (Dehn, 2008; Figure 10-1).

WM is the ability to manage, manipulate, and transform information drawn from either STM or LTM (Dehn, 2008) and is necessary for a wide range of cognitive functioning and academic tasks. WM is the "interface" between the input and output of information integrating STM and LTM. WM uses information available in STM or retrieves information from LTM or both. It accomplishes this task by performing an action on the information and then storing the new product in LTM or using it to construct a response.

In daily life, WM is the ability to keep information in the mind for a period of time and then use that information to think, problem solve, and understand texts. Notably, WM is where learning takes place and where problem solving occurs. Classroom performance and the development of academic skills are highly dependent on the proper functioning of WM (Dehn, 2008). As such, WM is an important predictor of reading and math performance in children who are struggling to read and/or having difficulty performing mathematical operations. In fact, Swanson and Zheng (2013) assert children who have difficulties solving word problems is due to a breakdown in WM. Moreover, their research also suggests WM plays a critical role in math computation. Similarly, Gersten et al. (2012) posit students with WM challenges may experience difficulties in mathematics because "students are not only asked to remember but also mentally 'juggle' several bits of abstract information (e.g., basic facts, the position of numbers on a mental line, computation procedures)" (p. 435).

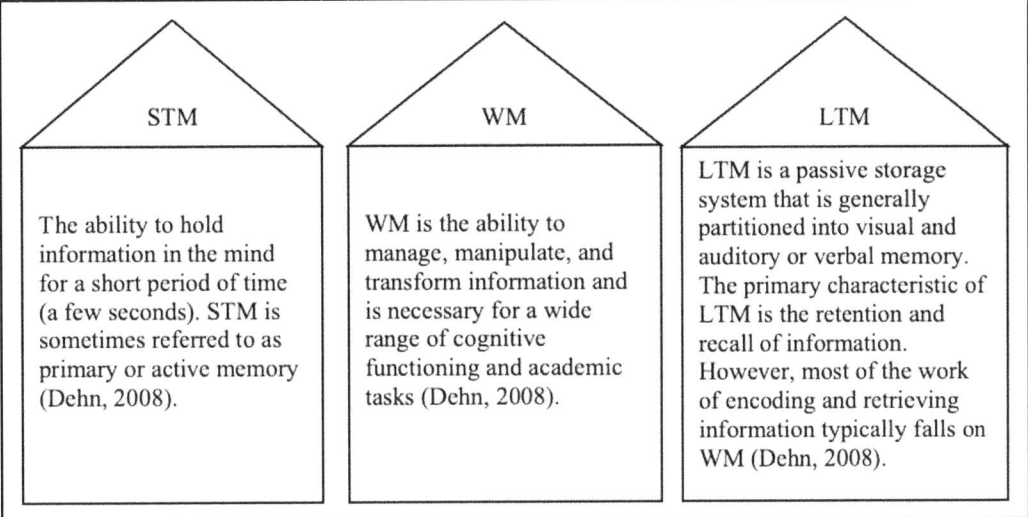

Figure 10-1. The Three Houses of Memory.

Executive Functioning

EF is the ability one uses to self-monitor by using WM, inner speech, attention, and recall of recent information (Swanson & Jerman, 2006). These skills are used to guide and control thought and actions. Miyake et al. (2000) noted EF is usually divided into three components: (1) WM, which is the ability to monitor and manipulate information and data held in the mind; (2) inhibition, which refers to the suppression of irrelevant information and inappropriate responses; and (3) shifting, which relates to switching attention between tasks.

An important indicator in mathematical performance is the ability to attend to instruction and to the task at hand (i.e., see *attention* in Swanson and Jerman [2006] definition). Maintaining and sustaining attention is a signpost of adequate EF. In fact, recent research suggests measuring attentiveness during academic instruction is a good predictor of future mathematical achievement for students who may be struggling with math concepts (Gersten et al., 2012). Accordingly, students who have difficulty sustaining attention to mathematical instruction and/or assignments, who process information more slowly, or who have memory-related problems (such as inhibition and WM) may experience difficulties with any number of skills necessary for success in mathematics (e.g., numeracy, automaticity of basic math facts, recalling steps to complete a word problem). Given the role of attention, a characteristic of EF, and its impact on mathematical achievement, Gersten and colleagues suggest interventions for students having problems in mathematics include a component for promoting attention to academic tasks (e.g., instruction, activities, assignments).

CHECK FOR UNDERSTANDING

WM and EF are fundamental cognitive processes that impact mathematical thinking.

Instructional Factors Impacting Mathematical Thinking

In addition to cognitive factors, there are instructional factors that may impact a student's mathematical ability. Teachers in today's classrooms are tasked with differentiating instruction to a diverse population of students. Preparing educators to understand and then teach complex content such as math and science is a difficult task (Kunter et al., 2013). Inadequate preparation is one factor that may impact a pre-service teacher's ability to provide appropriate instruction in mathematics. Maccini and Gagnon (2006) reported pre-service teachers' mathematical knowledge, as well as the number of methods courses they completed, helped predict the use of explicit instruction in mathematics. A related factor concerns math anxiety of the pre-service educator and its impact on mathematics instruction. Richardson and Suinn (1972) coined the term "math anxiety" as the fear and apprehension individuals feel when faced with the prospect of doing math. Math anxiety arises due to exposure to negative attitudes about mathematics (Wang et al., 2014), and the foundations for math anxieties are likely cemented early in a child's learning when a teacher or parent exposes their own fear of mathematics. Research shows when teaching pre-service teachers, the manner in which the math content is framed can have a marked effect on the math anxiety of the pre-service teacher (Beilock & Maloney, 2015).

Another instructional issue relates to insufficient opportunities to learn, practice, and master effective and efficient strategies. Too many primary classrooms teach mathematics through simple facts instead of advanced math concepts such as problem solving and reasoning (Clements & Sarama, 2016). It is important for educators to challenge students and provide opportunities for them to practice the content being taught. One way to provide support is through scaffolded instruction, which provides temporary assistance to students so they can complete a task successfully they are unable to achieve independently. These supports are provided visually, verbally, and through written communication. Teachers can also provide opportunities to practice and master strategies through explicit instruction (Archer & Hughes, 2011). Using explicit instruction, a teacher is able to identify the learning objectives, highlight important concepts, provide precise instruction, and connect to prior learning. To meet the unique needs of each student utilizing explicit instruction, a teacher must use informal and formal methods (Table 10-1) to assess a student's progress and to inform instruction.

Check for Understanding

Instructional issues related to mathematical thinking include the need to differentiate instruction and the need to provide sufficient opportunities to learn, practice, and master effective strategies.

Informal Classroom Assessment Strategies

Just as informal assessments are critical for understanding students' functioning in reading, they also provide valuable insights into students' mathematical abilities. As a reminder, informal assessments help teachers drive instruction. These assessments are routinely conducted in the classroom and occur in student–teacher interactions, whole class, small group, or one on one (Ruiz-Primo & Furtak, 2007). In this chapter, the following informal classroom assessment strategies for math are highlighted.

TABLE 10-1. INFORMAL MATHEMATICS STRATEGIES	
INFORMAL CLASSROOM ASSESSMENT STRATEGY	**DESCRIPTION**
Math curriculum-based measurements	M-CBM is a systematic approach for measuring mathematical skills consisting of short, simple measures that are used to monitor students' progress (Deno, 1985).
Observational data (observations, interviews, and work samples)	Information collected in the classroom such as student–teacher conversations, interviews with various stakeholders (students, teachers, parents, etc.), observations during academic tasks, and work samples also help to inform instruction.
Response cards	Although response cards come in many forms, typical response cards are dry erase boards that each student holds up to display responses to questions or problems that are posed by the teacher (Randolph, 2007).
Exit slips	Exit slips require students to respond in writing to a prompt given by the teacher and to give their written reflections to the teacher upon exiting the room. Moreover, the exit slip strategy is a great tool for incorporating writing in a variety of content areas (Allen Simon & Striegel, n.d.).
Statewide assessment information	Statewide assessment results identify specific skills that the child has mastered, skills the child is still working toward, or skills the child has not yet mastered. When combined with multiple sources of information, these results can provide insight and guidance to inform instruction.

Math Curriculum-Based Measurements: Informal Assessment Tools

Math curriculum-based measurements (M-CBM) are informal assessments tools that teachers can use to measure general math achievement (Thurber et al., 2002) and to monitor students' progress. However, the majority of the empirical research in monitoring mathematics performance has been focused at the elementary level with limited focus at the secondary level (Foegen et al., 2007). Foegen and colleagues also contend that progress monitoring tools such as M-CBM for secondary students should address particular areas of mathematics specific to the content demands: algebra and geometry.

Learning mathematics requires students to develop a differentiated set of skills and knowledge as they advance from grade to grade. Therefore, when selecting M-CBM, teachers must consider the "match" between the measure and the content being taught (Foegen et al., 2007). For example, young children might need a CBM that measures numeracy skills while a secondary student may need a CBM focused on algebraic concepts.

Examples of Math Curriculum-Based Measurements

In a review of the literature, Foegen et al. (2007) found that early mathematics measures with the most corroborating evidence included number identification, quantity discrimination, and missing numbers. Moreover, Jordan et al. (2010) found that *number sense,* as measured by the *Number Sense Brief Screen* (NSB) was a good indicator of later mathematic competencies at the end of first and third grade. Number sense includes numeric literacy skills such as counting, number knowledge, and numerical estimation. That said, depending on what type of mathematic skill is being measured, CBM can help teachers identify students who may be struggling with mathematical concepts.

A popular type of M-CBM at the elementary grade level includes 1-minute basic math fact probes (Jiban & Deno, 2007). These probes typically include single-digit by single-digit math problems from all four mathematic operations (i.e., addition, subtraction, division, multiplication). When administering these probes, teachers set a timer for 1 minute. At the end of the minute, the teacher counts the number of problems and/or digits the students completed correctly at the end of the time period (Jiban & Deno, 2007). However, the results of Jiban and Deno's study reported weak reliability scores for 1-minute math probes at third grade. As a result, they recommended more robust methods of measuring mathematic skills that are more closely aligned to the grade-level curriculum.

In the same study, Jiban and Deno (2007) investigated a combined approach, reading CBM (R-CBM) and M-CBM, and performance on the Minnesota Comprehensive Assessment (MCA), a statewide math test. The results indicate good predictors of performance for fifth graders on the MCA with the use of cloze math facts CBM in conjunction with maze R-CBM. In another example, Kiss and Christ (2019) examined the relationship between early reading skills as predictors of math achievement. Their findings suggest early math and reading are interrelated and both areas should be measured when screening students who may be at risk for academic failure.

OTHER TYPES OF INFORMAL ASSESSMENT STRATEGIES

As noted many times in this book, when assessing students who may be at risk for academic difficulties, collecting information from multiple sources of data provides a more accurate portrayal of a child's ability (McLeskey et al., 2017). Relying only on one data source or assessment strategy does not provide enough information for a teacher to make informed decisions regarding intervention. Other assessment strategies a teacher may want to use, along with M-CBM and R-CBM, when making instructional decisions are observational data, response cards, exit slips, statewide assessment results, and work samples from the classroom.

Observational Data

Sometimes overlooked as a trustworthy source of information, observational data collected from the classroom and other settings can provide important information about a child's academic abilities (McLeskey et al., 2017). Classroom observation data encompass a wide variety of behaviors. *For example, in Adi's case, Mr. Chang might tally the number of times Adi engages in avoidance behaviors during 10 minutes of independent practice. Avoidance behaviors might manifest themselves as the number of times Adi asks to go to the restroom, sharpen her pencil, or the number of minutes she spends rifling through her backpack.*

Observation data also include the teacher paying specific attention to how the child solves a problem, *for example, Mr. Chang's observations of Adi's calculation skills. Because Adi approaches addition problems left to right, she does not regroup and instead calculates each column of numbers individually (Figure 10-2).* He also notices that although Adi used her fingers to add 5 + 9, she obtained the incorrect answer. Accordingly, there are many observable behaviors to be noticed while a child is completing a task or responding to questions posed by the teacher.

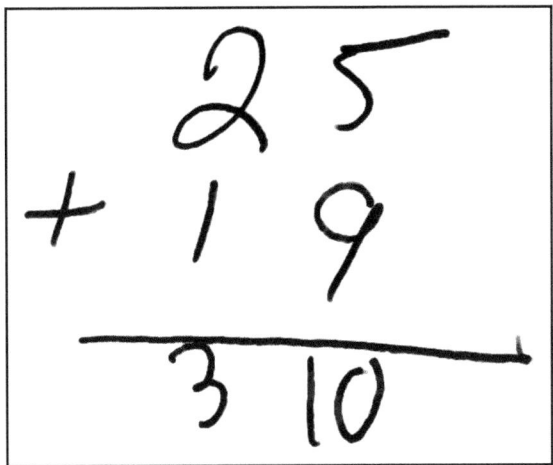

Figure 10-2. Observation example: Multi-digit addition problem calculated left to right.

Response Cards

Even though response cards are typically thought to be a strategy for increasing student engagement, they are often used to measure a child's skill level and whether they understand key concepts from the day's lesson. *Drawing upon the case study scenario, when Mr. Chang asks his class to respond to a problem that he poses for response card activity, he tallies responses based on the seating chart, scans student responses for correct answers, clarifies any misunderstanding, and provides feedback. This provides Mr. Chang with information he can use to inform instruction and assist him with identifying students requiring additional remediation.* As a review, response cards are an evidence-based, informal assessment strategy teachers can use when teaching children with and without disabilities. The benefits of implementing response cards in the classroom are increased student engagement and social change in the classroom (Randolph, 2007). Reluctant students or students who have disabilities are more likely to respond when teachers use response cards over traditional hand-raising (Owiny et al., 2018). *In the case of Adi, Mr. Chang notices Adi is very reluctant to provide a response when he calls upon her, but when given the opportunity to respond on her dry erase board, Adi responds even when she might solve the problem incorrectly (Figure 10-3).*

Exit Slips

Exit slips are an informal assessment strategy teachers can use to help guide instruction. When used properly, exit slips are relatively stress-free for the student while providing the teacher with key insights on what the student is thinking, understanding, or feeling (Albers, 2006). Although teachers can present exit slips in a variety of ways, a widely used method is the 1-minute reflection. During a 1-minute reflection, students respond to a short prompt provided by the teacher. Prompts may be categorized into three different subcategories: thinking, understanding, and feeling.

The purpose of thinking prompts is for the child to have some agency over their learning and to provide guidance for the teacher on future topics. "I wished I learned, but didn't" is an example of a thinking prompt. This prompt provides the teacher with insights on the topics or ideas the child would like to learn while also providing a sense of ownership of future topics for the child (Knight, 2013).

The second type of prompt that a teacher might pose is related to the child's understanding of key concepts from the day's lesson (Fisher & Frey, 2004)—"Write down or draw one thing you learned in class today," "Write down or draw one thing that was very clear to you from today's lesson," and "Write down or draw one thing from today's lesson that is still unclear to you." Prompts for understanding help the teacher measure what the child learned and which concepts the child is still struggling with.

Figure 10-3. Math response card example.

Figure 10-4. Feeling exit slip example.

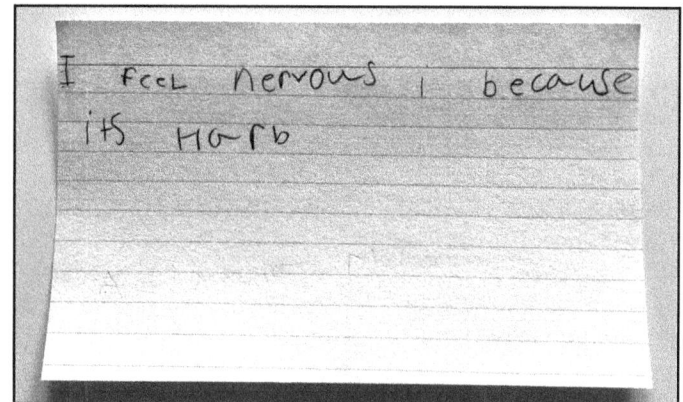

The third type of prompt a teacher might pose is related to the child's feelings about a topic (Reading Rockets, n.d.). These prompts typically ask the child to check in with their feelings about the lesson—"Write one sentence about how you feel when you see an addition problem that requires regrouping" (Figure 10-4). For students who struggle to write complete sentences, they might draw a smiley, frowny, or neutral face. Although these check-ins are drawn upon the case study example presented in this chapter, teachers can modify the prompts for their individual situations.

When choosing a prompt for an exit slip, teachers should select the type of prompt carefully based on the information that they are hoping to gain. Moreover, using a variety of prompts will help teachers obtain a deeper understanding of the child's strengths and weaknesses and will illuminate the child's feelings toward the lesson, topic, or concept (Albers, 2006). This is especially critical when working with students who are struggling with math such as Adi.

Statewide Assessment Information

When used as one data point in a child's assessment profile, statewide assessments can help teachers make instructional decisions. States and districts use statewide assessments to ascertain if students are meeting expected academic standards for their grade placement. However, when used punitively, results from statewide assessments can create an environment for teachers to "teach to the test" (Madus & Clarke, 2001; Nichols et al., 2012; Townsend, 2002). In some states, test results from statewide assessments are reported in ways that are not meaningful for instructional planning. For example, in some states the test data simply place students in categories such as below basic, basic, proficient, and advanced (Powell, 2019). These types of results do not provide data needed to make informed instructional decisions. In math, for example, the test results would not provide information about a student's understanding of place value, computation, or problem solving.

While statewide assessments give school leaders, administrators, and teachers a global view of student performance and may pinpoint curricular insufficiencies, they have little impact on overall student achievement. It is important for teachers to use the statewide data to develop formative and summative assessments to meet the individual needs of students. This collection of data gives teachers a method to understand student needs and provides a blueprint for individualized instruction and curricular choices.

Drawing upon the case study, Mr. Chang reviewed Adi's previous statewide assessment results and discovered that Adi has not mastered the single-digit addition problems and does not understand the steps needed to complete multidigit addition problems that require regrouping. Based on the data from the statewide assessment, Mr. Chang should review Adi's classroom formative and summative data and devise a new plan of action. While the statewide data are helpful, he can focus on the day-to-day assessments, including work samples, to make informed instructional decisions. These assessment measures serve to help Mr. Chang understand Adi's skill levels and may be used as benchmarks to provide evidence of growth.

CHECK FOR UNDERSTANDING

M-CBM, observational data, response cards, exit slips, and statewide assessment results are informal assessment strategies that teachers can use to gauge children's understanding of math concepts and to help drive instruction.

FORMAL ASSESSMENTS OF MATH

When combined with informal assessment procedures such as M-CBM, observations, interviews, and work samples, the results from formal assessment instruments can help stakeholders in targeting interventions, determining eligibility status for special education, and making programming and placement decisions. As noted in Chapter 4, formal assessments are administered in a one-to-one format. Three formal assessment measures of math will be highlighted in this chapter. Those assessments include the *Feifer Assessment of Mathematics* (FAM; Feifer, 2016), *KeyMath-3 Diagnostic Assessment* (KeyMath-3 DA; Connolly, 2007), and the *Test of Mathematical Abilities* (TOMA-3; Brown et al., 2012).

Feifer Assessment of Mathematics (FAM)

The FAM is a norm-referenced assessment designed to examine the underlying neurodevelopment processes supporting the acquisition of proficient math skills (Feifer, 2016). The FAM is comprised of 19 individual subtests measuring skills including math fact retrieval, numeric and spatial memory, perceptual estimation skills, linguistic math concepts, and core number sense development. This assessment is often used by examiners in determining if a specific subtype of dyscalculia may be present but is also used to determine if a student possesses a math learning disability. The FAM yields three scores representing each dyscalculia subtype: Verbal Index (measures automatic fact retrieval), Procedural Index (measures a student's ability to count, order, and sequence numbers), and Semantic Index (measure of visual-spatial and conceptual components). A Total Index Score represents total test performance. This assessment is applicable for ages 4 to 21 years.

TEST AT A GLANCE

Feifer Assessment of Mathematics (FAM)
- Type of assessment: Norm-referenced
- Type of administration: Individual
- Administration time: 35 to 60 minutes
- Age/grade level: PK–college
- Scores: Verbal Index, Procedural Index, and Semantic Index

KeyMath-3 Diagnostic Assessment (KeyMath-3 DA)

Another assessment used by school personnel is the KeyMath-3 DA (Connolly, 2007). The KeyMath-3 DA is an individually norm-referenced assessment that measures a range of mathematical skills from rote counting to solving linear equations. This assessment instrument is aligned to the content and process standards devised by the NCTM. The KeyMath-3 DA is arranged into 10 subtests including Numeration, Algebra, Geometry, Measurement, Data Analysis and Probability, Mental Computation and Estimation, Addition and Subtraction, Multiplication and Division, Foundations of Problem Solving, and Applied Problem Solving. The 10 subtests are organized into three broad categories: Basic Concepts, Operations, and Applications. The assessment provides scores including scale scores, standard scores, and percentile ranks. Data from the KeyMath-3 DA can be used to provide diagnostic information that can be used to develop individually tailored interventions for students with challenges in mathematics.

TEST AT A GLANCE

KeyMath-3 Diagnostic Assessment (KeyMath-3 DA)
- Type of assessment: Norm-referenced
- Type of administration: Individual
- Administration time: 30 to 90 minutes
- Age/grade level: 4:6 to 21:0
- Scores: Scale scores, standard scores, percentile ranks, and age/grade equivalents

Test of Mathematical Abilities, Third Edition (TOMA-3)

The final assessment that will be highlighted that pertains to formal assessment of mathematics is the TOMA-3 (Brown et al., 2012). The TOMA-3 is norm-referenced assessment administered individually or in a group and can be used to identify students who are significantly behind their peers in the area of mathematical knowledge. The TOMA-3 is comprised of four core subtests and one supplemental test. Those subtests include: Mathematical Symbols and Concepts, Computation, Mathematics in Everyday Life, Word Problems, and Attitude Toward Math (Supplemental). From the results of the four core subtests, a Mathematical Ability Index is calculated. Other scores that comprise the TOMA-3 include age/grade equivalents, scaled scores, percentile ranks, and standard errors of measurement.

TEST AT A GLANCE

Test of Mathematical Abilities, Third Edition (TOMA-3)
- Type of assessment: Norm-referenced
- Type of administration: Individual or group
- Administration time: 90 minutes
- Age/grade level: 8-0 to 18-11 years
- Scores: Age/grade equivalents, percentile ranks, scaled scores, and Mathematical Ability Index

Table 10-2 provides an overall summary of the purposes of the FAM, KeyMath-3 DA, and the TOMA-3.

SUMMARY

Understanding math concepts and the ability to apply these skills is an important life function for children and adults. Examples of daily math skills include calculating interest on a loan, using a tape measure to determine the length and width of an item or adapting the amount of an ingredient in a recipe. Although there is considerable debate regarding the terms "dyscalculia" and "math learning disability," the authors of this chapter contend that dyscalculia and math learning disabilities are interchangeable terms highlighting a breakdown of math calculation skills.

Children demonstrating challenges in mathematics may have deficits in cognitive abilities, specifically in WM or EF or both. Deficits in either of these areas are often characterized by the child's inability to retain basic math facts, recall steps needed to solve a problem, and self-monitor (Swanson & Zheng, 2013). In addition, students may experience challenges in mathematics related to instructional issues. Inadequate educator preparation, coupled with the lack of opportunity to learn, practice, and master effective strategies, contributes to mathematical deficits (Blevins-Knabe, 2012). The purpose of this chapter was to describe informal assessment strategies for math that can help classroom teachers in providing instruction for children who are struggling to understand and apply math concepts. Informal assessment strategies for math include M-CBM, response cards, exit slips, observations, statewide assessment results, and classroom work samples. When combined with formal assessments of math such as the FAM, KeyMath-3 DA, and TOMA-3, children who are struggling to understand math concepts can be identified and targeted interventions designed and implemented.

TABLE 10-2. Purpose of Selected Assessments of Mathematics

ASSESSMENT INSTRUMENT	PURPOSE
Feifer Assessment of Mathematics	The FAM identifies students from prekindergarten to college who may have mathematical learning difficulties. The results are reported in three math domains—procedural, verbal, and semantic. Assessment personnel can use the results from these three domains to help teachers in providing targeted interventions (Giella, 2019).
KeyMath-3 Diagnostic Assessment	The KeyMath-3 DA is an individually administered measure of essential mathematical concepts and skills and is aligned with the National Council of Teachers of Mathematics content and process standards. It is appropriate for grades kindergarten to 12th grade and covers the skills that are typically taught in kindergarten to 9th grade. It is comprised of 10 subtests that represent three math content areas: Basic Concepts, Operations, and Applications. The Key Math-3 DA can be used to identify students who may be struggling with mathematical concepts (Connolly, 2007).
Test of Mathematical Abilities, Third Edition	The TOMA-3 is a norm-referenced assessment instrument that can be used to identify, describe, and quantify children's mathematical deficits. It can be administered individually or in a group and is appropriate for ages 8 years, 0 months to 18 years, 11 months (Brown et al., 2012).

Case Study Wrap-Up

After consultation with the instructional math coach, Mr. Chang determined he needed to collect more information about Adi's basic math skills. As a result, Mr. Chang administered several types of M-CBM including 1-minute basic math probes and more complex probes evaluating Adi's problem-solving and calculation abilities. In addition, Mr. Chang examined Adi's work samples, exit slips, math journal, and the previous year's assessment results. Mr. Chang concluded Adi was not only having difficulty in regrouping while adding, but she lacked automaticity of basic math facts. Mr. Chang met with the school's student success team and recommended Adi be placed in Tier 2 of the response to intervention program.

Chapter Review

1. Design a lesson plan for math and describe the informal assessment strategies that you will use. Provide justification for selecting these strategies.
2. Interview a math teacher from elementary school, middle school, and high school. Discuss informal assessment strategies that they use in the classroom. Compare and contrast the different types of assessment strategies used by the teachers.
3. Create a variety of questions, prompts, or problems you would use as response cards for a math lesson.

REFERENCES

Albers, P. (2006). Imagining the possibilities in multimodal curriculum design. *English Education, 38*(2), 75-101.

Allen Simon, & Striegel, P. (n.d.). Strategy guide: Exit slips. *National Council of Teachers of English.* http://www.readwritethink.org/professional-development/strategy-guides/exit-slips-30760.html

Archer, A. L., & Hughes, C. A. (2011). *Explicit instruction: Effective and efficient teaching.* Guilford.

Beilock, S. L., & Maloney, E. A. (2015). Math anxiety: A factor in math achievement not to be ignored. *Policy Insights form Behavioral and Brain Sciences, 2*(1), 4-12. http://dx.doi.org/10.11177/2372732215601438

Blevins-Knabe, B. (2012). Fostering early numeracy at home. *Encyclopedia of language and literacy development* (pp. 1-9). Western University.

Brown, V., Cronin, M. E., & Bryant, D. P. (2012). *Test of Mathematical Abilities* (3rd ed.). Pro-Ed.

Clements, D. H., & Sarama, J. (2016). Math, science, and technology in the early grades. *The Future of Children, 26*(2), 75-94. http://dx.doi.org/10.1353/foc.2016.0013

Connolly, A. J. (2007). *KeyMath-3 Diagnostic Assessment: Manual forms A and B.* Pearson.

Daucourt, M. C., Erbeil, F., Little, C. W., Haughbrook, R., & Hart, S. A. (2020). A meta-analytical review of the genetic and environmental correlations between reading an attention-deficit/hyperactivity disorder symptoms and reading and math. *Scientific Studies of Reading, 24,* 23-56. http://dx.doi.org/10.1080/1088843.2019.1631827L

Dehn, M. (2008). *Working memory and academic learning: Assessment and intervention.* Wiley and Sons.

Deno, S. L. (1985). Curriculum-based measurement: The emerging alternative. *Exceptional Children, 52,* 219-232.

Duncan, G. J., Dowsett, C. J., Claessens, A., Magnuson, K., Huston, A. C., Klebanov, P., Pagani, L. S., Feinstein, L., Engel, M., Brooks-Gunn, J., Sexton, H., Duckworth, K., & Japel, C. (2007). School readiness and later achievement. *Developmental Psychology, 43*(6), 1428-1446. https://doi.org/10.1037/0012-1649.43.6.1428

Feifer, S. (2016). *Feifer Assessment of Mathematics.* PAR.

Fisher, D., & Frey, N. (2004). *Improving adolescent literacy: Strategies at work.* Pearson Prentice Hall.

Foegen, A., Jiban, C., & Deno, S. (2007). Progress monitoring measures in mathematics: A review of the literature. *The Journal of Special Education, 41*(2), 121-139.

Gersten, R., Clarke, B., Jordan, N. C., Newman-Gonchar, R., Hammond, K., & Wilkins, C. (2012). Universal screening in mathematics for the primary grades: Beginnings of a research base. *Exceptional Children, 78*(4), 423-445. http://dx.doi.org/10.1177/001440291207800403

Giella, A. K. (2019). *Utilizing skills, error, and behavior analyses with the Feifer Assessment of Reading (FAR) and the Feifer Assessment of Math (FAM): Hidden gems that bring detailed strengths and weaknesses to light* (white paper). PAR.

Individuals with Disabilities Education Act. Sec. 300.8 (c) (10). (2004). https://sites.ed.gov/idea/regs/b/a/300.8/c/10

Jiban, C. L., & Deno, S. L. (2007). Using math and reading curriculum-based measurements to predict state mathematics test performance: Are simple one-minute measures technically adequate. *Assessment for Effective Intervention, 32*(2), 78-89. http://dx.doi.org/10.1177/15345084070320020501

Jordan, N. C., Glutting, J., & Ramineni, C. (2010). The importance of number sense to mathematics achievement in first and third grades. *Learning and Individual Differences, 20,* 82-88. https://dx.doi.org/10.1016/j.lindif.2009.07.004

Kiss, A. J., & Christ, T. J. (2019). Screening for math in early grades: Is reading enough? *Assessment for Effective Intervention, 45*(1), 38-50. https://doi.org/10.1177/1534508418766410

Knight, J. (2013). *High-impact instruction: A framework for great teaching.* Corwin Press.

Kunter, M., Klusmann, U., Baumert, J., Richter, D., Voss, T., & Hachfeld, A. (2013). Professional competence of teachers: Effects on instructional quality and student development. *Journal of Educational Psychology, 105,* 805-820. http://dx.doi.org/10.1037/a0032583

Little, C. W., Lonigan, C. J., & Phillips, B. M. (2020). Differential patterns of growth in reading and math skills during elementary school. *Journal of Educational Psychology, 113*(3), 462-476. http://dx.doi.org/10.1037/edu000635

Lyons, I. M., & Ansari, D. (2015). Foundations of children's numerical and mathematics skills. The roles of symbolic and nonsymbolic representations of numerical magnitude. In J. B. Benson (Ed.), *Advances in child development and behavior* (Vol. 48, pp. 93-116). Academic Press.

Maccini, P., & Gagnon, J. C. (2006). Mathematics instructional practices and assessment accommodations by secondary special and general educators. *Exceptional Children, 72,* 217-234. http://dx.doi.org/10.1177/001440290607200206

Madus, G. F., & Clarke, M. (2001). The adverse impact of high-stakes testing on minority students: Evidence from 100 years of test data. In G. Orfield & M. Kornhaber (Eds.), *Raising standards or raising barriers? Inequality and high-stakes testing in public education.* The Century Foundation.

Mazzocco, M. M., & Thompson, R. E. (2005). Kindergarten predictors of math learning disability. *Learning Disabilities Research & Practice, 20,* 142-155. http://dx.doi.org/10.1111/j.1540-5826.2005.00129.x

McLeskey, J., Barringer, M-D., Billingsley, B., Brownell, M., Jackson, D., Kennedy, M., Lewis, T., Maheady, L., Rodriguez, J., Scheeler, M. D., Winn, J., & Ziegler, D. (2017). *High-leverage practices in special education.* Council for Exceptional Children & CEEDAR Center.

Miyake, A., Friedman, N. P., Emerson, M. J., Witzki, A. H., Howerter, A., & Wager, T. D. (2000). The unity and diversity of executive functions and their contributions to complex "frontal lobe" tasks: A latent variable analysis. *Cognitive Psychology, 41*(1), 49-100.

National Council of Teachers of Mathematics. (2000). *Principles and standards for school mathematics.* Author.

National Research Council. (2009). *Mathematics learning in early childhood: Paths toward excellence and equity.* The National Academies Press. https://doi.org/10.17226/12519.

Nichols, S. L., Glass, G. V., & Berliner, D. C. (2012). High-stakes testing and student achievement: Updated analyses with NAEP data. *Education Policy Analysis Archives, 20*(20), 1-35. http://dx.doi.org/10.14507/epaa.v20n20.2012

Owiny, R. L., Spriggs, A. D., Sartini, E. C., & Mills, J. R. (2018). Evaluating response cards as evidence based. *Preventing School Failure, 62*(2), 59-72. https://doi.org/10.1080/1045988X.2017.1344953

Powell, S. (2019). *Your introduction to education: Explorations in teaching.* Pearson.

Randolph, J. J. (2007). Meta-analysis of the research on response cards: Effects on test achievement, quiz achievement, participation, and off-task behavior. *Journal of Positive Behavior Interventions, 9*(2), 113-128. https://doi.org/10.1177/10983007070090020201

Reading Rockets. (n.d.). *Exit slips.* https://www.readingrockets.org/strategies/exit_slips

Richardson, F. C., & Suinn, R. M. (1972). The mathematics anxiety rating scale: Psychometric data. *Journal of Counseling Psychology, 19*(6), 551-554. https://doi.org/10.1037/h0033456

Rittle-Johnson, B. (2017). Developing mathematics knowledge. *Child Development Perspectives, 11*, 184-190. https://dx.doi.org/10.1111.cdep.1229

Ruiz-Primo, M. A., & Furtak, E. M. (2007). Exploring teachers' informal formative assessment practices and students' understanding in the context of scientific inquiry. *Journal of Research in Science Teaching, 44*(1), 57-84. https://doi.org/10.1002/tea.20163

Siegler, R. S., & Lortie-Forgues, H. (2014). An integrative theory of numerical development. *Child Development Perspectives, 8*, 144-150. http://dx.doi.org/10.1111/cdep.12077

Soares, N., Evans, T., & Patel, D. R. (2017). Specific learning disability in mathematics: A comprehensive review. *Translational Pediatrics, 7*(1), 48-62. http://dx.doi.org/10.21037.08.03

Swanson, H. L., & Jerman, O. (2006). Math disabilities: A selective meta-analysis of the literature. *Review of Educational Research, 76*(2), 249-274.

Swanson, H. L., & Zheng, X. (2013). Memory difficulties in children and adults with learning disabilities. In H. L. Swanson, K. R. Harris, & S. Graham (Eds.), *Handbook of learning disabilities* (2nd ed., pp. 214-238). Guilford Press.

Thurber, R. S., Shinn, M. R., & Smolkowski, K. (2002). What is measured in mathematics tests? Construct validity of curriculum-based mathematics measures. *School Psychology Review, 31*(4), 498-513.

Townsend, B. (2002). "Testing while black": Standards-based school reform and African American learners. *Remedial & Special Education, 23*(4), 222-230.

Wang, Z., Hart, S. A., Kovas, Y., Lukowski, S., Soden, B., Thompson, L. A., Plomin, R., McLoughlin, G., Bartlett, C. W., Lyons, I. M., & Petrill, S. A. (2014). Who is afraid of math? Two sources of genetic variance for mathematical anxiety. *The Journal of Child Psychology and Psychiatry, 55*(9), 1056-1064.

Appendix

Full Individual Initial Evaluation

Date of Report: October 5, 2020

Name: Ava Long	**School:** Your Private School
Birth Date: August 23, 2012	**Parents:** Ashley and Stuart Long
Grade: 2nd	**Age at Time of Testing:** 8.0

Sources of Data:	**Dates of Assessment:**
WISC-V (Primary Intellectual Instrument)	September 16, 2020
KABC-II (Secondary Intellectual Instrument)	September 17, 2020
KTEA-3 (Achievement Instrument)	September 16, 2020
GORT-5 (Diagnostic Reading Instrument)	September 16, 2020
CTOPP-2 (Diagnostic Reading Instrument)	September 17, 2020
WRMT-III (Diagnostic Reading Instrument)	September 17, 2020
Conversations with Mrs. Long (Phone & Text Messages)	August 27, September 14, 16, & 17
Interview with Sarah Houston (Phone)	September 23, 2020
Interview with Melody Stephens (Zoom)	September 23, 2020
Interview with Lisa Martinez (Phone)	September 24 & 28, 2020
Interview with Ava (Face to Face)	September 16 & 17, 2020
Review of Classroom Information (Teacher Provided)	September 28, 2020
Review of Cumulative File (School Provided)	September 28 & 29, 2020

> **Explanation of the Sources of Data**
>
> In the sources of data, remember to list informal and formal data sources that you used as part of the assessment.

Reason for Referral:

The reason for this referral is to conduct a private evaluation at the request of Ava's parents, Mr. and Mrs. Long. The secondary purposes of this evaluation are to identify Ava's strengths and weaknesses and educational needs, provide diagnosis of a reading disability (or lack thereof), and provide Ava's teachers with educational recommendations for the classroom.

> **Explanation of the Reason for Referral**
>
> State the reason why the child was referred and the concerns of the parent and/or school. Write the reason for referral in complete sentences.

Background Information
Ava is an 8-year-old girl who is a second grader at Your Private School in Far From Here, Texas. Ava resides with her biological parents and younger sibling. Mr. and Mrs. Long are involved in Ava's educational programming and are concerned about her academic progress. Parents report a family history (paternal) of learning difficulties and dyslexia respectively.

Health History
According to Mrs. Long, Ava met all her developmental milestones at age-appropriate rates, developed language appropriately, and has had no significant health issues. In addition, Ava passed the vision and hearing screening, conducted by Your Private School, unaided.

Educational History and School Information
Ava attended Your Private School beginning in PK and has had access to high-quality instruction. According to Ms. Houston, Ava's kindergarten teacher and private tutor, Ava was retained in kindergarten because she was a "young kindergartner" and needed time to develop. The second time in kindergarten, Ava was able to identify the initial sounds of all the letters in the alphabet. However, Ava had difficulty grasping concepts (in comparison to her peers) and was not able to identify the complex sounds of the alphabet. Ms. Houston also reported that a typical kindergartner should know 30 sight words and Ava only recognized 10 to 12 sight words on the Fry's 100 Sight Word List. At this point, Ms. Houston began to have concerns that there might be more than "developmental issues" and started to suspect a reading disability. As such, Mr. and Mrs. Long hired Ms. Houston as Ava's private tutor. Tutoring was conducted after school for 30 to 45 minutes one time a week. The focus of these tutoring sessions was on the alphabetic principle.

Ava was then promoted to first grade where she still struggled to obtain grade-level standards even though private tutoring continued one afternoon weekly and accommodations were being made (i.e., reduced spelling tests, tests in Learning Enrichment Center [LEC]). Moreover, Ava also began "Pre-Flight" dyslexia training in the LEC with Mrs. Melody Stephens, a Certified Academic Language Therapist (CALT). Mrs. Stephens noted that Ava has difficulty retaining and recalling information and struggles with phonemic awareness but is making slow progress. In March 2020, COVID-19 interrupted traditional face-to-face programming and intensive support programs and services.

In August 2020, Ava began face-to-face instruction as a second grader and is continuing dyslexia training, "Take Flight," in the LEC. Ava also continues to receive private tutoring with Ms. Houston. The duration of these tutoring sessions increased to two afternoons per week for 1½ hours each for a total of 3 hours weekly. The primary focus of these tutoring sessions is on the alphabetic principle, sight word instruction, vocabulary development, and book chats. Moreover, Ava continues to receive accommodations such as reduced spelling tests, testing in the LEC, and oral accommodations for reading tasks in the classroom.

Ms. Martinez is Ava's second-grade teacher. Ms. Martinez noted that Ava has a great personality, takes responsibility, and shows personal initiative. However, Ava continues to struggle with grade-level demands. Ms. Martinez's chief concern is Ava's reading skills. Ava is reading at a Rigby Level 5 (beginning of first grade). Typically developing second graders are reading at Rigby Levels 17–18. On a recent Renaissance STAR Reading assessment, Ava was estimated to be reading at the Pre-Primer level as she was not allowed to continue past the practice assessment because she scored too low. Although Ava is obtaining passing marks in the classroom and on her report cards, Ms. Martinez noted that Ava receives a modified curriculum (reduced spelling tests, oral accommodations, etc.) and would not be passing had the curriculum not been modified.

> **Explanation of the Background Information**
>
> The background information tells the story of the family and child. This section describes important health history and the educational history of programing and services. Curriculum-based measures and present level of academic functioning are also described in this section.

Language

Ava is a monolingual speaker of English. The home language of the Long family is English. According to informal measures, Ava's expressive language is average. Ava was administered Listening Comprehension on the *Woodcock Reading Mastery Tests, Third Edition* (WRMT-III) and scored within the average range, suggesting that her receptive language abilities are in the average range of functioning.

> **Explanation of Language**
>
> In this section, formal and informal language should be explained along with receptive and expressive abilities. If a child is non–native English speaker, language dominance must be addressed here, including basic interpersonal language communication skills (BICS) and cognitive academic language proficiency (CALP).

Testing Sessions and Behavioral Observations

Ava approached the testing situation easily, and rapport was quickly established. Ava appeared to give her best effort and displayed prosocial behaviors such as maintaining eye contact, leaning toward the examiner, and adequate attention to most tasks. However, she struggled to maintain sustained attention and became somewhat distracted during reading tasks. For example, Ava would want to engage in lengthy oral conversations during the reading activities. Testing was conducted over a period of two testing sessions on two different days. Each testing session consisted of multiple hours in a conference room at the Number One University. Ava was provided frequent breaks (every 45 minutes) with each break lasting 10 to 15 minutes in duration and 30-minute lunch breaks.

All standardized test administration procedures were followed according to the instruments' manuals with the exception of Word Comprehension on the WRMT-III. On this subtest, the examiner read the words aloud to Ava so that she could demonstrate her understanding of synonyms and antonyms without the interference of depressed decoding/word recognition skills.

To ensure the safety of Ava and the examiner, the following safety procedures were in place: The examiner wore a face mask, as did Ava, provided frequent breaks to sanitize hands, frequent cleaning of writing surfaces and pencils with disinfectant wipes, and appropriate social distancing as subtest allowed during the testing sessions. These safety procedures did not adversely affect Ava's participation in the assessment process.

> **Explanation of the Testing Sessions and Behavioral Observations**
>
> This section describes the following:
> - Rapport
> - Child's approach to task and behavior during the testing sessions
> - Duration of the testing sessions
> - Standardized testing procedures or any modifications to the procedures

Cognitive Assessments

Wechsler Intelligence Scale for Children, Fifth Edition

The WISC-V consists of 21 subtests and has four levels of interpretation: (1) Full Scale IQ, (2) Primary Index Scales, (3) Ancillary Index Scales, and (4) Complementary Index Scales. Each interpretation level is composed of one or more scales. Thus, depending on the nature of the referral and reason for assessment, clinicians have a variety of options regarding the selection of subtests that they choose to administer.

Description of Scores

Standard scores are scores that have a mean of 100 and a standard deviation of 15. The average range of standard scores for the WISC-V assessment falls between 90 and 110.

Scaled scores have a mean of 3 and a standard deviation of 10. The average range of scaled scores range between 8 to 12.

Confidence intervals are considered to be the true index scores with 90% confidence. This allows for the error of measurement expected in all standardized instruments. A confidence interval gives an estimated range of values, which is likely to include a reported value: estimating the probability that the true score lies within a range around the reported score.

Percentile ranks are scores that indicate performance against the norm population. They indicate the percentage of children that an individual outperformed in their age group. For example: A 14-year-old who scores at the 25th percentile on a particular subtest performed better than 25% of the 14-year-olds on that subtest.

TABLE OF SCORES

SCALE	STANDARD SCORE	CONFIDENCE INTERVAL (90%)	PERCENTILE RANK	DESCRIPTIVE CATEGORY
Full Scale IQ (FSIQ)	96	91-101	39	Average
Verbal Comprehension Index (VCI)	106	99-112	66	Average
Visual Spatial Index (VSI)	Nonunitary			
Fluid Reasoning Index (FSI)	94	88-100	34	Average
Working Memory Index (WMI)	Nonunitary			
Processing Speed Index (PSI)	95	88-103	37	Average

Subtest	Scaled Score	Percentile Rank
Verbal Comprehension Index		
Similarities	8	25
Vocabulary	14	91
Visual Spatial Index		
Block Design	6	9
Visual Puzzles	10	50
Fluid Reasoning Index		
Matrix Reasoning	10	50
Figure Weights	8	25

Working Memory Index		
Digit Span	11	63
Picture Span	7	16
Processing Speed Index		
Coding	9	37
Symbol Search	9	37

> **Explanation of the Introduction to the Cognitive Assessments**
>
> In this part of the cognitive assessment section, introduce the cognitive instruments that were administered and describe their purpose and what they measure. Also provide descriptions of the scores and provide scoring information in a table.

Nonunitary and Statistical Significance defined—to be able to say that one score is meaningfully higher or lower than another score, the examiner must determine that the two scores did not occur by chance. The first prong of determining statistical significance is through the analysis of critical values, the process of analyzing scores mathematically. Critical values are validated statistically and printed in the administration manual for each area. The second prong is through base rates or the probability of occurrence. Sattler, Dumont, and Coalson suggest using a base rate of 15% or less of the normative sample. When two subtests are compared to one another and meet the first and second prong of statistical significance, the index for these subtests cannot be used as a reliable measure of the child's overall abilities for that area. This is the case that happened in Ava's cognitive profile for the indexes Visual Spatial and Working Memory. Because the scores at the subtest level for each of these indexes vary significantly from one another, the overall index score for each area cannot be used as a good estimate of her abilities and are noted as "nonunitary."

The Full Scale IQ is an estimated measure of overall intelligence. Ava obtained a standard score of 96 with 90% confidence that the true score lies between 91 and 101. A standard score of 96 is within the average range of functioning and suggests that Ava has cognitive abilities that are typical for a child her age.

The Verbal Comprehension Index (VCI) is designed to measure verbal reasoning and concept formation. It is thought to be the best indicator of success in schools. Ava obtained a standard score of 106 with 90% confidence that the scores are likely to range between 99 and 112. A standard score of 106 is within the average range of functioning. Relative to performance among the cognitive processes that were measured on the WISC-V, the VCI presents as a significant strength (i.e., the score did not occur by chance and was rare in the norming population). Strengths in this area suggest that Ava should be able to rely on her knowledge of verbal information and language development to help her succeed academically.

Visual Spatial Index (VSI) measures the ability to perceive, analyze, synthesize, and think with visual patterns, including the ability to store and recall visual representations. On this index, Ava obtained scores at the subtest level that vary significantly from one another. Thus, the overall VSI index score is not an accurate measure of her abilities in this area. Analyzing each subtest that make up the VSI will provide insight into her abilities in this area. Two subtests make up the VSI: Block Design and Visual Puzzles. On Block Design, Ava obtained a scaled score of 6. A scaled score of 6 is within the below average range of functioning. On Block Design, Ava was asked to build a model using red and white blocks in a specified time period that matched a target design. Although Ava attempted each item and tried different options, she was inconsistent in noticing that her model did not match the target design. If she did notice that her model did not match the target design, it was after she had completed her model and the next item was being ready to be administered. It was only then that Ava would fix her mistake, but the item was not able to be counted as correct. This might indicate that Ava needs to be taught self-regulation strategies such as taking time to double-check her work before she turns in an assignment. On Visual Puzzles, Ava obtained a scaled score of 10. A scaled score of 10 is within the average range of functioning and indicates that she has intact visual spatial reasoning skills.

Fluid Reasoning Index (FRI) is the ability to reason, form concepts, and solve problems using unfamiliar information or novel procedures. On this index, Ava obtained a standard score of 94 with 90% confidence that the true score ranges between 88 and 100. This demonstrates that Ava has higher-order level thinking and reasoning abilities. Thus, she should be able to complete higher-order tasks in the classroom such as drawing inferences from text, reasoning with quantitative information, and written expression tasks.

Working Memory Index (WMI) is the ability to perform cognitive operations and manipulate information stored in short-term memory. It is important in higher-order thinking, learning, and achievement. Working memory can tap concentration, planning ability, cognitive flexibility, and sequencing skill, but is sensitive to anxiety. Moreover, it is an important component of learning and achievement, and ability to work effectively with ideas as they are presented in classroom situations. Ava obtained scaled scores at the subtest level that significantly differ from one another. Thus, the WMI is not an accurate measure of Ava's overall working memory abilities. Two subtests make up the WMI: Digit Span and Picture Span.

Ava obtained a scaled score of 11 on Digit Span, an auditory working memory task. A scaled score of 11 is within the average range of functioning and indicates that when receiving information auditorily Ava is better able to remember the information. In contrast, Ava obtained a scaled score of 7 on Picture Span. A scaled score of 7 falls in the below average range of functioning. Picture Span measures visual working memory and working memory capacity. This suggests that Ava's ability to remember information provided to her auditorily is better developed than her visual working memory abilities. This is not a surprise given the emphasis on phonemic awareness instruction in Take Flight and private tutoring and that the bulk of lessons provided in school are via the auditory modality.

Processing Speed is the ability to perform automatic cognitive tasks quickly and efficiently. Ava obtained an index score of 95 with 90% confidence that the true score ranges between 88 and 103. A standard score of 95 is within the average range of functioning. Processing speed is an important cognitive process as it allows individuals the ability to free up cognitive energy for other more complex cognitive activities such as working memory.

Although Auditory Processing is not represented on the WISC-V as a cognitive processing ability, when combined with the KTEA-3, measures of auditory processing can be obtained via the Sound-Symbol Composite. On the Sound-Symbol Composite, Ava obtained a standard score of 88, which is in the average range of functioning. Although within the average range of functioning on the KTEA-3, Ava scored at the 21st percentile for the Sound-Symbol Composite, indicating that 79% of the children outperformed Ava in this area. It is 90% likely that if Ava was tested again in this area on the KTEA-3, she would obtain a score that ranges between 84 and 92. These scores are consistent with the diagnosis of dyslexia in that children who struggle with sound-symbol tasks have difficulty with reading.

Kaufman Assessment Battery for Children, Second Edition

Ava was administered selected subtests from the *Kaufman Assessment Battery for Children, Second Edition* (KABC-II), which is an individually administered norm-referenced instrument designed to measure the processing and cognitive abilities of children and adolescents aged 3 through 18. The subtests administered for this assessment were in the area of Learning (i.e., Long-Term Retrieval). Although the WISC-V includes measures of long-term retrieval, the examiner determined that the KABC-II would represent a more accurate portrayal of Ava's abilities in this area.

Description of Scores
Standard scores are scores that have a mean of 100 and a standard deviation of 15. The average range of standard scores is based on the distribution of the bell curve of +1 and −1 SD. Thus, the average range is between 85 and 115.

Scaled scores are scores that have a mean of 10 and a standard deviation of 3. The average range of scaled scores is based on the distribution of the bell curve of +1 and −1 SD. Thus, the average range is between 7 and 13.

Confidence intervals are considered to be the true index scores with 90% confidence. This allows for the error of measurement expected in all standardized instruments. A confidence interval gives an estimated range of values, which is likely to include a reported value: estimating the probability that the true score lies within a range around the reported score.

Percentile ranks are scores that indicate performance against the norm population. They indicate the percentage of children that an individual outperformed in their age group. For example: A 14-year-old who scores at the 25th percentile on a particular subtest performed better than 25% of the 14-year-olds on that subtest.

TABLE OF SCORES

SCALE	STANDARD SCORE	CONFIDENCE INTERVAL (90%)	PERCENTILE RANK	DESCRIPTIVE CATEGORY
Learning Index	89	85-93	23	Average

Subtest	Scaled Score	Percentile Rank
Atlantis (Learning)	10	50
Rebus (Learning)	6	9

Interpretation of Test Scores
The Learning Index is a measure of long-term retrieval. This is the ability to store and retrieve information (names, concepts, ideas) from long-term memory. It is the efficiency with which information is initially stored in and retrieved from long-term memory. Ava obtained a standard score of 89 with 90% assurance that her true scores range between 85 and 93. A standard score of 89 is considered to be in the average range of functioning.

Two subtests comprise the Learning Index. The first is Atlantis. On this subtest, Ava obtained a scaled score of 10. A scaled score of 10 is within the average range. Ava appeared to be careful and deliberate in her selections. Ava may have used auditory repetition skill to help remember the names of the pictures.

The second subtest administered was Rebus. Rebus was developed to measure a child's ability to learn a new language bit by bit until they are able to read long sentences in this new language. This subtest has direct relevance to the reading process. The child is given a word or concept associated with a particular rebus (i.e., drawing), and then the child reads aloud phrases and sentences composed of these rebuses. On this subtest, Ava obtained a scaled score of 6. A scaled score of 6 is within the below average range of functioning. Moreover, Ava did not recognize that each sentence was a story, and she did not use any context clues while reading.

> **Explanation of the Cognitive Assessment Data**
>
> This section provides in-depth analysis and explanation of the cognitive assessment data and implications for classroom performance. This section is the link between the assessment data and the classroom.

Adaptive Behavior

"Adaptive behavior is the performance of daily activities required for personal and social sufficiency." It is age-related, defined by the expectations or standards of other people, and defined by typical performance, not ability.

Ava's adaptive behavior was evaluated through informal measures (interviews, observations, and a review of her educational records). Based on the information obtained, it appears that Ava's adaptive behavior skills and abilities are what is expected for a child her age.

> **Explanation of Adaptive Behavior**
>
> The adaptive behavior section describes the daily activities (e.g., self-care, communication, social, school and home living) of the child. These areas can be addressed through informal or formal measures depending on the reason for referral.

Summary of Cognitive Assessments

Ava was administered the WISC-V and selected subtests from the KABC-II. On these assessments, Ava exhibited a relatively consistent cognitive profile. Of particular note is Ava's abilities within the VCI. Abilities in this area suggest that Ava has intact language and vocabulary skills and should be able to succeed in school. Conversely, Ava presented working memory abilities that were statistically significant from one another. The results of the assessment indicate that Ava's auditory working memory is better developed than her visual working memory. This has important implications in that visual working memory has direct impact on orthographic processing, an important reading area. Further, Ava also struggled when asked to read rebuses. This reveals that Ava is experiencing difficulties associating symbols with words, an important skill when asked to read.

> **Explanation of the Summary of Cognitive Assessments**
>
> The cognitive assessment summary synthesizes the data from the cognitive instruments, adaptive behavior, qualitative observations during the testing sessions, and implications for the classroom.

Achievement Information

Kaufman Test of Educational Achievement, Third Edition

Ava was administered Form A of the *Kaufman Test of Educational Achievement, Third Edition* (KTEA-3), which is an individual norm-referenced achievement test that is appropriate for individuals aged 4.5 through 25 years.

Description of Scores
All scores reported on the KTEA-3 are the same as scores described on the KABC-II.

Table of Scores

COMPOSITE	STANDARD SCORE	CONFIDENCE INTERVAL (90%)	PERCENTILE RANK	DESCRIPTIVE CATEGORY
Reading Composite	73	68-78	4	Below Average
Letter and Word Recognition	70	66-74	2	Below Average
Reading Comprehension	78	69-87	7	Below Average
Written Language Composite	87	82-92	19	Average
Written Expression	97	89-105	42	Average
Spelling	79	75-83	8	Below Average
Sound-Symbol Composite	88	84-92	21	Average
Phonological Processing	94	88-100	34	Average
Nonsense Word Decoding	87	82-92	19	Average
Decoding Composite	77	74-80	6	Below Average
Orthographic Processing Composite	73	65-81	4	Below Average
Word Recognition Fluency	66	55-77	1	Low
Letter Naming Facility	86	69-103	18	Average

Reading Composite

The Reading Composite consists of two subtests: Letter and Word Recognition and Reading Comprehension. Ava obtained a standard score of 73, which is within the below average range of functioning. There is a 90% chance that the true score actually ranges between 68 and 78.

Letter and Word Recognition: The student identifies letters and pronounces words of gradually increasing difficulty within an acceptable time (i.e., 3 seconds or less). Most words on this subtest are irregular to ensure that the subtest measures word recognition (reading vocabulary) more than decoding ability. On this subtest Ava obtained a standard score of 70 with 90% confidence that the true score ranges between 66 and 74. A standard score of 70 is in the below average range of functioning. When Ava was asked to read words that were unfamiliar, such as *apple,* she would try to break the word into parts and then blend the parts together.

Reading Comprehension: The student reads passages of increasing difficulty and answers literal or inferential questions about them. On this subtest Ava obtained a standard score of 73 with 90% confidence that the true scores range between 68 and 78. A standard score of 73 is within the below average range of performance. Ava was administered Item Set B (Grade 1). Ava was able to associate a word when given picture cues. However, when the picture cues were extinguished, she was not able to consistently read words such as *farm, pin,* etc. Moreover, when presented with a picture cue and asked to read a word, Ava would look at the word and notice the initial letter, then pick the picture that started with the sound. Because Ava was unable to read the increasingly difficult sentences without pictures, the subtest was suspended early.

Written Language Composite

The Written Language Composite consists of two subtests: Written Expression and Spelling. On this composite, Ava obtained a standard score of 87 with 90% confidence that the true score ranges between 82 and 92. A standard score of 87 is within the average range of functioning.

Written Expression: The student completes writing tasks in the context of a storybook format. Tasks include writing sentences from dictation, adding punctuation and capitalization, filling in missing words, completing sentences, combining sentences, writing compound and complex sentences, and writing an essay based on the story the student helped complete. On the written expression subtest Ava obtained a standard score of 97 with 90% confidence that the true score ranges between 89 and 105. A standard score of 97 is in the average range of functioning. Ava was administered Level 2 (Grades 1 and 2). Ava was able to write a three-word simple sentence and was able to apply a period as an ending punctuation mark. She was also able to demonstrate discernment for the different types of sentences and application of appropriate ending punctuation marks of these sentences (i.e., question mark, exclamation mark). As part of the written expression subtest, the student is asked to retell the story. The student is given a 5-minute time limit to retell the story. Ava wrote for 2 minutes and 36 seconds. The story that Ava produced was an accurate retelling of the main parts of the story, and she demonstrated good thoughts when writing. However, Ava's writing was largely unrecognizable for a child her age, and she used phonetic spelling to represent words. For example, she wrote "felawt ov . . ." (i.e., *fell out of*). Although Ava demonstrated emerging writing abilities, she struggled with getting her thoughts on paper. She used a significant amount of cognitive energy to write a sentence by saying the sentence aloud before she wrote it and by erasing and rewriting multiple times. Specifically, she may use this as a coping strategy because writing is so difficult for her.

Spelling: The student writes words dictated by the examiner from a steeply graded word list. On this subtest Ava obtained a standard score of 79, which is in the below average range. There is a 90% chance that the true score ranges between 75 and 83. When spelling unknown words, children use their phonological knowledge to segment words into their individual phonemes. Once this is completed, they can then apply orthographic and morphological knowledge to represent those sounds. Ava demonstrated an overreliance on auditory features when spelling words.

Sound-Symbol Composite
The Sound-Symbol Composite consists of Phonological Processing and Nonsense Word Decoding. On this composite, Ava obtained a standard score of 88, which is in the average range of functioning. It is 90% likely that if Ava was tested again in this area on the KTEA-3, she would obtain a score that ranged between 84 and 92. Although within the average range of functioning, Ava scored at the 21st percentile, suggesting that 79% of the children who this composite was normed on outperformed Ava.

Phonological Processing: The primary focus of phonological processing tasks is to manipulate sounds. Phonological processing on the KTEA-3 consists of Blending, Rhyming, Sound Matching, Deleting Sounds, and Segmenting. On this subtest, Ava obtained a standard score of 94, which is in the average range of functioning with 90% confidence that the true score ranges between 88 and 100. Although within the average range, phonological processing on the KTEA-3 is a general indicator of phonemic awareness and should be viewed with a degree of caution. As such, in-depth measures that specialize in phonological processing are a more accurate portrayal of abilities in this area. Ava's phonological processing will be discussed in the CTOPP-2 and WRMT-III sections of this report.

Nonsense Word Decoding: The student applies phonics and structural analysis skills to decode invented words of increasing difficulty. On this subtest, Ava obtained a standard score of 87, which is in the average range of functioning with 90% confidence that the true score ranges between 82 and 92. It was obvious that Ava applied skills she learned to attack words that were unfamiliar to her. The main strategy that Ava employed was letter-by-letter.

Decoding Composite
The Decoding Composite consists of Letter and Word Recognition and Nonsense Word Decoding. On this composite, Ava obtained a standard score of 77, which is in the below average range. There is a 90% chance that the true score ranges between 74 and 80.

Orthographic Processing Composite

The Orthographic Processing Composite consists of spelling, letter naming facility, and word recognition fluency. Orthographic Processing uses the visual system to form, store, and recall words. On this composite, Ava obtained a standard score of 73 with 90% assurance that the true score actually ranges between 65 and 81. A standard score of 73 is within the below average range of functioning and is aligned with the low score on Picture Span, a visual working memory task. Students with weak orthographic processing skills are not able to make a mental picture of words in their brains. These students rely completely on phonics to read and write words. Because they decode all words instead of learning words by sight, their reading sounds choppy and is not fluent. Even letter shapes can be easily confused because their brains do not retain the memory of specific letter forms. They may mistake "b" and "d" often, or substitute known words for unknown words because they start with the same letter. For example, *house* and *home*—relying on the first letter "h" to guess the word.

Word Recognition Fluency: The examinee reads a list of words aloud as quickly as possible during two 15-second trials. On this subtest, Ava obtained a standard score of 66 with 90% assurance that the true score actually ranges between 55 and 77. A standard score of 66 is within the low range of functioning and is consistent with the diagnosis of dyslexia. Ava attempted to read 9 words in 30 seconds and was able to read words such as *cat*, *go*, *at*, and *fan*.

Letter Naming Facility: The examinee names a combination of upper- and lowercase letters as quickly as possible. Letter Naming Facility is a measure of Rapid Automatic Naming (RAN), a key indicator of developmental dyslexia. On this subtest, Ava obtained a standard score of 86 with 90% assurance that the true score actually ranges between 69 and 103. A standard score of 86 is within average range of functioning, but is at the 18th percentile, indicating that 82% of the children that this subtest was normed on outperformed Ava.

Diagnostic Reading Instruments

Gray Oral Reading Test, Fifth Edition (GORT-5)

Ava was administered the *Gray Oral Reading Test, Fifth Edition* (GORT-5). The GORT-5 is an individually administered measure of oral reading ability. The GORT-5 reports four Index Scores and an overall Oral Reading Index.

Description of Scores Unique to GORT-5

Rate—the amount of time taken by a student to read a story

Accuracy—the student's ability to pronounce each word in the story correctly

Fluency—the student's Rate and Accuracy Scores combined

Comprehension—the appropriateness of the student's responses to questions about the content of each story read

Oral Reading Index—a composite score formed by combining students' fluency (i.e., Rate and Accuracy) and Comprehension scaled scores

Rate, Accuracy, Fluency, and Comprehension are reported as scaled scores with a mean of 10 and a standard deviation of 3. The overall oral reading composite score is reported as a quotient, a statistical score with a mean of 100 and a standard deviation of 15. Percentile ranks are also provided.

	RATE SCORE	ACCURACY SCORE	FLUENCY SCORE	COMPREHENSION SCORE	ORAL READING INDEX
Scaled/Standard Score	2	3	2	*Not administered*	52
Percentile Rank	<1	1	<1		<1
Qualitative Description	Very Poor	Very Poor	Very Poor		Very Poor

Interpretation of Scores:

Rate

The Rate Score is derived from the amount of time in seconds taken by the student to read a story out loud. Ava obtained a scaled score of 2, which falls in the very poor range of functioning. On Story 1, Ava was asked to read 17 words. Ava read these 17 words in 1 minute and 8 seconds. On Story 2, Ava was asked to read 41 words. She read 41 words in 3 minutes and 8 seconds. While reading it was obvious that Ava was expending a significant amount of energy to decode the words and sentences. Ava's strategy for reading was phoneme by phoneme and then blending the phonemes together. She was unable to read common sight words in either passage.

Accuracy

The Accuracy Score is the number of words the student pronounces correctly when reading a story. Ava obtained a scaled score of 3, which falls in the very poor range of functioning. On Story 1, Ava was asked to read 17 words. She made 6 errors. On Story 2, Ava was asked to read 41 words and made 11 errors. This is a 35% and 26% error rate, respectively. Testing was suspended after Story 2.

Fluency

The Fluency Score is found by combining the student's rate and accuracy scores. Ava obtained a fluency scaled score of 2, which falls in the very poor range of functioning. Ava's rate and accuracy are poorly developed. That is, she is a slow reader, and she is not very accurate.

Comprehension

Per the GORT-5 manual guidelines, the comprehension questions were not given to Ava because she was provided more than 20% of the words in the passage.

Oral Reading Index

Because Ava was unable to respond to the Comprehension questions, an Oral Reading Index score was not obtained.

Comprehensive Test of Phonological Processing, Second Edition (CTOPP-2)

Ava was administered the *Comprehensive Test of Phonological Processing, Second Edition* (CTOPP-2), which is an individually administered, norm-referenced test that is appropriate for individuals of ages 5 years, 0 months through 24 years, 11 months. It is intended to assess phonological awareness, phonological memory, and rapid naming. A deficit in one or more of these areas is often associated with reading difficulties. The following table lists the scores that were obtained.

Description of Scores Unique to CTOPP-2

Scaled scores are scores with a mean (average) of 10 and a standard deviation of 3 as distributed on the normal bell curve. The average range for the CTOPP-2 falls within the range of 8 to 12 with standard deviations of +1 and –1 on the bell curve.

Composite scores are calculated from the sum of subtest scaled scores and have a mean (average) of 100 and a standard deviation of 15. These composite scores indicate an examinee's ability relative to phonological awareness, phonological memory, and rapid naming.

TABLE OF SCORES

COMPOSITE	COMPOSITE SCORE	%ILE RANK	DESCRIPTIVE TERM
Phonological Awareness	86	18	Below Average
Phonological Memory	92	30	Average
Rapid Symbolic Naming	79	8	Poor

SUBTEST	SCALED SCORE	%ILE RANK	DESCRIPTIVE TERM
Elision	5	5	Poor
Blending Words	11	63	Average
Phoneme Isolation	7	16	Below Average
Memory for Digits	8	25	Average
Nonword Repetition	9	37	Below Average
Rapid Digit Naming	6	9	Below Average
Rapid Letter Naming	7	16	Below Average

Interpretation of CTOPP-2 Scores

Phonological Awareness Composite

The Phonological Awareness Composite Score (PACS) consists of three subtests: Elision, Blending Words, and Phoneme Isolation. The PACS measures an individual's phonological awareness. Ava obtained a composite score of 86 and is in the below average range of functioning. The true score is likely to fall between 82 and 90.

Ava was able to orally identify words when asked to drop part of the target word within a compound word. For example, when asked to say *cowgirl* without saying *girl*, she was able to say *cow*. However, Ava struggled when asked to say a new word after dropping part of the target word: "Say *farm*. Now say *farm* without saying /f/." In addition, Ava did not fare much better at manipulating sounds with Phoneme Isolation. Although she was able to identify the initial and ending sounds, she struggled with the medial sounds. Moreover, Ava expended a significant amount of energy to identify sounds by sounding out each sound in the word, saying it aloud, then identifying the target sound.

On Blending Words, Ava was successful at blending words of one to five syllables but began to struggle at six syllables. Ava's likely success on Blending Words with a scaled score of 11 is most likely attributed to her vocabulary skills. That is, she is able to recognize enough sounds to blend words together.

Phonological Memory Composite

The Phonological Memory Composite Score (PMCS) consists of two subtests: Memory for Digits and Nonword Repetition. The PMCS represents the examinee's ability to code information phonologically for temporary storage in working or short-term memory. Ava was able to successfully repeat up to five digits in the correct order and successfully repeated nonwords up to five syllables in this area. She obtained a composite score of 92, which is the average range of functioning. The true score likely ranges between 86 and 98. This is consistent with the scores on the WISC-V Digit Span subtest.

Rapid Symbolic Naming Composite

The Rapid Symbolic Naming Composite Score (RSNCS) consists of two subtests: Rapid Digit Naming and Rapid Letter Naming. The RSNCS measures efficient retrieval of phonological information from long-term, or permanent, memory and quick and repeated execution of sequence operations. Efficient retrieval of phonological information and execution of sequences of operations are required when readers attempt to decode unfamiliar words. Because of the timed nature of the subtests that make up the RSNCS, individuals who perform poorly commonly have problems with reading fluency. Ava obtained a composite score of 79, which is in the poor range of functioning. The true score likely falls within 75 and 83. The scores obtained on RSNCS are relatively consistent with the naming speed scores obtained on the KTEA-3 and indicate that Ava has difficulty with RAN tasks, a key characteristic of children with developmental dyslexia.

Woodcock Reading Mastery Tests, Third Edition

The *Woodcock Reading Mastery Tests, Third Edition* (WRMT-III) is a comprehensive battery of individually administered tests that measure reading achievement in individuals aged 4 years, 6 months through 79 years, 11 months. Ava was administered selected subtests from the WRMT-III for the purposes of supplementing the information obtained from the GORT-5 and CTOPP-2.

Description of Scores Unique to the WRMT-III

Standard scores are scores that have a mean of 100 and a standard deviation of 15. The average range of scores is between 85 and 115 and is based on the distribution of the bell curve of +1 and −1 SD.

Confidence intervals are considered to be the true index scores with 90% confidence as all instruments have a margin of error.

Percentile ranks are scores that indicate performance against the norm population. They indicate the percentage of children that an individual outperformed in their age group. For example, a 14-year-old who scores at the 25th percentile on a particular subtest performed better than 25% of the 14-year-olds on that subtest.

TABLE OF SCORES

SUBTEST/CLUSTER	STANDARD SCORE	CONFIDENCE INTERVAL (90%)	DESCRIPTIVE TERM
Phonological Awareness	86	78-94	Average
Rapid Automatic Naming	79	69-89	Below Average
Word Identification	75	69-81	Below Average
Word Attack	80	75-85	Below Average
Basic Skills Cluster	**76**	**72-80**	**Below Average**
*Word Comprehension	96	89-103	Average
Passage Comprehension	63	55-71	Well Below Average
Reading Comprehension Cluster	**78**	**72-84**	**Below Average**
Listening Comprehension	109	100-118	Average
Oral Reading Fluency	Unable to administer		
*Nonstandard administration.			

Basic Skills Cluster
The Basic Skills Cluster consists of word attack and word identification subtests and provides an overall measure of basic reading skills. Ava obtained a standard score of 76 with 90% confidence that the true score actually ranges between 72 and 80. A standard score of 76 is within the below average range of functioning. Ava struggles with the basic foundations of reading, which is impacting fluency and comprehension tasks.

Reading Comprehension Cluster
The Reading Comprehension Cluster consists of Word Comprehension and Passage Comprehension. It is intended to measure a child's understanding of what they have read. Ava obtained a reading comprehension standard score of 78 with 90% confidence that the true score actually ranges from 72 to 84. A standard score of 78 is within the below average range of functioning. However, this should be taken with a degree of caution. Because the examiner wanted to examine Ava's knowledge of words (specifically synonyms and antonyms), the examiner administered Word Comprehension outside the bounds of the manual guidelines. That is, the examiner read the items to Ava and Ava responded with a synonym or antonym for each item. This produced an average standard score of 96. Had Ava been required to read the target words and then respond with a synonym or antonym, it is very likely that the standard score would be commensurate with Ava's performance on passage comprehension and other reading measures.

Listening Comprehension
Listening Comprehension is a measure of a child's receptive language abilities. On this subtest, Ava obtained a standard score of 109 with 90% accuracy that the true score ranges between 100 and 118. A standard score of 109 is within the average range of functioning. This indicates that Ava's receptive language abilities are average and typical for a child her age. Notably, Word Comprehension, with nonstandard administration, and Listening Comprehension fell within the average range as these subtests do not require reading.

> **Explanation of the Academic Achievement Data**
>
> This section provides in-depth analysis and explanation of the academic achievement instruments and implications for classroom performance. This section is the link between the assessment data and the classroom.

Academic Achievement Summary
Ava was administered a variety of reading measures. These instruments ranged from general measures to diagnostic measures of reading. Importantly, the data reveal that Ava is a young lady who is experiencing profound difficulties with all aspects of reading and is expending a significant amount of cognitive energy to read even simple words. Ava's overreliance on sounding out individual phonemes and blending phonemes together as her main strategy for identifying unknown words is likely to adversely impact her ability to attack more complex or irregular words as the content demands increase. Moreover, it will also adversely impact her ability to read fluently and is requiring a great deal of energy and effort on her part.

Ava's weakness with visual working memory (Picture Span on the WISC-V) and orthographic processing is also negatively impacting her ability to read fluently. As noted previously, children with weak orthographic processing skills are not able to make a mental picture of words in their brains. These students rely completely on phonics to read and write words. Because they decode all words instead of learning words by sight, their reading sounds choppy and is not fluent. Even letter shapes can be easily confused because their brains do not retain the memory of specific letter forms. They may mistake "b" and "d" often, or substitute known words for unknown words because they start with the same letter, for example, *house* and *home*—relying on the first letter "h" to guess the word.

Finally, it appears that Ava has developed a couple of coping mechanisms to help her compensate for the breakdown in reading. First, Ava relies on her auditory working memory and expressive language skills to help bypass her difficulties with reading. Although this works for now, as the content demands increase with each grade, Ava's reliance on auditory working memory and expressive language will cease to work as effectively. Second, Ava appears to be more distracted and inattentive during reading tasks. It is the examiner's expert opinion that because reading is so challenging for Ava, she is using this as a way to escape some of the cognitive dissonance she is experiencing during the task of reading. Most importantly, Ava may not even realize that she is distracted and not maintaining appropriate attention to the reading task.

> **Explanation of the Summary of Academic Achievement Assessments**
> The academic achievement summary synthesizes the data from the academic achievements instruments, qualitative observations during the testing session(s), and implications for the classroom.

Summary

Ava was administered the WISC-V and selected subtests from the KABC-II. On these assessments, Ava exhibited a relatively consistent cognitive profile. Of particular note is Ava's abilities within the VCI. Abilities in this area suggest that Ava has intact language and vocabulary skills and should be able to succeed in school. Conversely, Ava presented working memory abilities that were statistically significantly different from one another. The results of the assessment indicate that Ava's auditory working memory is better developed than her visual working memory. This has important implications in that visual working memory has direct impact on orthographic processing, an important reading area. Further, Ava also struggled when asked to read rebuses. This reveals that Ava is experiencing difficulties associating symbols with words, an important skill when asked to read.

Ava was administered a variety of reading measures. These instruments ranged from general measures to diagnostic measures of reading. Importantly, the data reveal that Ava is a young lady who is experiencing profound difficulties with all aspects of reading and is expending a significant amount of cognitive energy to read even simple words. Ava's overreliance on sounding out individual phonemes and blending phonemes together as her main strategy for identifying unknown words is likely to adversely impact her ability to attack more complex or irregular words as the content demands increase. Moreover, it will also adversely impact her ability to read fluently and is requiring a great deal of energy and effort on her part.

Ava's weakness with visual working memory (Picture Span on the WISC-V) and orthographic processing is also negatively impacting her ability to read fluently. As noted previously, children with weak orthographic processing skills are not able to make a mental picture of words in their brains. These students rely completely on phonics to read and write words. Because they decode all words instead of learning words by sight, their reading sounds choppy and is not fluent. Even letter shapes can be easily confused because their brains do not retain the memory of specific letter forms. They may mistake "b" and "d often, or substitute known words for unknown words because they start with the same letter, for example, *house* and *home*—relying on the first letter "h" to guess the word.

Finally, it appears that Ava has developed a couple of coping mechanisms to help her compensate for the breakdown in reading. First, Ava relies on her auditory working memory and expressive language skills to help bypass her difficulties with reading. Although this works for now, as the content demands increase with each grade, Ava's reliance on auditory working memory and expressive language will cease to work as effectively. Second, Ava appears to be more distracted and inattentive during reading tasks. It is the examiner's expert opinion that because reading is so challenging for

Ava, she is using this as a way to escape some of the cognitive dissonance she is experiencing during the task of reading. Most importantly, Ava may not even realize that she is distracted and not maintaining appropriate attention to the reading task.

Explanation of the Summary of Assessments

This section summarizes the assessment information. It is often the only section that is ever read, so be sure to describe the important points that were noticed during the assessment.

Eligibility Statement
As defined by Texas Education Code §38.003(1), "Dyslexia means a disorder of constitutional origin manifested by a difficulty in learning to read, write, or spell, despite conventional instruction, adequate intelligence and sociocultural opportunity."

Based on multiple measures of assessment (formal and informal), Ava is exhibiting difficulty in learning to read, spell, and write even though she has had high-quality instruction, adequate sociocultural opportunities, and intellectual functioning. Ava demonstrated average performance on the WISC-V indicating that she has adequate intelligence. Despite average cognitive abilities and access to high-quality instruction (private tutoring, Take Flight, etc.), Ava is experiencing significant disruptions in reading specifically in phonological awareness and reading related tasks such as spelling and writing.

Therefore, Ava meets the criteria as a child with dyslexia, a specific learning disability in the area of reading.

Explanation of the Eligibility Statement

This section addresses the eligibility of the child for specialized programming and services. It is the responsibility of the examiner to determine eligibility and state if the child meets the legal requirements for special education services.

Recommendations
Although Ava can learn to read, the progress is going to be slow. It is critical that Your Private School teachers and staff, Mr. and Mrs. Long, and private tutors understand that Ava will learn at a rate that is appropriate for her, and this rate will be much slower than her typical age-mate peers. Celebrate the progress Ava makes.

Dyslexia Programming/Instruction
1. Ava should continue to receive dyslexia services from a highly qualified dyslexia teacher who understands development of reading skills.
2. Ava should continue Take Flight, dyslexia training, as provided by Your Private School.
3. Coordinate Ava's private tutoring with Take Flight instruction and be consistent about the instructional focus in each setting.
4. Ava requires specific sight word instruction through multisensory methods such as building words with magnetic tiles, writing words in a variety of mediums, and so on. This instruction needs to be scaled up during Ava's instructional day (i.e., reading, private tutoring). It is important that the private tutor and Ava's teachers (classroom teacher and LEC teacher) work together to provide this instruction so that there is no disconnect between what is happening at school and what is occurring in the tutoring sessions.

5. Set reasonable goals that is based on Ava's rate of learning—not what is expected for typical age-mate peers. For example, if Ava is only able to read 20 sight words consistently as a beginning second grader (and has been provided high-quality instruction and private tutoring), it is not reasonable that she will read 50 to 100 words by the end of the school year.
6. Progress monitor Ava's performance (words correct per minute, sight words that she learns and masters, etc.). This is easily accomplished through graphing. Involve Ava in creating the graphs and graphing her progress.

_____   _____
Signature   Date

Explanation of the Recommendations

This section provides evidence-based recommendations from the assessment information that can be implemented in the child's classroom. Recommendations provided should be strategic, observable, and measurable. A report must also be signed and dated by the examiner.

INDEX

Adaptive Behavior Assessment System, Third Edition (ABAS-3), 65–66
age equivalents, 14
alphabetic principle, 136
antecedent, 108
assessment, 1–12
    anecdotal, 2
    assessment, 2
    bias, 2
    case study, 2
    case study wrap-up, 10
    cultural bias in assessment, 8–9
    curriculum-based assessment, 2
    curriculum-based measurement, 2
    defining, 2–3
    formal assessment, 8
    history of educational assessment, 3–5
    history of intelligence testing, 5–6
    informal assessment, 6–7
        curriculum-based assessment, 6–7
        curriculum-based measurement, 7
        portfolio assessment, 7
    multidisciplinary assessment, 2, 9–10
    portfolio assessment, 2
    probe, 2
    purposes of, 3
    test, 2
        distinguished, 8
authentic assessment, 72

baseline, 90
basic reading skills, 136, 141–143
    assessing basic reading skills, 141–142
    assessing spelling, 142–143
behavior assessment, 107–134
    antecedent, 108
    behavior defined, 110–113
    behavior intervention plan, 108, 130–132
    case study, 109
    case study wrap-up, 133
    direct data, 108
    duration, 108
    event recording, 108
    frequency count, 108
    functional behavior assessment, 108, 123–125
        comprehensive, steps to completing, 125–130
    indirect data, 108
    interval recording, 108
    interviews, 108
    latency recording, 108
    measuring behavior examples, 116–123
        direct, 119–123
            ABC observation, 119–120
            duration, 120
            frequency count, 120
            latency, 120–121
            scatterplot, 121–123
        indirect, 116–119
            interviews, 116
            rating scales/surveys/questionnaires, 118–119
            records, 116–118
    multi-tiered system of support, 109–110
    positive behavioral interventions and supports, 108
    predicting behavior, 113–114
    purpose of behavior, 114–116
    rating scale/surveys/questionnaires, 108
    records, 108
    scatterplot, 108
behavior defined, 110–113
behavior intervention plan, 108, 130–132
blending, 136

central tendency, applying measures of, 19–22
    normal distribution, 20–22
        percentage of population/normal curve, 20–21
        standard deviations/normal curve, 20
        uses of normal curve, 21–22
central tendency reliability measures, 23–24
    equivalent forms reliability, 23
    internal consistency, 24
    interrater reliability, 23
    test-retest reliability, 23
Cognitive Abilities Test (CogAT), 57
cognitive processes, 170–171
    executive functioning, 171
    working memory, 170–171
concurrent validity, 14
confidence intervals, 14
construct validity, 14
constructs related to reliability, 25–27
    confidence intervals, 25
    obtained/true scores, 25
    standard error of measurement, 25
    validity, 26–27
        construct validity, 27
        content validity, 26
        criterion-related validity, 26
content validity, 14
correlation, 14

correlation coefficient, 14
court cases, 33
criterion-related validity, 14
cultural bias in assessment, 8–9
curriculum-based measurements, 90, 136

data-based decision making, 90
de facto, 32
de jure, 32
de minimis, 32
defining assessment, 2–3
derived scores, 14
development of math skills, 169–170
direct behavior, measuring, 119–123
    ABC observation, 119–120
    duration, 120
    frequency count, 120
    latency, 120–121
    scatterplot, 121–123
direct data, 108
duration, 108
dyscalculia, 169
dysgraphia, 152
dyslexia, 136
    characteristics of, 154
dyslexia/reading disabilities, defining, 138–139

Education for All Handicapped Children Act of 1975, 44
Education of the Handicapped Act of 1970, 44
educational assessment, history of, 3–5
educational diagnostician, 14
educational/programming history, 16
Elementary and Secondary Education Act of 1965, 44
eligibility statement, in reading assessment, 148
equivalent forms reliability, 14
evaluation, appropriate, 32
event recording, 108
examiner, 14
exams, state assessments, 80–81
exit slips, 72

federal involvement, 44–49
field testing, 54
formal assessment, 8
formal math assessments, 177–179
    Feifer Assessment of Mathematics (FAM), 178
    KeyMath-3 Diagnostic Assessment (KeyMath-3 DA), 178
    Test of Mathematical Abilities, Third Edition (TOMA-3), 179
formal reading assessments, 136, 147
formative assessments, 72
formative/summative assessments, 71–88
    authentic assessment, 72
    case study, 72
    case study wrap-up, 85

exit slips, 72
formative assessments, 72–80
    exit slips (written evidence), 76–77
    features, 73–75
        feedback, 74
        frequent, 74
        student involvement, 73–74
    graphic organizers (graphic evidence), 77
    introduction, 73
    observations of student learning behaviors (practical evidence), 77–79
    response cards (nonverbal evidence), 79
    summary, 80
    Think-Pair-Share (oral evidence), 75–76
graphic organizers, 72
performance-based assessments, 72
portfolio assessments, 72
response cards, 72
rubric, 72
rubrics, 83–84
    general design principles, 84
    purpose of, 84
summative assessments, 72, 80–83
    exams, state assessments, 80–81
    performance-based assessments, 82
    portfolio assessments, 82–83
    summary, 83
Think-Pair-Share, 72
free appropriate public education, 32
frequency count, 108
functional behavior assessment, 108, 123–125
    comprehensive, steps to completing, 125–130

grade equivalents, 14
graphic organizers, 72, 77
group assessment, 54
group assessments, 57–58
    Cognitive Abilities Test (CogAT), 57
    Iowa Assessments, 58
    Otis-Lennon School Ability Test (OLSAT), 58

handwriting, 153–158. *See also* writing
    formal assessment of, 156–158
    informal assessment of, 154–156
health history, 15
high-leverage practices, 136
high-stakes testing, 54, 67–68
history of educational assessment, 3–5
history of intelligence testing, 5–6

indirect behavior, measuring, 116–119
    interviews, 116
    rating scales/surveys/questionnaires, 118–119
    records, 116–118
indirect data, 108
individual assessment, 54
Individualized Education Program, 32

Index 203

individually administered assessment, 59–66
    Adaptive Behavior Assessment System, Third Edition (ABAS-3), 65–66
    Kaufman Test of Educational Achievement, Third Edition (KTEA-3), 64–65
    Wechsler Intelligence Scale for Children, Fifth Edition (WISC-V), 59–61
    Woodcock-Johnson IV Tests of Cognitive Abilities (WJ IV COG), 61–63
Individuals with Disabilities Education Act, 32, 45–46
    disability categories under, 46
informal assessment, 6–7
    curriculum-based assessment, 6–7
    curriculum-based measurement, 7
    portfolio assessment, 7
informal math assessment, 174–177
    classroom, 172–174
        examples of measurements, 174
        math curriculum-based measurements, 173–174
    exit slips, 175–176
    observational data, 174–175
    response cards, 175
    statewide assessment information, 177
informal reading assessments, 139
informal reading inventories, 136
initial evaluation, full individual, 183–200
instructional factors, mathematical thinking, 172
intelligence testing, history of, 5–6
internal consistency, 14
interrater reliability, 14
interval recording, 108
interviews, 108
Iowa Assessments, 58
item pool, 54

Kaufman Test of Educational Achievement, Third Edition (KTEA-3), 64–65

landmark court cases, 33–38
    Board of Education of the Hendrick Hudson Central School District v. Rowley (1982), 41
    Brown v. Board of Education (1954, 1955), 33–36
    court cases involving assessment issues, 38–44
    Diana v. State Board of Education (1970), 39
    Endrew F. v. Douglas County School District (2017), 42–44
    Hobson v. Hansen (1967), 38–39
    Honig v. Doe (1988), 37–38
    Larry P. v. Riles (1979), 39–40
    Luke S. and Han S. v. Nix et al. (1981), 40–41
    Mills v. Board of Education of the District of Columbia (1972), 36–37
    Pennsylvania Association for Retarded Children v. Commonwealth of Pennsylvania (1972), 36–37
    Timothy W. v. Rochester, New Hampshire, School District (1988), 42

latency recording, 108
least restrictive environment, 32
legal issues, 31–52
    appropriate evaluation, 32
    case study, 32–33
    case study wrap-up, 49
    court cases, 33
    de facto, 32
    de jure, 32
    de minimis, 32
    Education for All Handicapped Children Act of 1975, 44
    Education of the Handicapped Act of 1970, 44
    Elementary and Secondary Education Act of 1965, 44
    federal involvement, 44–49
    free appropriate public education, 32
    Individualized Education Program, 32
    Individuals with Disabilities Education Act, 32, 45–46
    disability categories under, 46
    landmark court cases, 33–38
        Board of Education of the Hendrick Hudson Central School District v. Rowley (1982), 41
        Brown v. Board of Education (1954, 1955), 33–36
        court cases involving assessment issues, 38–44
        Diana v. State Board of Education (1970), 39
        Endrew F. v. Douglas County School District (2017), 42–44
        Hobson v. Hansen (1967), 38–39
        Honig v. Doe (1988), 37–38
        Larry P. v. Riles (1979), 39–40
        Luke S. and Han S. v. Nix et al. (1981), 40–41
        Pennsylvania Association for Retarded Children v. Commonwealth of Pennsylvania (1972), 36–37
        Timothy W. v. Rochester, New Hampshire, School District (1988), 42
    least restrictive environment, 32
    manifestation determination, 32
    parent participation, 32
    procedural safeguards, 32
    six principles of the Individuals with Disabilities Education Improvement Act, 47–48
        appropriate evaluation, 47
        free appropriate public education, 47
        Individualized Education Program, 48
        least restrictive environment, 48
        parent participation, 48–49
        procedural safeguards, 49

manifestation determination, 32
mastery measurement, 90
mathematics, 167–182
    case study, 168
    case study wrap-up, 180
    cognitive processes, 170–171
        executive functioning, 171
        working memory, 170–171
    development of math skills, 169–170
    dyscalculia, 168–169
    executive functioning, 168
    explicit instruction, 168
    formal assessments, 177–179
        Feifer Assessment of Mathematics (FAM), 178
        KeyMath-3 Diagnostic Assessment (KeyMath-3 DA), 178
        Test of Mathematical Abilities, Third Edition (TOMA-3), 179
    full individual initial evaluation, 183–200
    informal assessment, 174–177
        classroom, 172–174
            examples of measurements, 174
                math curriculum-based measurements, 173–174
        exit slips, 175–176
        observational data, 174–175
        response cards, 175
        statewide assessment information, 177
    instructional factors, mathematical thinking, 172
    long-term memory, 168
    principles of mathematics, 169
    short-term memory, 168
    working memory, 168
mean, 14
measurement, 14–15
    age equivalents, 14
    basic concepts, 13–30
    case study, 15–16
    case study wrap-up, 28–29
    central tendency
        applying measures of, 19–22
            normal distribution, 20–22
            normal distribution, percentage of population/normal curve, 20–21
            normal distribution, standard deviations/normal curve, 20
            normal distribution, uses of normal curve, 21–22
        measures of reliability, 23–24
            equivalent forms reliability, 23
            internal consistency, 24
            interrater reliability, 23
            test-retest reliability, 23
    choosing, 24
    concurrent validity, 14
    confidence intervals, 14
    construct validity, 14
    constructs related to reliability, 25–27
        confidence intervals, 25
        obtained/true scores, 25
        standard error of measurement, 25
        validity, 26–27
            construct validity, 27
            content validity, 26
            criterion-related validity, 26
    content validity, 14
    correlation, 14
    correlation coefficient, 14
    criterion-related validity, 14
    derived scores, 14
    educational diagnostician, 14
    educational/programming history, 16
    equivalent forms reliability, 14
    examiner, 14
    grade equivalents, 14
    health history, 15
    importance of, 16
    internal consistency, 14
    interrater reliability, 14
    mean, 14
    measures of central tendency, 14
    median, 14
    mode, 14
    normal distribution or curve, 14
    obtained score, 14
    percentile ranks, 14
    predictive validity, 14
    raw scores, 14
    reason for referral, 15
    reliability, 14
        validity, distinguishing, 27
    scaled scores, 15
    score types, 16–19
        age/grade equivalency, 18
        central tendency/normal curve, measures of, 18–19
        derived scores, 17
        percentile ranks, 17–18
        raw score, example of calculating, 17
        raw scores, 16–17
    scores, summary of, 28
    standard deviation, 15
    standard error of measurement, 15
    standard scores, 15
    standardized assessments, 15
    technical adequacy, terms of, 22–23
        correlation, 22–23
        reliability, 22
    terms of technical adequacy, 15
    test-retest reliability, 15
    true score, 15
    validity, 15
measures of central tendency, 14

measuring behavior examples, 116–123
median, 14, 90
Mills v. Board of Education of the District of Columbia (1972), 36–37
mode, 14
multi-tiered system of support, 109–110
multidisciplinary assessments, 9–10

norm-referenced assessments, 53–69
    case study, 54
    case study wrap-up, 68
    construction of, 55
    defining, 55
    field testing, 54
    group assessment, 54
    group assessments, 57–58
        Cognitive Abilities Test (CogAT), 57
        Iowa Assessments, 58
        Otis-Lennon School Ability Test (OLSAT), 58
    high-stakes testing, 54, 67–68
    individual assessment, 54
    individually administered assessment, 59–66
        Adaptive Behavior Assessment System, Third Edition (ABAS-3), 65–66
        Kaufman Test of Educational Achievement, Third Edition (KTEA-3), 64–65
        Wechsler Intelligence Scale for Children, Fifth Edition (WISC-V), 59–61
        Woodcock-Johnson IV Tests of Cognitive Abilities (WJ IV COG), 61–63
    item pool, 54
    norm-referenced assessment, 54
    norm-referenced assessments, 66
    norms, 54
    protocol, 54
    rapport, 54
    standardized test administration procedures, 56
normal distribution or curve, 14
norms, 54

observations of student learning behaviors (practical evidence), 77–79
obtained score, 14
occupational therapy, 152
oral reading, informal assessments of, 143–147
    curriculum-based measurement, 145–147
        charting curriculum-based measurement data, 146–147
    running records, 144–145
orthographic awareness, 136
    informal assessments of, 143
orthography, 136
Otis-Lennon School Ability Test (OLSAT), 58

parent participation, 32
past/present assessment practices, 91–92

Pennsylvania Association for Retarded Children v. Commonwealth of Pennsylvania (1972), 36–37
percentile ranks, 14
performance-based assessments, 72, 82
phonics, 136
phonological awareness, 136
    informal assessments, 139–141
        bleeding, 140
        segmenting, 140–141
portfolio assessments, 72, 82–83
positive behavioral interventions and supports, 108
predicting behavior, 113–114
predictive validity, 14
principles of mathematics, 169
procedural safeguards, 32
programming history, 16
progress monitoring, 90, 95–104
    curriculum-based measurement in classroom, 101–103
    implementation of progress monitoring, 97–101
    mastery measurement, 103–104
progress monitoring/response to intervention, 89–106
    baseline, 90
    case study, 90–91
    case study wrap-up, 104
    curriculum-based measurement, 90
    data-based decision making, 90
    mastery measurement, 90
    median, 90
    past/present assessment practices, 91–92
    progress monitoring, 90, 95–104
        curriculum-based measurement in classroom, 101–103
        implementation of progress monitoring, 97–101
        mastery measurement, 103–104
    response to intervention, 90, 92–95
        assessment practices within response to intervention framework, 94–95
        implementation, 93–95
        tier 1, 93
        tier 2, 93–94
        tier 3, 94
protocol, 54
purpose of behavior, 114–116
purposes of assessment, 3

rapport, 54
rating scale/surveys/questionnaires, 108
raw scores, 14
reading assessment, 135–150
    alphabetic principle, 136
    basic reading skills, 136, 141–143
        assessing basic reading skills, 141–142
        assessing spelling, 142–143

blending, 136
case study, 137–138
case study wrap-up, 147
curriculum-based measurements of reading, 136
defining dyslexia/reading disabilities, 138–139
dyslexia, 136
eligibility statement, 148
formal reading assessments, 136, 147
high-leverage practices, 136
informal assessments of phonological awareness, 139–141
informal reading assessments, 139
informal reading inventories, 136
oral reading, informal assessments of, 143–147
    curriculum-based measurement, 145–147
        charting curriculum-based measurement data, 146–147
    running records, 144–145
orthographic awareness, 136
    informal assessments of, 143
orthography, 136
phonics, 136
phonological awareness, 136
    informal assessments of bleeding, 140
        segmenting, 140–141
reading fluency, 136
running records, 136
segmenting, 136
sight word recognition, 136
structural analysis, 136
reading disabilities, defining, 138–139
reading fluency, 136
records, 108
referral, reason for, 15
reliability, 14
    validity, distinguishing, 27
response cards, 72
response cards (nonverbal evidence), 79
response to intervention, 90, 92–95
    assessment practices within response to intervention framework, 94–95
    implementation, 93–95
    tier 1, 93
    tier 2, 93–94
    tier 3, 94
rubric, 72
running records, 136

scaled scores, 15
scatterplot, 108
score types, 16–19
    age/grade equivalency, 18
    central tendency/normal curve, measures of, 18–19
    derived scores, 17
    percentile ranks, 17–18
    raw score, example of calculating, 17
    raw scores, 16–17
scores, summary of, 28
segmenting, 136
    in phonological awareness, 140–141
sight word recognition, 136
six principles of the Individuals with Disabilities Education Improvement Act, 47–48
    appropriate evaluation, 47
    free appropriate public education, 47
    Individualized Education Program, 48
    least restrictive environment, 48
    parent participation, 48–49
    procedural safeguards, 49
spelling, assessing, 142–143
standard deviation, 15
standard error of measurement, 15
standard scores, 15
standardized assessments, 15
standardized test administration procedures, 56
structural analysis, 136
structural error analysis, 152
summative assessments, 72

technical adequacy, terms of, 22–23
    correlation, 22–23
    reliability, 22
terms of technical adequacy, 15
test, assessment, distinguished, 8
test-retest reliability, 15
Think-Pair-Share, 72
true score, 15

validity, 15
    reliability, distinguishing, 27
visual-motor integration, 152

Wechsler Intelligence Scale for Children, Fifth Edition (WISC-V), 59–61
Woodcock-Johnson IV Tests of Cognitive Abilities (WJ IV COG), 61–63
writing, 151–166
    case study, 152
    case study wrap-up, 164
    dysgraphia, 152
    dyslexia, characteristics of, 154
    handwriting, 153–158
        formal assessment of, 156–158
        informal assessment of, 154–156
    occupational therapy, 152
    structural error analysis, 152
    visual-motor integration, 152
written expression, 152, 158–164. *See also* writing
    defining, 152–153
    formal assessment of, 162–164
    informal assessment of, 159–162

Printed in the USA
CPSIA information can be obtained
at www.ICGtesting.com
LVHW081108260824
789277LV00015B/1065